THEY THREW TOMATOES AT US THE FIRST DAY
WE ARRIVED AT THE "WHITE" SCHOOL

EVERYDAY RACISM IN AMERICA AND THE POWER OF FORGIVENESS

Wilma Jean Turner, Ed.D.

WESTBOW
PRESS®
A DIVISION OF THOMAS NELSON
& ZONDERVAN

Unless otherwise marked, all Scripture quotations are taken from the Kings James Version of the Bible.

Scripture quotations marked NIV are taken from THE HOLY BIBLE, NEW INTERNATIONAL VERSION®, NIV® Copyright © 1973, 1978, 1984, 2011 by Biblica, Inc.® Used by permission. All rights reserved worldwide.

Scripture quotations marked NLT are taken from the Holy Bible, New Living Translation, copyright © 1996, 2004, 2015 by Tyndale House Foundation. Used by permission of Tyndale House Publishers, Inc., Carol Stream, Illinois 60188. All rights reserved.

WestBow Press books may be ordered through booksellers or by contacting:

WestBow Press
A Division of Thomas Nelson & Zondervan
1663 Liberty Drive
Bloomington, IN 47403
www.westbowpress.com
1 (866) 928-1240

ISBN: 978-1-9736-3469-0 (sc)
ISBN: 978-1-9736-3470-6 (e)

Library of Congress Control Number: 2018908565

Print information available on the last page.

WestBow Press rev. date: 08/02/2019

Contents

ACKNOWLEDGMENTS

First, "thank you" to my Lord and Savior, Jesus Christ, giving thanks to God the Father through Him, for allowing me to see my dream of writing a book to share my life experiences with everyday racism in America, come true. I thank Him for my mother who was brave enough to allow me to venture into a place where I, at sixteen years of age, learned that I could do anything I set my mind to, and to stand up for my human and civil rights as an African American born in and living in the United States of America. I would like to thank specifically, Dr. Richard Streedain for his faith in my ability and his cheerful encouragement always and Dr. Norman Weston for his understanding, support and unwavering optimism throughout my doctoral internship and the writing of my dissertation which led to this book. I would also like to thank each and every one of my National Louis University professors for rekindling my desire to learn even after retirement from twenty-seven years in the classroom as an elementary school teacher. Thank you also to Dr. Carl Whiting for his conscientious work in reading and discussing my drafts, and to Dr. Allen Bearden for having faith in my ability to make a difference for teachers and students as a professional development facilitator in the Chicago public schools. My deepest gratitude to Dr. Catherine Morgan, confidant and spiritual advisor, and to Attorney Clyde J. Cahill, Jr. (posthumously) for his indefatigable work on the court case against segregation in the Charleston, Missouri public schools in 1962. Thanks also to Attorney Robert Sedler who assisted Mr. Cahill. "To God be the glory for the things He has done" (Crouch 1996).

DEDICATION

To my mother, Emma, and
For Troy, Tanya, Tia and Teddy

Who shall separate us from the love of Christ? Shall tribulation, or distress, or persecution, or famine, or nakedness, or peril, or sword? ... Nay, in all these things we are more than conquerors through Him who loved us. For I am persuaded that neither death, nor life, nor angels, nor principalities, nor powers, nor things present, nor things to come, nor height, nor depth, nor any other creature, shall be able to separate us from the love of God which is in Christ Jesus our Lord. Romans 8: 35, 37-39, KJV, Holy Bible.

PREFACE

This is the story of my experiences as an African American born and raised in the United States of America, who from the time I realized I was Black at the age of ten, until the present day, more than a half-century later, has experienced racism either overtly or covertly, on a daily basis. I first explore my days as a sixteen-year-old high school girl involved in a court desegregation case in Charleston, Missouri in 1962, and the trauma I experienced in a hostile environment where White students openly showed their racial hatred for the Black students who would dare to enroll in "their school."

I also tell of my life as a college student in Alabama, at the height of the Civil Rights Movement and my participation in non-violent protests, especially the famous Selma to Montgomery march led by Dr. Martin Luther King, Jr., eventually resulting in the 1965 Voters' Rights Act. Through a series of short stories I analyze how these experiences have influenced my racial identity development, outlook on life, pedagogy as an elementary school teacher and future life endeavors as an advocate for racial equity and social justice which still eludes us as a country to this day.

It is my prayer that this story of my experiences with racism will help its readers to have a better and deeper understanding of what hatred and racism does to the psyche of an individual and to the heart of a nation. The Edmund Pettis Bridge, between Selma and Montgomery Alabama, was the site where one of the bloodiest events of the Civil Rights Struggle of the 1960's took place. Bloody Sunday, as it is called, happened on the bridge on March 7, 1965 when peaceful protestors tried to cross the bride to Montgomery in order to "sit-in" at the State Capitol for the first time. They were attacked by the Alabama state troopers with billy clubs and tear gas and many of the protestors sustained significant injuries. Twice they were not allowed to cross the bridge. The leaders of the movement went to court to seek federal protection for a third march and won. Marchers again set out from Selma and sympathizers joined them all along the way. I was one of those who waited anxiously and defiantly for the protestors, and joined them on the other side of the bridge, in Montgomery, a little scared but ready and determined to be a part of *whatever* might happen next ...

INTRODUCTION

This book is a product of an autoethnographic study of my experiences with racial hatred. It is my hope that this work will serve as a resource for teachers, students and curious and courageous people of all races and nationalities as they learn about the history of racial hatred and segregation in America, particularly as it relates to the 1954 *Brown v. Board of Education* Supreme Court decision and the 1960's Civil Rights Movement. For the purpose of this study I have indicated several definitions of racism that coincide with my experiences. Sue (2003, xii) defines racism as "any attitude, action, or institutional structure or any social policy that subordinates persons or groups because of their [skin] color." Racism is further defined by Singleton and Linton (2006) as "beliefs and an enactment of beliefs that one set of characteristics is superior to another set (e.g., white skin, blonde hair and blue eyes are more beautiful than brown skin, brown eyes and brown hair" (39). Pollack et al. (2008) define racism as "any act that, even unwittingly, tolerates, accepts, or reinforces racially unequal opportunities for children to learn and thrive; allows racial inequalities in opportunity as if they are normal and acceptable; or treats people of color as less worthy or less complex than 'white' people" (xxii).

This account is authentic in that it was written by someone who actually participated in civil rights demonstrations and marches, one of which was led by civil rights leader, Dr. Martin Luther King, Jr. in Montgomery, Alabama, in 1965, and who lived through racial segregation and discrimination of the ugliest kind from an early age.

I would like for this study of my life experiences to serve as a catalyst to encourage people to talk more about race and racism and to help foster cross-cultural and cross-racial understandings. I believe if we can learn to talk about race openly and honestly, change is possible, especially for future generations and young people today of all races when they learn how hurtful and traumatizing experiencing racism can be. It is my hope that they will gain knowledge of how to avoid the mistakes their parents and grandparents made in the past. The historical data which I have included will serve to help my story come alive and place it in the annals of American history. My hope is that this study will also be a legacy to my grandchildren who will grow up Black in America and that it will serve as a guide to show them and others who read it that no matter what the challenge; with God all things are possible. My legacy to them will not be a legacy of houses and land, but of a life lived with integrity and fortitude and the ability to overcome immense obstacles. They will know through my story that it is possible to triumph over racism and not become bitter, possible to love and forgive those who hurt or mistreat you, possible to see the "heart" of another person regardless of their skin color, and possible to follow your dreams and succeed, if you are willing to hold fast, dig in and claim your victory.

My personal encounter with racism began as a teenaged African American high school student who left an all-Black high school, along with thirteen others, to help integrate a "White" (except for one "token" Black girl) high school in Charleston, Missouri in 1962. A formula, later found unconstitutional in *Davis v. Charleston Bd. Of Ed.,* was created by the Charleston Board of Education to "allow" Black Charleston students to enter CHS in their junior or senior year to show that the schools were "integrated." A court order got seven of us who lived outside the Charleston District, in the Wyatt School District, into the school, but what we suffered on the inside could only be understood if you were there. That same year seven Black students, who lived in Charleston, entered CHS. (The names of all the Black students in attendance in 1962 are listed in the court documents.) It was what Payne (2008) describes as "crude racism", unsophisticated racism where you could see the disdain on their faces, no pretenses. I would like to share how the experiences of being called hateful, demeaning names, having tomatoes thrown at me and the other Black students, and having to face racial hatred every day for a number of years in that school, has impacted my life.

There is a derogatory term which carries with it a history of hate and violence and death. Some say it was the last word heard by many Black men before they were lynched by a hate-filled White mob, pre-Civil Rights Era. It was used by the students at Charleston High School to make the Black students, who had come there and "messed up" their school, feel less intelligent, less human and less in every way than the White students. As Eleanor Roosevelt's (1937) famous quote says, "No one can make you feel inferior without your consent." They did not have my consent, and what it did for me was make me stronger and more determined to stay there. The Merriam-Webster Dictionary online (2010) indicates that the so-called, "N-word" now ranks as possibly the most inflammatory and offensive racial slur in the English language; an expression of hatred and bigotry.

I also explore how the racism I encountered in high school—the name-calling, the insults, the feelings of indignation by the way we, and Black people in general, in America were being treated, led to my participation in the Civil Rights Movement as a college student while attending Tuskegee Institute in Tuskegee, Alabama, at the peak of the Movement. I was not fortunate enough to see Dr. Martin Luther King up close, or shake his hand, but I heard him speak as we shared the same space on two occasions, first as a graduation speaker at Tuskegee and then in Montgomery, Alabama at the culmination of the famous Selma-Montgomery march in 1965. A group of students from Tuskegee, including me, met up with the marchers from Selma and completed the march to the Alabama Capitol Building. Dr. King, who had led the voting-rights march, spoke that day while my friends and I sat on the lawn with thousands of others, some of whom were White, and like us were putting themselves in serious peril, not knowing what to expect—vicious attack dogs, water hoses—but being willing to sacrifice *whatever* was necessary including our own lives, for the cause. The route the marchers took has since been designated a US National Historic Trail (http://www.nps.gov./nr/trave;/civilrights/al4.htm 2010).

I believe this account has significance today because the same racism that existed in the 1960s continues to exist. Racism has led to the re-segregation of many of America's schools nearly sixty years after what some consider the most "significant ruling" on education of all time, *Brown v. Board of Education*. In the *Brown* (1954) lawsuit the United States Supreme Court asked and answered this question:

> Does segregation of children in public schools solely on the basis of race, even though the physical facilities and other tangible factors may be equal, deprive children of the minority group of equal educational opportunities? We believe it does.

Through a series of vignettes, my story chronicles the racism I experienced in high school as well as my participation in the Civil Rights Movement and through self-analysis explores the influences those events have had on my life as a student, as a mother, as an educator, and on my daily existence as an African American living in the United States of America for more than a half century.

As I write this story of my life and the racist culture in which I live, I have twenty-seven years of experience as an elementary classroom teacher, seven years as a central office administrator in the Chicago Public Schools and seven combined years as an educational consultant, instructional coach, student-teacher supervisor, and staff-developer. In each and every personal and professional situation, I have always been aware that I am a Black person in America and the struggles that blackness brings with it in this country.

Ellis and Bochner (2000) stated that some of the common approaches to qualitative research may consist of "short stories, poetry, fiction, novels, photographic essays, personal essays, journals, fragmented and layered writing, and social science prose" (739). In that vein, I have chosen to write the following poem in the styling of one of my favorite African American writers, Nikki Giovanni, to introduce and give background to my story. Giovanni writes mostly about the Black experience and is a not so quiet voice, in her own way, in the fight for civil rights and equality. She believes in each individual's power to make a positive difference in self and in the lives of others (http://nikki-giovanni.com).

Who I Am

2011

I am a child of God.
A Black woman in America is who I am.
If you know even a little bit of my history
These few words tell you a story of
Racism, segregation, discrimination!
Some things you already realize, like
My African ancestors were brought here by force
Women raped by their White slave masters,
Men stripped of their dignity.
They survived the Middle Passage.
I have their inner strength.
Born of modest means
in a farming town, gravel roads.
Clothed, fed, nurtured, loved by my mother
Daddy died before I knew him,
I was only three.
We lived in a place where Blacks and Whites
experienced two different worlds.
They owned the stores
and worked in the post office
where "colored" folks had no place.
They thought us not intelligent enough

for that kind of job!
So we moved to a city where
Mama could find work.
Stayed there for a little while
Long enough for me to think
I was a "city girl."
Then we moved back to the small town with gravel roads.
Why I don't know.
Lord, I didn't wanna go.
Maybe because the house was there
waiting for us.
I graduated salutatorian in my eighth grade class.
Started to think of myself as "smart"
Then high school at the "all-Black" high school
segregated and unequal to
the White school a few blocks away.
Imagine 100 old, *raggedy* books in the library
Couldn't get what I needed for college there
So we went to court and I
Was one of 14 who integrated
the White high school in Charleston, Missouri.
Was that exciting? Thrilling? A new adventure?
Guess again!
Everyday they called us out of our names,
And wrote unkind words on our lockers,
I wasn't much for fighting
But I learned to cuss like a sailor.
I thought it was my only defense …
"Don't push me, boy!"
I remember Lizzy
She fought nearly every day
when someone called her a name or
pushed her in the hallway!
I was sixteen then and even today
it makes me sad when I think of

the trauma we experienced ...
Hated because of the color of our skin
I fought back by showing
all of my White teachers
and all of the White kids
How brilliant I was—just because
They thought Blacks were incapable, dumb, stupid!
A's on all of my papers
Highest honors on the Honor Roll
that first semester!
Blackened up the Glee Club
My friend, Betty and I.
I won 2nd place in the Oratory Contest.
"*Gossiping Gertie*", was the monologue.
Should have been first place
But they couldn't give it to
one of us, Please!
Still they knew I was exceptional.
"How you like me now?"
You! Can't! Stop! Me!
I have a right to be here!
Everyone deserves to be treated with dignity
Why are you more special than I?"
Remember when JFK was shot!
When he died ...
We forgot for a moment that we were
different—Black and White.
We were just humans—feeling loss and sadness!
I remember exactly where I was in the White school ...
Singing in Glee Club, and
how we all cried together.
College was a better place.
Accepted, respected, and appreciated.
Historical, Black college—
Tuskegee University

Booker T. and George Washington C.
Work study is a marvelous thing!
Whatever you think I can't do—
only motivates me more.
Alabama, Governor Wallace,
Sit-ins, demonstrations, water hoses, attack dogs!
Civil rights, non-violence, Dr. King!
I was there at the Montgomery State House.
My mother feared I would go to jail,
but a fire inside me had been started
when they threw tomatoes at us that first
day at the White high school.
I was not afraid.
Do what you will to me—
I will not be moved!
College graduation would take
five years on the work-study plan, but
I was determined to achieve my goal.
Make myself and my mother proud
And then surprisingly,
a little baby boy!
My Mama loved him so much
and cared for him as her own.
When he was growing into a size twelve shoe
and feeling unhappy that his
feet were getting so big, I told him
"Don't worry; all really intelligent people have big feet!"
Guess he believed me …
Now he's a lawyer, a family man
and a fine human being—
a contributing member of society.
Made me grandma,
Such joy unspeakable they bring!
Mom to their mommy too.
And what about being a teacher?

I guess teaching chose me—.
I never planned to be a teacher, but
discovered I liked it and was good at it.
Stayed there for a very long time
So many lives touched …
I thought it my obligation to teach them well,
these kids who looked like me
and shared my history.
Told them of my experiences,
taught them "freedom songs"
I learned in the Movement
for their civil rights and mine
Built up their self-esteem
talking about African kings and queens
and how "A mind is a terrible thing to waste."
Tried to show them that they
could be anything and do anything they set
their minds to.
I saw one of them just the other day.
He's a preacher now.
And did I tell you?
God has always been there
no matter what the experience –
even when my behavior did not honor Him.
He always forgives.
He's the only One who knows for sure who I am.
I am His creation.
With the gift of song He gave me,
I sang in the college choir
and in rock 'n roll bands—
in the classroom when nothing else worked
Soloist in the church choir
Sing girl, sing!
Hallelujah! Jesus, you are my saving grace!
My sins are forgiven and

"I am redeemed!"
There's so much more to tell—
new experiences every day make you who you are
Different today than yesterday.
How wonderful it is to grow, to experience--
Tomorrow I'll have a new story to tell,
but I will still be
wanting, needing, love—
Wanting to trust my fellow man
Wanting to know you accept
and believe in me
Just the way I am.
Who am I?
I am Black. I am blessed.
I am prosperous. I am healthy.
I am talented. I am creative. I am wise.
Wise enough to know
that "forgiveness is freedom."
I am forever changing.
Seeing the world through a new lens,
understanding some things differently.
Knowing that change is difficult to come by.
I still believe that all is not lost,
and I too have the "audacity" of never-ending hope.
Hope that one day,
As a *Kingly* messenger once said,
No one will be judged or hated or dishonored
because of the color of their skin.
But will be judged justly by the substance of
their character.
And I know I have won the greatest battle
by the love I still have in my heart.

———————————

By using autoethnography as a qualitative research method, I explore and tell the story of how my lived experiences with blatant racism as a high school student and experiences as a non-violent participant in the 1960s Civil Rights Movement as a college student, have impacted my life experiences—self image, racial identity development, spiritual development, intra and inter-personal relationships, academic achievement, career choice, professional practices, doctoral internship and daily life as an American citizen. Etherington (2004) in *Becoming a Reflexive Researcher: Using Ourselves in Research* referenced Frank (1995) who made this statement about the significance of each of us telling our own personal story:

> The very act of forming stories requires us to create coherence through ordering our own experiences, and provides us with an opportunity for reclaiming ourselves and our histories. New selves form within as we tell and re-tell our stories and when we write them down. When we use our own stories ... we give testimony to what we have witnessed, and that testimony creates voice (9).

Chapter One

RACE AND THE RIGHT TO LEARN

In this chapter I review the literature which examines the historical context of racism in the United States as it impacts the right to learn for every child within its borders. This includes my own experience as a Black high school student who, by court order, forcibly entered a high school which was considered just "for Whites."

Eight years after the 1954 US Supreme Court case, *Brown v. Board of Education,* which ended the legal segregation of schools, I became a student at Charleston High School (CHS), along with thirteen other Black students. As before stated, at the time there was only one African American student there. She had enrolled in CHS in her junior year. The other three to four hundred students were White. Sometimes I wonder what she experienced. Perhaps one "token" Black student wasn't seen as a threat, unlike fourteen. Black high school students who lived in the city of Charleston, Missouri, unlike the Black students who were bussed to school from throughout the district, were *on paper* allowed to enter CHS in their junior or senior year. But by that time Black high school students had completed two years of their high school program at the ill-equipped Black high school they were *required* to attend for at least two years. Most did not want to transfer and suffer through the isolation of being one of a few Blacks or the only Black in a White environment.

I also look at the literature of the historical 1960s Civil Rights Movement, of which I was a participant. In addition, literature related to racial identity development is examined and its impact on my culturally relevant pedagogical practices as an elementary school teacher is explored. Next, I survey the literature that speaks to the inequities of academics, tracking as it relates to the re-segregation of a large metropolitan high school in the Midwest a half-century after *Brown v. Board of Education*, which declared racial segregation in America's schools illegal. Jonathan Kozol, long-time educator, researcher, and writer, stated in *Shame of the Nation: The Restoration of Apartheid Schooling in America* (2005) that he could not see "the slightest hint that any vestige of the legal victory embodied in *Brown v. Board of Education* or the moral mandate that a generation of unselfish activists and young idealists lived and sometimes died for has survived …" (10). I utilize the Critical Race Theory framework to understand and analyze how race impacts the "…ways [in which] people of color are ordered and constrained in the United States" (Trevino, Harris and Wallace 2008, 7) on every turn, including in our schools. And lastly, I examine literature which speaks to how we can begin to fix the inequity and racism problems in our communities, in our schools, and in our country.

W. E. B. DuBois, born in 1868, was an African American educator, civil rights activist, and intellectual scholar. In 1895 he became the first African American to graduate from Harvard University with a PhD. Aldridge (2008) paints DuBois as "a pragmatic educational theorist who developed original ideas and adopted and adapted many ideas of his time to forge educational strategies aimed at improving the social, economic, and political conditions of African Americans" (1).

DuBois was one of the founders of and the first to head the National Association for the Advancement of Colored People (NAACP) and was considered one of the most influential African American leaders of his time (Appiah and Gates 2003). In a 1949 speech entitled "Freedom to Learn" he said the following which resonates with me deeply and helps provide a foundation for the telling of my story. These words speak to the racism I encountered as a high school student simply seeking the "freedom to learn." Darling-Hammond (2010) opens Chapter 2 (27) of *The Flat World and Education: How*

America's Commitment to Equity Will Determine Our Future with this same quote from DuBois. In addition, Singleton and Linton (2006) begin Chapter 1 (1) of *A Field Guide for Achieving Equity in Schools: Courageous Conversations about Race* with these words as well. I believe DuBois is so widely quoted at this time in history because his message, although delivered in 1949, is still profound and timeless. He said,

> Of all the civil rights for which the world has struggled and fought for 5,000 years, the right to learn is undoubtedly the most fundamental ... The freedom to learn ... has been bought by bitter sacrifice. And whatever we may think of the curtailment of other civil rights, we should fight to the last ditch to keep open the right to learn ... We must insist upon this to give our children the fairness of a start which will equip them with such an array of facts and such an attitude toward truth that they can have a real chance to judge what the world is and what its greater minds have thought it might be.

Writer and teacher bell hooks, who does not capitalize her name, in *Teaching to Transgress* (1994) speaks of education as being about the "practice of freedom"—freedom that would uplift the Black race. She believes that education is politically rooted in the antiracist struggle and that to Black folks learning is a "counter-hegemonic" means to resist White privilege and domination (2).

What Price Equity?
2012
What was the price of seeking equity for Martin?
What price for Medgar?
Imagine how Rosa felt

the day she was hauled off to jail
for taking a stand
by sitting down.
Harriet suffered a blow to the head
that would wound her for life.
Sammie, killed by a White racist
at a gas station not far from campus,
over his right to use
a public restroom,
was buried in his Navy uniform.
Think about the price of equity for Ruby,
a little girl with the weight of the prejudiced South on her shoulders
as she tried to go to school,
just to school.
Wasn't that her unalienable right, along with
life and liberty?
Or was that for someone
of a different race and nationality?
Viola was a White woman.
A civil rights activist who left five children when
she was killed by the KKK.
The price of being beaten about the head
with a cop's bully/billy stick?
Ask John Lewis about it.
For the educators who for years have fought
for equality in funding
and resources
for minority students
all over this country ...
What has been the cost
of equity for those who
have lost their jobs and
because they refuse to give in?
And for others who have been
humiliated by having

another human being
spit in their faces
because they chose
to fight for
what is right for them
and future generations just like them?
What price the deep hurt and pain
that will never truly go away?
And for the countless men and women
who will remain faceless
and nameless for eternity long,
Who were tortured
physically and mentally
for standing up to racial prejudice
and discrimination?
What was the price
of seeking equity for them?
What has been the
price of equity
for our country
and for those of us
who call ourselves members of the
greatest country on earth?

Okun (2010) offers an additional definition of racism as "race prejudice plus social and institutional power, a system of advantages based on race, a system of oppression based on race, a white supremacy system ... more than personal prejudice; to qualify as racism, thoughts, behaviors, or acts must be systematically supported by institutional and cultural power" (xiv). By telling my story, I am able to share how it felt to know you are hated and confronted with racism not because of anything you have done but because you were born into a political system that sets people apart according to skin color. "Racism is the systematic mistreatment of certain groups of people … [who have been negatively pre-judged] on the basis of skin color or other physical characteristics" [alone] (Singleton and Linton 2006, 266). How many people have actually looked in the face of racial hatred?

I write about my participation in the Civil Rights protests in the 1960s. I know how it felt to walk on a picket line and sit in at the Capitol in Montgomery, Alabama, knowing that at any time someone could spit on me, vicious dogs could be let loose to attack me or I could be hauled off to jail for protesting the wrongs that were being done to African Americans in this country at that time. I prayed, "Lord, please don't let anyone spit on me," because I wasn't sure how I would respond. Would I be strong? Would I cry? Would I fight back? We were told by demonstration leaders that to fight back would destroy the non-violent movement. Thank God, I never had to make that decision.

Unfortunately, today, racism is still alive. It has a strong pulse and is by no means dead. Many improvements in race relations have been made since the Civil Rights Movement began, but there is still a mountain of equity work to be done in our schools, in our communities, and in our nation. In 2002, President George W. Bush made what I consider the most insightful statement of his presidency. He said, "Education is the great civil rights issue of our time." Singleton and Linton (2006) offer that racial discrimination has a history dating back to the founding of the nation. Although the Declaration of Independence holds that "all men are created equal," Singleton and Linton reference historian James Horton as having said,

> We are a society based on principles literally to die for, principles that are so wonderful that it brings tears to your eyes. But we are a society that so often allows itself to ignore those principles. We live in a kind of heightened state of anxiety because we know we are not what we could be or what we say we are (164).

In "*Brown v. Board of Education* at 50: An Update on School Desegregation in the U.S.", Russo (2004) calls attention to the fact that there were two *Brown v. Board of Education* cases known as *Brown I* and *Brown II. Brown I* was a class action suit which called for an end to segregated schooling because racial segregation violated the Equal Protection Clause of the Fourteenth Amendment to the Constitution. This case served as a "catalyst for systemic change that influenced just about every facet of American society ranging from the legislation effectuating the Civil Rights Movement of the 1960s to gender equity, to protecting the rights of children with disabilities" (183). In "Is Brown Dying? Exploring the Resegregation Trend in our Public Schools", D.R. Holley (2004) looked at many district court cases and called them "resegregation" cases. He noted that in *Brown I* (1954) the Supreme Court failed to explain how schools should be desegregated and in *Brown II* (1955) it said schools should be desegregated "with all deliberate speed." Many school districts took "all deliberate speed" to mean they were on their own time table and that desegregation was not urgent. Local school boards actively resisted the Supreme Court's decision in *Brown II* (Holley 2004, 1089), causing a lack of crucial progress toward desegregation.

My first assignment as a doctoral student was to read *Crash Course* (2005) by Christopher Whittle. I remember thinking that he was talking about me and what I had experienced as a high school student in an inadequately equipped all-Black high school when he said, "We are sending 15 million of our children, mostly poor and of color, to schools that, by government statistics, are significantly failing to deliver on a promise this democracy proudly makes to all of its citizens: an equal start" (10). He further captured my attention right away on the inside front cover of the book when he wrote,

> Imagine that upon your arrival at an airline ticket counter, you are told that only 70% of the flights to your intended destination actually arrive. The remainder crash en route. And, if you are a child of color, or poor, you are required to fly on special,

poorly maintained planes—of which a much smaller percentage makes it (front cover, 16).

Albert Einstein is quoted as having said, "The world is too dangerous to live in—not because of the people who do evil, but because of the people who sit and let it happen" (Sue 2003, 14). This too is Whittle's perception of the American public education system. He talks about the public outrage it would cause if this crash potential were a true occurrence in the airline industry and yet in the public education system there is no outcry, no outrage while fifteen million, mostly Black and Brown children are below basic "literacy and numeracy" levels and are being failed by the poor performance of the nation's schools. He believes that we as the public are in denial and that our educational system (K-12) is a "national embarrassment." He poses the question, "Why does the greatest nation in the history of mankind allow roughly 30% of its children to languish in functional illiteracy?" (16). Jonathan Kozol (2005) calls this failure to educate its children the "shame of the nation." Whittle proposes another question which I too have contemplated with a few additional rhetorical questions such as, who would clean our houses, open doors for us, polish our shoes, and do those other things for us that we don't care to do for ourselves if we educated everyone to their highest potential? He asks,

> Is it just accidental that virtually all the children in failing schools in America are children of color and poverty? Is it possible that somewhere inside us we don't want everyone one to be well educated? Is it possible that we're actually worried about how America would function with 100 percent literacy? If everyone read well would that somehow destabilize the hierarchy we now have? (22).

Racial Identity Development

I think I only realized I was Black when my mom and I moved back to Missouri after living in Ohio for a few years. I was about ten years old then and just beginning to notice how people who were Black like me were treated differently than Whites. Dissimilarly, in *Growing Up White* (2008), Julie Landsman posited, "I am not sure when children realize they are black, but I do know I never learned I was 'white' in a sense of being 'raced' until I was in my forties" (9). In Ohio I attended an integrated school. There were Black kids and White kids, but we were all just "kids" and I don't recall feeling that I was being treated any differently than other children. In Missouri the school I attended in 1956, was all Black. Every teacher was Black and every student was Black. Clearly *Brown v. Board of Education* (1954), which called for an end to segregated schooling, was being ignored. At that time, Blacks in my hometown were pretty much powerless to change anything regarding their concerns with the school system and Whites didn't seem to care about what was happening to Black children. I believe my mother later signed me up to attend an all-White high school because she was the kind of parent that Tatum (2010) describes here—

When African American parents pressed for an end to legalized school segregation in the years leading up to the 1954 *Brown v. Board of Education of Topeka* decision, it was not the companionship of white children they were seeking for their children: It was access to educational resources. The schools white children attended had better equipment and supplies, more curricular options, and often … more highly trained teachers than those serving black children. Black parents believed that equal access to those publicly funded resources was their children's birthright. Attending the same schools that white children did seemed the most likely means to achieve it (30).

After coming back home to southeast Missouri, where my home town could just as well have been the deepest, darkest, racist parts of Mississippi, it was just a given—we were Black and expected to take an inferior role to the White people who lived in the area. I specifically remember a truck stop on an Interstate Highway within walking distance from my house where the restaurant would not serve Blacks unless they went around to the back kitchen door and ordered from there. Black people were not allowed to go inside the restaurant from the front door where you might want to sit down like a normal human being and eat your food. I guess the "old folks" were accustomed to being treated like second-class citizens. Most of the kids my age, however, moved away to Chicago or Detroit or some other city where they could find work and hopefully a better way of life, and a little more dignity, as soon as they finished high school.

Goodman (2008) in "Exposing Race as an Obsolete Biological Concept" asserts that race is a social construct created or "made up" by humans, not a biological reality. I recall learning in church that we are "all God's children" and we sang a song in Sunday school with these lyrics: "…black and white—we're all precious in His sight. Jesus loves the little children of the world." It was meant to teach us that we should love everybody regardless of their race or skin color. Ponterotto, Utsey and Penderson (2006), citing Jones (1997) enters this profound statement about the impact of race:

> Race—this four-letter word has wreaked more havoc on people in the world than all the four-letter words banned by censors of the U.S. airwaves. Race divides human beings into categories that loom in our psyches. Racial differences create cavernous divides in our psychological understandings of who we are and who we should be (6).

There is biologically no clear marker to tell where one race ends and another begins.

My daughter-in-law is Black/White biracial. She and millions of people of color who have a "divided inheritance" (Obama 1995) have been designated "Black" through means of a system created by the "White privileged" in American society. She proudly claims her Blackness and very much teachers her children to do the same. But, isn't it unfair to force her to "deny" one-half of her ancestral background? I remember a story she told me about her White female gynecologist's facial expression when she discovered my daughter-in-law was married to a Black man, my son. The doctor seemed to be shocked and even had the audacity to say to her, "I thought you were married to a White man." Skin color falsely distinguishes racial groups, but in America we seem to be convinced that it rightly does (Goodman, 2008). We as a nation are obsessed with race. Although most White Americans would not admit it, some may not even be aware of it because racism is institutionalized and so common in America, " ...so wide-spread and deep-seated, that it is invisible because it is so normal" (Singleton and Linton 2006, 266) —but for African Americans in this country race drives everything we do and for the most part, the lives we live—our politics, the schools our children attend, our career opportunities, the salaries we earn, the neighborhoods we live in, the cars we drive, the insurance premiums we pay, the churches we attend, the gas prices we pay, how we are treated by police and even salesmen in stores, and on and on.

DuBois (1903) opened his book, *The Souls of Black Folk*, by stating, 'The problem of the 20th Century is the problem of the color line' (Trevino, Harris and Wallace, 2008). Singleton and Linton (2006) make this assertion about the "color line":

> Race continues to create confusing and often
> polarizing relationships among and between people
> of all racial groups ... It is clear ... that few people of
> color have been able to or allowed to fully transcend
> a deficit racial identity imposed by society ... Second

we struggle to find White Americans who have not
benefited, to some degree, by having White skin. At
the least, they have not had to think about race, much
less worry about being mistreated because of it (167).

Beverly Daniel Tatum (2004) uses Cross's (1971) model to
analyze racial identity development. According to Cross there are
"five stages of the racial identity development process: pre-counter,
encounter, immersion/emersion, internalization, and internalization-
commitment." Tatum explains each of these processes and relates
each to her findings "in a previous interview study of Black families
living in predominantly White and prosperous suburbs of California
(Tatum 1987, 1992)" where she found that most of these parents were
concerned about the impact of living in a White community and
attending a majority White school would have on their children's
racial identity development. Out of this concern some parents became
very "race conscious." Others adopted a "race-neutral", "class-
conscious" or "race-avoidant" approach (Tatum 2004, 118). In my
household, which was in an all-Black community, we were very race
conscious. We lived in segregated housing so there was no question
that White people and Black people each had their place and "never
the twain" should meet except when Blacks had to shop for essentials,
like groceries, or visit the post office. I recall the White waiting room
and the Black waiting room at the doctor's office when I was a small
child in Missouri. We had to trust our care to a person who possibly
thought us inferior. There were no Black doctors anywhere close
to where we lived and so we had no choice but to wait in the Black
waiting room. White Christians and Black Christians worshipped
in segregated churches—just as some do today in many cities. In my
private moments, sometimes I think about how mind-boggling the
whole racial thing is and dealing with it in a humorous manner helps
for a brief time. I remember thinking: *Black believers would probably
be okay with finding out on Judgment Day that Jesus is actually White
because that's the way we've seen Him in pictures all of our lives, but
if White believers found out He is actually Black, it might take some*

time to wrap their heads around that. Some might even consider taking heaven's alternate route (not seriously). Tatum (2004) submitted these findings about racial identity development:

> While those young people raised in race-conscious families seem to have been given a good foundation on which to build a positive racial identity, the educational experiences of all of the participants suggest that White-dominated schools, which formally and informally perpetuate the racial order, can work to undermine that foundation. In all the cases presented, the perception that teachers did not expect excellence from their Black students (in fact, were surprised by it) ... and the stereotypical expectations of ... White peers hindered the development of a positive Black identity (132).

The two traumatic years I spent in the majority White high school and the racially hostile environment where I spent the greatest part of my childhood, made it hard for me to develop a positive racial identity. My Black classmates and I were trying to fit into a culture which had already been established to exclude Blacks and with no Black teachers or Black administrators in the school; we felt we were on our own. Being able to attend a (Historical Black College and University) HBCU helped to renew my self-confidence and helped me to stand proud as a Black American. Truly, race has occupied a central role in my life experiences and has significantly affected my understanding of what it means to be Black in the United States (Lee 2005). I am reminded here and encouraged by what the *Holy Bible* says in 2 Corinthians 4: 8-9 (KJV): *"We are troubled on every side, yet not distressed; we are perplexed, but not in despair; persecuted, but not forsaken; cast down, but not destroyed."* At Tuskegee I began to feel better about and discover who I really was. Tatum (1999) comments, "As students get older and reach puberty, young people, regardless of race, are starting to ask, 'Who am I?' For young people of color, greater awareness starts to emerge about their racial group membership (42)."

The Civil Rights Movement

The Civil Rights Movement had its roots in the Constitutional amendments enacted during the Reconstruction era. The Thirteenth Amendment abolished slavery, the Fourteenth Amendment expanded the guarantees of federally protected citizenship rights, and the Fifteenth Amendment barred voting restrictions based on race ... the Civil Rights Act of 1964 and the Voting Rights Act of 1965 reinforced the guarantees of full citizenship provided for in [these] amendments nearly a century earlier, and marked the end of the Jim Crow system in the South" (Appiah and Gates 2003, 135).

I believe I became aware of the Civil Rights Movement as a teenager. I remember the Student Non-violent Coordinating Committee (SNCC), pronounced "snick", holding meetings in Charleston, Missouri where I attended high school. In his article "The Tribe of SNCC", Tom Hayden (2010) describes US Attorney Eric Holder's speech at SNCC's 50th year celebration in which he credited the organization's sit-in movement, which began in Greensboro, North Carolina in the 1960s, with "paving the way for Barack Obama's presidency" (6). Holder is cited as saying, "There is a straight line from those lunch counter sit-ins to the Oval Office today, and a straight line to the sixth floor of the Justice Department, where I serve" (6). African American civil rights' leaders such as Julian Bond, John Lewis and Stokely Carmichael came out of the SNCC movement. Carmichael, who died in 1998, had ties to the so-called "militant" Black Panther Party. Bond and Lewis both later ran for public office and Lewis continues to serve as a member of the US Congress. In 2005 while Bond was serving at the chairman of the NAACP, he eulogized Rosa Parks who has been called the "Mother of the Civil Rights Movement" and the catalyst to the introduction of a new civil rights leader, Dr. Martin L. King (*The Crisis*, 2005). [*The Crisis* magazine is the official magazine of the NAACP founded by W. E .B. DuBois in 1910]. John Lewis presided over SNCC from 1963-1966. In 1965, he helped to lead more than 600 non-violent protestors across the Edmund Pettis Bridge in Selma, Alabama. State troopers attacked the marchers in a conflict known as "Bloody Sunday." Lewis was beaten in the head with a trooper's billy club and survived. That march and subsequent protests led to the passage of the Voting Rights Act of 1965 (*The New Crisis Magazine*, 2002). James T. Patterson, in his introduction to *Debating the Civil Rights Movement, 1945-1968*, by Lawson and Payne (1998) said:

> Few developments of twentieth-century United States history are as controversial—or as important—as the quest for racial justice, or the civil rights movement, as we often call it, that gathered strength in mid-century and peaked in the 1960s. The struggle against white supremacy, as Charles Payne labels racial segregation, featured a host of angry activists, well-meaning white liberals, and determined defenders of the old ways. It produced soaring rhetoric, acts of astonishing personal courage, and a fair amount of violence and bloodshed. All Americans today live in a society that is much affected by these ... polarizing events (1).

I recall that in Charleston, Missouri in the 1960s, there was one movie theater and when it first opened Blacks were not allowed in, but perhaps for monetary reasons the owners changed their minds and decided that "Negroes", as we were called then, could come, but had to sit in the balcony—the main floor was reserved for Whites. I was a pubescent adolescent then and a few of my friends and I decided to go to the movies to check it out. (I vaguely remember that my mother was a little uneasy, but allowed me to go anyway). Oddly enough, we had so much fun that night!! Fun could have turned into disaster at any time. What we decided to do to show our anger at being told we had to sit in the balcony was throw popcorn down on the White people who sat in what management decided was the "best" place in the theater. I don't think we even watched the movie; we just bought popcorn to throw on the people below. It's a wonder that we didn't get arrested, but no one could tell who actually "did the deed" because the theater was dark. I don't recall if we were asked to leave, but I would venture to guess we were. I rejected the idea of someone telling me where I could and could not sit and for that reason that was my first and last time at the movies until years later when I came to live in Chicago. In college free movies were shown on campus for those of us who cared to go. The town of Tuskegee was just as racist as Charleston and I never even considering going to the movies there.

I first became aware of Tuskegee Institute through three of my Black teachers at Lincoln High School where all of the Black students were sent during their freshmen year. They told me how it would be possible for me to attend college even with lack of funds to pay for it. Tuskegee had a 5-year work study program for students like me who wanted to attend college and were willing to work their way through. That was when I began to question and care about the quality of the education I was receiving or rather not receiving at Lincoln, not because the Black teachers were any less qualified, but because of the scarcity of resources with which they had to work and poor leadership by the Black administration, " …meager materials, the inadequate facilities, the unequal funding of schools and teachers … and the failure of [white] school boards to respond to black parents requests …" (Walker 1996, 1) all speak to the inferior education African Americans received in public schools during the period of legal segregation. "The blatant lack of equality in school facilities and resources was, of course, a reflection of the unequal treatment of blacks in all aspects of American life" (2). My life was changed forever because these three teachers cared about me and my future. I didn't know it then, but they would be the only teachers throughout my years as a high school student to do so.

Critical Race Theory

Critical Race Theory (CRT) was developed in the 1970s by legal scholars Bell, Freeman and Delgado, as a way of adequately addressing the effects of race and racism on society while bringing about changes that would implement social justice (Decuir and Dixson 2004). Ladson-Billings and Tate (1995) are cited by Decuir and Dixon as arguing that by using the Critical Race Theory tenets to analyze inequity in education, it is easy to see how access to a highly rigorous curriculum "has been almost exclusively enjoyed by White students" (28). Critical Race Theory has become a method by which to analyze problems of the "color line." Trevino, Harris and Wallace (2008) see the "race" label as the manner by which people of color are controlled and restricted in American society (7).

Scientists have confirmed that Homo sapiens (human beings) are about 99.9% alike. According to Genesis: Chapters 1 and 2, in the King James Version of the Holy Bible, all human beings originated with the first man, Adam, and the first woman, Eve. Based on years of research, today archeologists say that life for all mankind began on the continent of Africa. Does that make us all sisters and brothers? Some would like to think so; others would cringe at the thought. Goodman (2008) noted the idea of "race categories", with some races being superior to others, "was a part of the dominant European world view." He goes further to say,

> This idea fit wealthy Europeans' belief in their own essential superiority to other peoples around the globe. It stuck because ideologies about racial superiority and inferiority supported their policies of taking away land (in the Americas) and wealth in Asia [and Africa] and rationalized the enslavement of Africans (5).

Singleton and Linton (2006) list several definitions related to race and racism. They describe the term *race* as the "socially constructed meaning attached to a variety of physical attributes including but not limited to skin and eye color, hair texture and bone structures of people in the United States and elsewhere" (39). In addition, Linton and Singleton "believe that *racism* is the conscious or unconscious, intentional or unintentional enactment of racial power, grounded in racial prejudice, by an individual or group against another individual or group perceived to have lower racial status" (40). I am reminded of the book, *The Help* (2009), written by Kathryn Stockett, which gives a fictional account of Black maids in Mississippi in the early 1960s during the time of the Civil Rights Movement, and how they were trusted to virtually raise "White folk's children", the most precious of all possessions, but were not allowed to use the indoor toilets in those homes. Yet these families did not think of themselves as racists. This story, though fictional, was accurate in its historical account of the Jim Crow laws which "enforced segregation and discrimination throughout the United States, especially the South, from the late nineteenth century to the 1960s" (Appiah and Gates 2003, 478), under the pretense of separate but equal. These laws stripped African Americans of "all social forms of respect." There were signs indicating "Whites Only" and "Colored Only" over water fountains and on restroom doors. Blacks were expected to "show deference" to Whites while Black men, young and old, were further humiliated by being referred to as "boys." Blacks faced housing and job discrimination and were denied the right to vote. Jim Crow eventually became an embarrassment to America, but it wasn't until the NAACP began to experience successful litigation in the 1950s challenging *Plessy v. Ferguson* that the Jim Crow laws and customs were struck down (Appiah and Gates, 2003). The US 1896 landmark Supreme Court decision in *Plessey v. Ferguson*—

> permitted states to institute racially separate public accommodations despite the Constitution's Fourteenth Amendment, which guarantees all citizens equal protection under the law. It would take nearly 60 years for the court to reverse itself in *Brown v. Board of Education* (1954), and over turn the

judicial precedent for segregation (Appiah and Gates 2003, 755).

According to Ladson-Billings (2006), almost everything in our society deals with race ix). As I write this dissertation there is a discussion in the mainstream media concerning the fact that the Mark Twain "classic", Huck Finn, has been republished (2010) and the "N-word", which appeared over 200 times, has been taken out. It seems the book, in recent years, has been taken off many public schools' reading lists because of the word which carries with it images of hatred and bigotry, and republishing the book is an effort to have the book returned to the shelves. Some say the word should be kept in because it takes away the authenticity of the work and it becomes historically incorrect. I don't believe racism will change in America by taking the word out of books if it is still in the hearts of men and women. The disease of racism shows up in every aspect of US life and even when we try to avoid it we are engaging it (Ladson-Billings 2006).

Culturally Relevant Pedagogy

I walked into Baker Elementary School (pseudonym) with "Angela Davis hair" for the first time as a substitute teacher. I was met at a side door by an African American man who I later learned was a teachers' aide. Before he even knew my name he told me "Female teachers don't wear pants." I had worn my best professional outfit, a brown pantsuit with a jacket that came down to my knees, and wondered what he was talking about. I had a big, beautiful afro hair style that I was very proud of, and I could tell by the way he looked at me that he didn't like that either. No one at the Board of Education Office had mentioned a dress code when I applied for the substitute teacher position. I learned later that he thought he was the "person in charge" of everything. It had taken me a long time to get my hair back to its "natural" state after using harmful chemicals to straighten it. During my last year of college, I shampooed my hair with anything and everything anyone suggested—vinegar, eggs, mayonnaise, because I wanted to get my hair back to its "nappiness" as a celebration of my culture, my Blackness, my rebelliousness. While I was participating in the civil rights demonstrations, I discovered that I no longer wanted to straighten my hair to look like White women's hair, but to wear it the way God gave it to me, kinky and bold—part of my racial identity development. In her study on why African American women try to obtain 'good hair' Bellinger (2007) remarked,

> [African Americans] ... in the 1960s began viewing hair as a political statement and a symbol of the Black Power Movement. Hair was used as a resistant strategy of White beauty standards (White 2005) and women such as Angela Davis became emblems of power and the struggle to overcome racism and challenge White supremacy. People showed their racial pride by wearing thick tall afros on their heads to attempt to alter racist stereotypes insisting Black people are monstrously ugly, undesirable, or even evil (hooks 1995). Hair became a symbol of power and recognition. In the 1990s, however, instead of being a symbol of power, afro hairstyles have to an extent become a symbol of delinquency for males and once again of lower status for females ... Straight hair is still the North American norm and is often needed to secure employment for African American women (65).

For more than twenty years I was a classroom teacher in a high-poverty Chicago public school where the student population was 100% African American. I never planned to be a teacher, but after working as a substitute teacher for a few months and discovering that teaching was a fulfilling job where I could earn a living and make a positive impact on these students' lives, I decided to return to school to take methods of teaching classes which I had never taken as a Political Science major in college. In this account I will take the reader on a journey of how experiencing the horrors of racism traumatized me and have had a life-long effect on my intrapersonal and interpersonal relationships, especially as it relates to my professional and instructional practices as an elementary school teacher.

One thing that was always very important to me was to help my students see their own beauty and strength, and see themselves capable of doing anything they set their minds to despite what they had heard on television or read in magazines about the non-abilities of Black folk. Irvine (2010) stated, "Culturally relevant teaching may indeed boost your students' self-esteem, but that's not why you should adopt it. You should adopt it because it will maximize student learning" (58). I let my students know that I had high expectations of them, and that even though my mother didn't have the money to send me, I had gone to college, and they could too. We talked about the history of Black people in America and Africa as a constant theme and not just because it was Black History month. I told them of my experiences of fighting racial injustice in high school and college and how I was able overcome the obstacles that were in my way, attend college and become a contributing member of society. "...culturally relevant teachers must also assist students in changing our society. When teachers promote justice they directly confront inequities such as racism, sexism, and classism" (61).

Throughout my years as a teacher my students were always made aware of their cultural heritage. We studied the kings and queens of ancient Africa and for one assembly my students modeled African clothing which I borrowed from an African clothing store. They took on the persona of kings and queens themselves that day. I signed up for a summer institute, "Teaching about Africa", to improve my knowledge of African history. "Culturally relevant teaching requires teachers to possess a thorough knowledge of the content and employ multiple representations of knowledge that use students' lived experiences to connect new knowledge to home, community, and global settings" (Irvine 2010, 59). By teaching my students about the continent of their ancestry, I developed a deep love for Africa and its people as well as African art and clothing. What I was teaching I was also learning and it affected me in a huge way. I decided that one day I would travel to West Africa, the place from which most Black Americans' ancestors came. And even though I was extremely afraid of flying then, I knew the only way I could get there would be to get over that fear. With a lot of prayer and affirmations I released that fear and visited the countries of Ghana and Côte d'Ivoire. A few years later I traveled to South Africa. Visiting Robben Island where Nelson Mandela, the first Black president of South Africa was imprisoned for twenty-seven years for speaking out against apartheid was especially moving for me.

My students and I learned the seven principles of Kwanzaa and performed them for assemblies. (Kwanzaa is not a religious holiday, but a celebration of African American heritage). Each year another class would learn the Swahili-named principles (Umoja-unity, Kujichagulia-self-determination, Ujima-collective work and responsibility, Ujama-collective economics, Nia-purpose, Kuumba-creativity and Imani-faith) and how they applied in their community and daily lives (Appiah and Gates 2003). It was encouraging that my efforts towards culturally relevant pedagogy were always supported by parents, administration and other teachers in the school. One day a little girl at school said to me in her tiny voice, "Teacher, I like the way you teach about Africa." She must have been in first or second grade and had been to one or several of the assemblies where my students lit Kwanzaa candles or modeled African clothing. I was proud that something I had done mainly for my class had carried over to other children—I knew I was doing the right thing. Hyland (2009) points out—

> Culturally relevant teachers share a belief that children are capable of academic excellence, which is matched with classroom practices that insure high academic performance. They view knowledge as socially constructed and teach their students to critically analyze information ... they root learning in issues relevant to the students' lives and help students

> make connections between their home community
> and broader national and global issues (97).

I believe my experiences in high school and college and the connection I felt with my own African heritage led to my strong advocacy for the children in my classroom and in my school. My life experiences impacted my teaching in numerous ways. In 1987 when the Chicago Teachers Union went on strike for nineteen days I started a "freedom school" for the students who went to the school where I taught. Although I believed in the strike, and I took my turn on the picket line in front of the school, I felt students had been out of school too long and we didn't know when the strike would end. I spoke to the pastor at a neighborhood church about holding classes there for students who wanted to come. He agreed and I convinced a few of my colleagues to join me and we held classes in the church basement until the strike ended. I believed then and now, as Hinchey (1998) related, "However cynical many Americans have become, critical theorist argue that it is still reasonable to work towards a more just, ethical, and moral world" (140).

Because of my religious upbringing, I was taught that the color of one's skin is not important, but what is important is what one harbors in his heart. While, in essence, I still believe that to be true, I can understand the view of Lindsey, Robins and Terrell in *Cultural Proficiency* (2009), when they say, "As a result of many educators' blindness to the cultural differences among students, many students feel discounted or invisible in school" (117). And while as an elementary school teacher I mostly taught African American children who had been raised with values similar to mine, when Haitian children became a part of several of my classes, I still saw them as Black children, but I was cognizant that their cultural background was different than mine and their classmates, and I did what I could to honor their culture. I developed a good rapport with the Haitian bilingual teacher whom I knew was on the staff but had had no previous relationship with, and asked him to assist me in serving the educational needs of my Haitian students. More details regarding the instructional practices focused on my Haitian students are chronicled in the autoethnograpic vignettes portion of this work.

Tracking and Re-segregation

In my studies as a doctoral student I discovered a large, urban high school where students were being racially segregated as a result of the school's academic tracking system. Students at this school are tracked from the moment they make application to the high school, and most students stay with those groups throughout their four years in high school. According to Oakes (2005),

> ... tracking is something more than a flawed schooling practice—an anomaly that might be rooted out or reformed out of schooling's structural repertoire. Indeed, it is the social consequences of tracking—sorting students according to preconceptions based on race and social class and providing them with different and unequal access—as much as the organizational or pedagogical details that matter most (xi).

And so, although in this school when students walk down the hallways on their way to classes there is a beautiful multiculturalism mix of students, when the bell rings most of the students of color go into the lower track rooms and White students go into the higher track rooms. Darling-Hammond (2010) addresses this problem in *The Flat World of Education* when she states:

> In racially mixed schools, curriculum tracks are generally color-coded. Honors or advanced courses are reserved primarily for White students, while the lower tracks (basic, remedial, or vocational) are disproportionately filled with students of color. Unequal access to high-level courses and challenging curriculum explains much of the difference in achievement between minority students and

> White students, as coursetaking is strongly related
> to achievement, and there are large race-based
> differences among students in coursetaking from an
> early age, especially in such areas as mathematics,
> science, and foreign language (52).

One of the requirements of my doctoral program was an internship with a sitting superintendent to learn how to carry out the day-to-day responsibilities should I desire to take on that position after receiving my doctorate degree. I sought out the superintendent of the aforementioned high school because of the school's connection to my own story as a high school student. I learned of the superintendent's courageous efforts to de-track the school with both equity and excellence as the focus beginning in the 2012 school season, and he was open to my request to serve as an intern in his school to watch the process unfold. And although it is called academic tracking in that school, the results are same as what I had experienced as a teenager— racially segregated schooling. According to Rubin (2006),

> Tracking has frequently been critiqued as providing
> inadequate and inequitable education to students in
> lower ability tracks, for separating students along race
> and class lines, and for perpetuating unequal access to
> a college-bound curriculum. De-tracking is a reform
> in which students are placed intentionally in mixed-
> ability, heterogeneous classes, in an attempt to remedy
> the negative effects of tracking (4).

At Middleton District High School (MDHS), (pseudonym), the administration recognizes that teaching practices and expectations are different for White students than for African American and Latino students in some classrooms. For White students it is a great school, but many of the Black and Brown students are failing. Although it has its critics, thanks to *No Child Left Behind* (NCLB) "good schools" can no longer hide their failure to educate minority students. Rubin in Pollack's *Everyday Racism* (2008) states:

> Researchers argue that students in lower tracks, often low income students and students of color are denied well-taught, challenging college preparatory curricula, while students in the higher tracks, who often are mainly White and middle class, take part in a rigorous curriculum taught by more experienced and skilled teachers. When classes are detracked, diverse students are brought together in an attempt to remedy the inequalities caused by tracking. However, students can bring damaging ideas about one another from broader societal contexts, as well as differences in academic preparation resulting from years of difference in instructional quality (90).

At the high school in the 2010-2011 school year, all meetings, all professional development training and anything that had to do with students was being filtered through the race and equity lens. Many of the teachers seemed to be on board with improving the school for all students, but there was much work to be done. The superintendent plans were to begin de-tracking with the ninth grade in the next school year to make MDHS more equitable for non-Whites and a better school overall. Jeannie Oakes, said to be the country's leading expert on tracking, states in *Keeping Track: How Schools Structure Inequality* (2005),

> In our quest for higher standards and superior academic performance we seem to have forgotten that schools cannot be excellent as long as there are groups of children who are not well served by them. In short, we cannot have educational excellence until we have educational equality (xvi).

The school community surrounding MDHS has a long history of strained racial relations and the superintendent will more than likely have a political fight on his hands trying to bring about this change. I would like those who read my work to know and understand that the current struggle to provide a quality education for African American, Latino and other minority students is in a different time period, but sadly not much different than it was when I was a high school student more than fifty years ago; it's just that it's not politically correct today to be as obviously racially prejudiced as it was back then.

The origins of tracking in the United States (Darling-Hammond 2010) can be traced by to the early 1900s as an effort by the privileged and powerful in society to separate Italian, Polish and other immigrants, along with Indians, Blacks and Mexicans—those who were lower on the socioeconomic ladder and therefore thought to be less "intelligent", from the masses of the White advantaged, and to assign them to vocational and industrial training. And so schools became sorting institutions where privileged students were selected to be taught to think critically, while the more disadvantaged students who were not taught to think for themselves, learned to just regurgitate information, and eventually fell into the unskilled labor ranks. According to Oakes (2005),

> The assumptions about the native abilities and appropriate future places of the poor and minorities that so influenced the form of the high school at the turn of the century may have changed considerably, but the mechanisms we use for sorting and selecting students for school programs and instructional groups have remained the same. So have the results (39).

"Towards a Single Nation", Coffin (1968), was written the year Dr. Martin Luther King, Jr. was assassinated, but could have been written in 2011, with very minor changes. In the article he addressed the failure of the White community to understand the depth and intensity of the institutionalized racism that existed in the schools. Coffin challenged parents to thumb through their children's textbooks, and not just the reading books, but other textbooks as well. "It is all white—not just white people, but white situations, white institutions, white frames of references, and 'white is right' conclusions." He noted that change is always difficult and that people are resistant to "changing the status quo", moreover White parents are fearful and emotional when it comes to the integration of White kids and Black and Brown kids in the same school or classroom. They run scared and ask, "Will my property value go down? [This is one of the products of institutionalized racism]. Will my children's habits, morals, language, and personal values be affected? Will the quality of my children's education be diminished?" (144-146). Some parents are still asking the same questions today. They have not realized that their children live in a multicultural world and as adults will need to know how to navigate a multicultural global society. The stereotypes still exist that Blacks are not as intelligent as Whites; Black parents don't care about their children, etc. Sadly, the stereotypes are perpetuated by tracking which mostly minority students experience. Students know what their track placement says about them; that the adults in the school don't have much faith in their ability, usually based on one test taken somewhere in their past. In an October 1992 article for *Educational Leadership* magazine entitled "On Tracking and Individual Differences: A Conversation with Jeannie Oakes", Jon O'Neil interviews Oakes who describes tracking as a harmful practice where students are publicly placed in groups which say they are in the top, middle or low group in the hierarchy of the school's culture. She states, "And often in the culture of the schools, the 'top group' quickly becomes the 'top kids', in a very value-laden way. So the students take their place in the hierarchy and the values associated with it" (1). She argues that this sorting can begin as early as kindergarten where some children are said to be "ready for kindergarten" and some are placed in "developmental" kindergarten. It is here that the disparities begin and different groups of children are taught in a very different way. In her decades of research on tracking, Oakes found that children in the top tracks are engaged in "hands-on and critical thinking activities" while students in the bottom tracks are flooded with low-level worksheets, teachers are passive and the curriculum is fragmented and disconnected.

At Middleton District High School administrators and staff worked feverously to have everything in place to begin de-tracking the ninth grade humanities classes in the 2012 school year. It will take a great deal of professional development, curriculum mapping and changing of mind sets to succeed, but they are well on their way led by a dynamic superintendent who has shown great courage and passion in this endeavor. Oakes, 2005, after twenty-five years of researching and writing about tracking in schools still believes that, "Public schools remain our best hope for achieving a free and democratic society in which all have decent lives and rich opportunities" (299). MDHS and schools like it which have begun the trek down the road to de-tracking may meet with opposition. As expected, some community members whose children attend the school have fought, during school board hearings, to keep the tracking system in place. Educators may be in for a tough fight which will require courageous leaders, and those willing to commit to staying in it for as long as it takes, to undo the injustices tracking has caused (Oakes 2005). "Today, not only have the gaps between the wealthy and poor Americans widened, but the neighborhoods and schools in most parts of the country are more segregated racially than they were in 1985 (299)." Those who think they are safe in their little corner of America are in for a rude awakening. Education for all its citizenry has become increasingly a crucial issue for the United States as a whole. The way other nations view us is as one nation, not a White nation or a Black nation—as a world leader we must do better when it comes to educating all of our children. Darling-Hammond (2010) offers this cautionary advice—

> For the United States to make progress on its long-standing inequities, we will need to make the case to one another that none of us benefits by keeping any of us ignorant, and as a society, all of us profit from the full development of one another's abilities ... The

path to our mutual well-being is built on educational opportunity. Central to our collective future is the recognition that our capacity to thrive ultimately depends on ensuring to all of our people what should be an unquestioned entitlement—a rich and inalienable right to learn" (328).

How Then Shall We Overcome?

Tatum's *Can We Talk about Race and Other Conversations in an Era of School Resegregation* (2007), as well as Singleton and Linton's *Courageous Conversations about Race* (2006), speak to the importance of educators and policy makers having conversations about racial relations in America. Race is the "elephant in the room" that most people, when in mixed-race environments, don't like to talk about. It makes for an uncomfortable situation in the corporate workplace, in schools and in classrooms, so we just don't talk about it.   As one African American community activist once said, 'Don't you realize how much better we could be, how much farther along we could be, if we didn't invest so much time and energy into racism'? (Singleton and Linton 2006, x). Perhaps the thinking is if we keep it "under the covers" we won't have to deal with race and the history of racism in America. Teachers have been encouraged in the past, not to see color and that they should be "color blind" when in fact one of the best things a teacher can do for a child is to see them as they truly are and accept that everyone, regardless of "race, creed or color" deserves to be treated with dignity and respect and that our children, all of them, deserve the best education we can provide. James A. Banks, as cited in Darling-Hammond's *The Flat World and Education* (2010) states: "If we can improve race relations and help all students acquire the knowledge, attitudes and skills needed to participate in cross-cultural interactions and in personal, social, and civic action, we will create a more democratic and just society" (xi). Those who are only concerned with the progress of their own non-minority children are in for a "big reveal." As a nation we are all connected in one way or another, if by nothing else but terrorists' threats and gas prices. "In the 30-year period between 1973 and 2004, the percentage of students of color in US public schools increased from 22 to 43 percent. If current trends continue, students of color will equal or exceed the percentage of White students in US public schools within two decades" (Sykes 2010, Darling-Hammond 2010, x). Accordingly, if we are to succeed as a nation ready to compete in a 21st Century global society, we must educate all of our children and educate them well. If we fail to rise to this challenge, we as a nation will suffer the consequences. Gergen (2009), in the foreword to Childress, Doyle and Thomas's *Leading for Equity* laments—

> We are kidding ourselves in not calling it [our failure to educate millions of students] a national scandal … by 2050—just over forty years from now—whites will compose less than half the population of the country. In most major urban systems, minorities are already well over half of all students. Yet the starkest differences in educational opportunity and achievement are those between African American, Hispanic, and other minority children (v).

In my experience much of the educational literature speaks of the achievement gap between minority and White students, but not enough researchers talk about the "opportunity and resources" gap and the gap that institutional racism perpetuates. Failure to educate all of our children to their highest potential can "do more harm to the country than any outside enemy could inflict" (Gergen 2009, v).

In "Integrated Schools: Finding a New Path", Orfield, Frankenberg, and Siegel-Hawley (2010) begin by stating that segregated schools are almost always separated by race and poverty. They argue that fifty years after *Brown v. Board of Education, Brown* still has not reached its goal even though some school districts have spent countless hours over the past 50+ years, trying to achieve equity in their schools and some are experiencing diversity for the first time, yet the US Department of Education, as well as the Office of Civil Rights has failed to provide support for those districts continuing to pursue integration. They found that the research continues to show separate is not equal and that segregated schools limit both minority and White students in their understanding of other cultures. In a 2007 National Academy of Education report, a committee lead by educational researchers Linn and Welner (2007) concluded "students in integrated schools are more likely to be exposed to challenging advanced courses and, as a result, are more likely to have higher test scores, graduate, and succeed in college" [and in the real world] (24).

"Re-segregation: What's the Answer", an article published in *Educational Leadership* magazine (2010), was co-written by educational researchers Jonathan Kozol, Beverly Daniel Tatum, Susan Eaton, and Patricia Gandara. Kozol, author of *The Shame of the Nation* (2005) and *Savage Inequalities* (1992) said that resegregation "is at its highest level since the death of Dr. Martin Luther King, Jr. in 1968." He believed the answers to resegregation lay with the White House and President Obama. He suggested that the government should create enticing incentives to encourage wealthy suburban schools to admit students of color from poor neighborhoods. He believed that charter schools, favored by the White House, were even more segregated than most public schools and that magnet schools had failed to advance diversity. He stated that we need to battle " … practices [such as zoning] that perpetuate residential segregation and consign the black and brown and poor to isolated neighborhoods in which they are intentionally sequestered so that they cannot contaminate the lives and education of the privileged" (29). In *The Shame of the Nation,* Kozol says that he holds out hope that all is not lost in classrooms where there are promising exchanges between caring teachers and eager children in schools he calls "treasured places." He argues that school segregation is still the rule for poor minorities and believes it may take a new Civil Rights Movement with "like-minded politicians, educators and advocates" to eliminate it.

Also offering her opinion, Beverly Daniel Tatum, past President of Spelman College in Atlanta, Georgia and the author of *Can We Talk*

About Race? And Other Conversations in an Era of School Resegregation (2008), posits that not much can be done about resegregation without "housing policies that encourage the development of racially integrated neighborhoods" (30). She says that after *Brown v. Board of Education* in 1954, desegregation of schools was largely a result of busing and other orders from the Supreme Court. However the courts could not stop White flight from urban schools and segregated housing patterns have caused many schools to remain segregated. She also believes that children of color should not be denied a quality education because of where they live. "The presence of white children should not be required to ensure students have adequate facilities, a challenging curriculum, well-qualified teachers, and a learning atmosphere conducive to success" (30). Tatum believes, as I believe, that the key to success for children of color is high expectations from teachers, administrators and parents, and that a multicultural learning environment teaches students to interact with others different from themselves. However, if the school climate is not one where White children and Black and Brown children are expected to perform at high levels a "reinforcement of racial hierarchies and ideology about assumed inferiority and superiority" is the lesson these children will learn. Her concluding thought is that we must invest in the potential of all children in order to compete in a global economy (Tatum 2008, Darling-Hammond 2010, Wagner 2008).

Susan Eaton, research director at the Huston Institute for Race and Justice at Harvard Law School and author of *The Children in Room E4: American Education on Trial* (2009), gave these thoughts on eradicating resegregation. She stated that concerned educators can begin by joining civil rights organizations that advocate for greater funding and commitment to racial diversity in federal policy. Her organization, the National Coalition on School Diversity (NCSD), calls for "increased funding for voluntary, public magnet schools to enroll a diverse student body ... and issue official guidance on how local school boards can legally achieve racial diversity (30)." Eaton suggests that educators should be supporters for fair and reasonable housing and work to change laws that foster segregation. She says that children in high-poverty segregated schools should be provided the same opportunities middle-class White children have in order to close the achievement gap.

Patricia Gandara, professor of education and the co-director of the Civil Rights Project at the University of California, says in the article, "it [resegregation] is harmful to all children who will need the skills and experiences to live and work in a multicultural nation" (31). She believes there are two factors driving the rise in resegregation of schools: 1) the political climate which has furthered the acceptance of school segregation by making it seem "un-American" to relocate students to schools for integration purposes and 2) housing practices which support segregated neighborhoods. (Yet many students ride buses everyday in order to attend their school of choice). She also suggests dual language immersion schools which naturally integrate students because middle-class parents want their children in classes which will help them become multilingual. In a final analysis, Gandara believes that integration is absolutely necessary for the future of public education.

DuBois asserted years ago that the utmost problem of the 20th century was the "color line." The challenge to us at the dawn of the 21st Century is to continue the fight for racial equity by eradicating the various color lines that divide us as a nation. A multicultural generation of students is now entering school. Most of these students are Latino, 25%, and Black, 16%, with the highest percentage of students identified as being multiracial, making the *Brown* decision more important now than any other time in history (Orfield, Frankenberg, and Siegel-Hawley 2010).

In the interest of global economic development and student achievement in the US, a May 2011 report was issued regarding a recent study entitled: *Standing on the Shoulders of Giants: An American Agenda for Education Reform,* by Marc S. Tucker and a research team from the National Center on Education and the Economy. This study set out to answer the question: "What would the education policies and practices of the United States be if they were based on the policies and practices of the countries that now lead the world in student performance" (3)? US Secretary of Education, Arne Duncan asked the Organization for Economic Cooperation and Development (OECD) to produce this report based on the countries that currently outperform the US in student achievement on international tests. Among the countries studied were "Canada (focusing on Ontario), China (focusing on Shanghai), Finland, Japan and Singapore (3)." The research approach the team took was as follows:

> We contrast [ed] the strategies that appear to be driving the policy agendas of the most successful countries with the strategies that appear to be driving the current agenda for education reform in the United States. We conclude[d] that the strategies driving the best performing systems are rarely found in the United States, and, conversely, that the education strategies now most popular in the United States are conspicuous by their absence in the countries with the most successful education systems (4).

The team acknowledged that there are pockets of excellence in education in the United States but not on the large scale required to compete as a nation globally. The US comes up lacking when it comes to "policy systems that make for effective education systems." Unlike researcher, Jonathan Kozol, who believes the shortcomings in educating America's children falls on the shoulders of the federal government, those who studied these high-performing countries "believe the main player has got to be state government. When we speak of changing the system, it is the states, not the national government, we have in mind" (4).

This report applauds the Congress and Obama Administration's *Race to the Top* program for states and the development of Common Core State Standards and Assessments as a great beginning toward improved student achievement in America's schools. The researchers credited Secretary Duncan with calling attention to the high-performing countries and studying how they get results.

Some of these countries have caught up to and exceeded US student performance. The report suggests that the US federal government provide assistance to states which lack the resources to execute the following:

- implement programs to improve teacher preparation,
- provide schools that are untracked and open to children of all races and socioeconomic levels,
- supply funds for capacity-building professional development for teachers and administrators,
- support school-to-work programs, and
- create a weighted school finance system to insure equity in school funding (40-42).

Our nation's major downfall, according to this report, is lack of teachers who are qualified to teach the students who, in the not too distant future, will be competing for jobs on the international stage. "Only those who can offer the world's highest skill levels and the world's most creative ideas will be able to justify the world's highest wages (5)." The report also recommends that teachers should be recruited from the best of college students, that there should be better pre-service programs for teachers, better professional training, more professionalism and reverence for those in the teaching field, (just as for those in law or medicine), competitive salaries, and greatly improved working conditions. If these recommendations are followed it will change everything: the standards for entering teachers colleges, the institutions which do the training, who is recruited, the nature of the training offered to teachers, the structure and the amount of their compensation, the way they are brought into the workforce, the structure of the profession itself, the nature of teachers' unions, the authority of teachers, the way they teach and much more. And then there's race and class which can never be forgotten when speaking about education in America's schools. Accordingly, *Standing on the Shoulders of Giants: An American Agenda for Education* offers this proposal:

> These [high-achieving] nations have also realized that this formulation means that very high wage nations must now abandon the idea that only a few of their citizens need to have high skills and creative capacities. This is a new idea in the world, the idea that *all* must have an education formerly reserved only for elites. It leads to abandonment of education systems designed to reach their goals by sorting students, by giving only some students intellectually demanding curricula, by recruiting only a few teachers who are themselves educated to high levels, and by directing funding toward the easiest to educate and denying it to those hardest to educate. It is this fundamental change in the goals of education that has been forcing an equally fundamental change in the design of national and provincial education systems (5).

Tony Wagner, author of *The Global Achievement Gap* (2008) and co-director of the Change Leadership Group at the Harvard Graduate School of Education, has listed seven abilities which he deems "survival skills" that our children need to compete in the 21st Century global job market, but are not getting from even the best schools in America. Those skills are: *"critical thinking and problem-solving, collaboration across networks and leading by influence, agility and adaptability, initiative and entrepreneurialism, effective oral and written communication, accessing and analyzing information and curiosity and imagination."* Wagner says that our schools are "dangerously obsolete" and that the number one problem in our schools is "the problem of practice" or teacher quality. He states, "… the quality of teachers' preparation, continuing professional development, and supervision is very low in our nation's schools" (52). His message is that to improve student learning we must improve teaching by agreeing on what "good teaching" looks like. Wagner offers this statement:

Focusing teaching and learning on the new survival skills, having better tests that assess the skills that matter most, and reinventing how we prepare educators, as well as how they work together, are all necessary if we are serious about eliminating the global achievement gap (166).

Wagner doesn't spend much time addressing equity in schools or the racial achievement gap, but he does say " ... closing the other achievement gap in this country—the gap between white middle class students' achievement and that of poor, predominantly minority students—requires a better understanding of each group and their needs" (200). While he believes this gap is mostly about race and class, he also thinks students are pre-programmed to succeed or fail by family circumstances, teachers who have low expectations, and the over-management or under-management of adult authority. Wagner affirms, "There are, of course, many students of color who are very successful, just as there are white students who struggle" (204). Wagner's goal seems to be to provide a roadmap for navigating our future as a successful nation where all students are taught the skills to survive in a global society and not just a few students in flourishing schools here and there. Paraphrasing what John Dewey spoke over a century ago and which still holds true today—*what the wisest want for their own children must be what the community wants for all its children.*

In concluding this chapter I quote author, bell hooks, who sums up what has to take place if we as a nation are ever to overcome racial injustice and transform our schools and our world: She says—

All of us in the academy and in the culture as a whole are called to renew our minds if we are to transform educational institutions—and society—so that the way we live, teach, and work can reflect our joy in cultural diversity, our passion for justice and our love of freedom (34).

Seemingly bell hooks has been influenced by Romans 12: 2 in the *Holy Bible* which says: "Be ye transformed by the renewing of your mind." King (1996) adds, "With hope above to inspire us, faith around to encourage us, convictions beneath us to sustain us, love within us to guide us, and with God in front of us to direct us, we will overcome (170).

CHAPTER TWO

METHODOLOGY

Why Autoethnography?

The research method which best fits my desire to tell the story of my personal experiences with Black/White racial hatred and prejudice, first as a teenager and then as an adult living in America, is autoethnography. What is autoethnography? Autoethnography is an emerging method of qualitative inquiry, while ethnography is said to be the oldest method of qualitative inquiry (Patton 2002). "... ethnography is 'devoted to describing ways of life of humankind'" (81). It is a branch of anthropology which studies human beings and their environment or culture (Patton 2002). The prefix "auto" is defined as "self"; accordingly autoethnography is "studying [describing] one's own culture and oneself as part of that culture and its many variations" (Patton, 85). Coia and Taylor (2007) contend that autoethnography focuses on the experiences of self in a larger social context. Racism in America, the theme that runs throughout my story, certainly fits into such a category. Holt (2003) references Reed-Danahay who describes autoethnography as a "genre of writing and research that connects the personal to the cultural, placing the self within a social context" (2).

I had not considered sharing my story in a dissertation format until two of my college professors suggested I should. It all started when I wrote an essay about my leadership journey in my first class as a doctoral student. I believe that journey began when I was sixteen years old. Had it not been for my National Louis-University instructors, who took the time to show interest and provide support, I probably would have written about some current trend in education, but I would not have had the passion that I have for the topic on which I now research and write. I was not aware that doctoral, but I would not have had the passion that I have for the topic on which I now research and write. I was not aware that doctoral students could write about their life experiences as a legitimate qualitative study until then. When I first heard that I could write an "autoethnography", my excitement grew that someone thought my story was an important one that should be told. I questioned what was said because I had thought my dissertation would have had some "lofty educational title" where no one really knew what I was talking about, but would let others know how "deep" I was when they asked what my dissertation was about.

I am forever grateful to have been given an opportunity through autoethnography to tell the story of my lived experiences with racial hatred and racial discrimination first as a high school student and then as a participant in the Civil Rights Movement as a college student. It's a story not unlike what was experienced by many African Americans who lived before my time, as well as those who lived through and perhaps participated in the Movement, and those who are still experiencing racism right now, today, this minute.

In two recent conversations with educators in my same age group, when they learned that my dissertation was about my experiences with racism, I learned that one of them participated in "sit-ins" in the 60s and helped to integrate the Woolworth's lunch counter in Jackson, Mississippi and the other attended a predominately White Catholic elementary school in Chicago where even though her parents paid tuition, she was still not welcomed and remembers being unhappy as a child because she was treated badly because of her race. Another colleague, who was born and raised in Alabama shared that he never had a "new" book in school until he went to high school. All of his books in elementary school were old books sent to his "Black" school from the "White" school. It is my hope that through my voice their voices and others, who have experienced racial hatred in America, will be heard and our struggle not forgotten, but read about and discussed and remembered as a time to which we, as a nation, do not wish to return.

As mentioned earlier in this account, my research problem addresses how my lived experiences with blatant racism as a high school student and experiences as a non-violent participant in the 1960s Civil Rights Movement as a college student, have impacted my life experiences—self image, racial identity development, spiritual development, intra- and inter- personal relationships, academic achievement, career choice, professional practices and doctoral internship. I chose this method of study because it is the one which will best allow me to share the narrative of my first personal experiences with racism as a sixteen year old high school student who, by court order, left a mediocre Black high school, along with thirteen others, to help integrate a first-rate White high school in Charleston, Missouri in 1962. A court order got us into the school, but what we suffered on the inside could only be understood if you were there. It was racism at its very best—a true oxymoron. I would like to share how the experiences of being called names on a daily basis, having tomatoes thrown at me and the other Black students, and having to face racial hatred everyday from one person or another for two whole years in that school, has impacted my life. Through my story, I will take the reader on a journey and let them see how experiencing "open, in-your-face" racism can traumatize and have a life-long effect on the relationships of those who experience it, and especially as it relates to my instructional practices and interpersonal, interracial relationships as an elementary school teacher. This exploration will also help me to develop a better understanding of myself and others with whom I interact. Chang (2008) says it this way:

> Given a clear understanding that autoethnography is
> a rigorous ethnographic, broadly qualitative research
> method that attempts to achieve in-depth cultural
> understanding of self and others, this inquiry has
> much to offer to social scientists, especially those

concerned with raising cross-cultural understanding in a culturally diverse society (57).

In autoethnography the researcher is the main character, the storyteller and narrator of personal experiences. The autoethnographer is both a "producer and a product" (Patton, 87) of the text. "...autoethnographers struggle to find a distinct voice by documenting their own experiences in an increasingly all-encompassing and commercialized global culture" (Patton, 91). In "Fitting the Methodology with the Research: An Exploration of Narrative, Self-study and Auto-ethnography" by Hamilton et al. (2008), Reed-Danahay is documented as speaking of autoethnography as a "postmodern" ethnography. In the postmodern outlook there are numerous ways of capturing knowledge as opposed to one method of inquiry as in the positivist approach where there is strict adherence to the scientific method, and the natural sciences are *the* paradigm for educational inquiry (Briggs and Coleman 2007). Patton (2002) further explains the postmodern era with this statement:

> Belief in science as generating truth was one of the cornerstones of modernism … Postmodernism attacked this faith in science by questioning its capacity to generate truth because, in part like all human communications, it is dependent upon language, which is socially constructed and, as such distorts reality. Postmodernism asserts that no language, not even that of science can provide a direct window through which one can view reality (100).

The history of qualitative research in North American literature can be explained in seven phases:

- Phase One—1900s traditional period when researchers aimed to present objective data from field experiences.

- Phase Two—the modernist phase (1970) which was concerned with qualitative research being as rigorous as quantitative research
- Phase Three—(1970-1986) concerned with maintaining a separation of the genres
- Phase Four—(mid 1980s) characterized by crises of "representation (writing practices) and legitimation (reliability, validity, objectivity)"
- Phase Five—experimental writing and participatory research
- Phases Six and Seven—post experimental and future, whereby fictional ethnographies and ethnographic poetry are taken for granted (Holt 2003, 3).

I also believe the autoethnographic method is the best choice for my study because it also allows options in writing styles and provides opportunity for non-traditional forms of query and expression (Wall 2006). It lends itself to creative and non-traditional writing which allows me to tell my story without the limitations of some other methodologies. It allows me to express my artistic, creative self. Ellis and Bocher (2000) maintain, as cited in Patton (2002), that "Usually written in first-person voice, autoethnographic texts appear in a variety of forms—short stories, poetry, fiction, novels, photographic essays, personal essays, journals, fragmented and layered writing, and social science prose" (86). I have chosen to include narrative, poetry and vignette in this study which speak to specific life events where I share my thoughts, feelings and emotions in that period of time. Autoethnography is autobiography with the author paying close attention to the "culture" connection (Patton 2002). Goodall (2000) sees autoethnography as a creative saga which comes from personal experiences inside a culture and addresses not only the academic community, but also the public (as cited in Patton 2002, 85). It also forces the researcher to ask: "How does my own experience of this culture connect with and offer insights about this culture, situation, event, and/or way of life" (Patton, 132)?

Autoethnography also calls for reflexivity—self-reflection and self-awareness—as an innermost premise while observing oneself. Reflexivity is a way of looking back on self and reflecting on relationships with others more deeply (Ellis and Bocher 2000, Chang 2008). Patton (2002) describes it this way—

> ... reflexivity [is] one of the central strategic themes of contemporary, postmodern qualitative inquiry. The term reflexivity has entered the qualitative lexicon as a way of emphasizing the importance of self-awareness ... and ownership of one's perspective. Reflexivity reminds the qualitative inquirer to observe herself or himself so as to be attentive to and conscious of the cultural, political, social, linguistic, and ideological origins of her or his own perspective and voice ... (299).

My autoethnography is a study of the life and times of one person, along with others I have met along the way. It also speaks to the culture of a people and the national climate in which it is set. "Culture [includes] evidence of shared patterns of thought, symbol, and action typical of a particular group" (Hamilton, Smith and Worthington 2008, 22).

It is my expectation that this writing will serve as a resource to teachers and students of all races and nationalities as they learn about race and racism in America, particularly as it relates to the *Brown v. Board of Education* Supreme Court decision (1954), the 1960s Civil Rights Movement and the everyday experiences of African Americans in the USA. "Studying others invariably invites readers to compare and contrast themselves with others in the cultural texts [and contexts] they read and study, in turn discovering new dimensions of their own lives" (Chang 2008, 34.)

It is my wish for those who read my work to know that the struggle over how to educate minority students is not much different today than it was nearly 6 decades ago when I was a high school student; they don't call you "that word" *out loud* and throw tomatoes at you anymore, but as Tatum (2002) states it " …Racism still systematically provides white people with greater access to education, employment, housing, quality health care, and media representation, just to name a few examples"(216). And some educational systems still use high school tracking as a means of separating the students who they think "can learn and be successful", from the ones who can't and probably won't—in other words, the Black and Brown students from the White students. The fight for equity in schooling is far from over—reason enough to believe it is important to tell my story. No one can tell this exact story; it is uniquely mine. Perhaps it will shine a light and offer a perspective that some have never seen or thought of in quite this way before. Someone once said, "When we know better we do better." If only that statement proves to be true. Professor Terry Jo Smith (National Louis University, 2010) renders this perspective on new insights:

> For what is researching really, but active and intentional learning with the hope of making the world, including the world of the classroom, a more interesting, challenging, just and loving place … When teachers spin experiences into stories about schooling, they create text that can provide insight into dimensions of education which have often been overlooked. Stories have morals, beliefs, concerning what is good and what is not. Through story we can address moral dimensions of education from within the contexts of particular lives; lives that have feelings, lives that have histories, lives that exist within culture and community, lives that have gender, and lives that are connected to other lives through relationships which are multiple, complex, paradoxical and fascinating (Smith, 2010 PowerPoint on Epistemology, slide 42 & 44).

Epistemology

> Epistemology … is a branch of philosophy that
> investigates the origin, nature, methods, and
> limits of human knowledge. Such beliefs influence
> the development of knowledge because they are
> considered to be the central values or theories that
> are functionally connected to most other beliefs
> and knowledge (Hofer & Pintrich 1997).Our own
> personal [educational] epistemology influences our
> own theories of learning, and consequently, how we
> approach, design, and deliver our classes. The terms
> used to describe epistemological positions vary,
> depending on whether it's describing the origin or
> the acquisition of knowledge (http://www.ucdoer.
> ie/index. php/Education Theory/Epistemology and
> Learning Theorie).

I have discovered through my doctoral work at National Louis
University that I am a critical theorist at my core. Patton's (2002)
explanation of critical theory resonates with me clearly when he says:

> The 'critical' nature of critical theory flows from a
> commitment to go beyond just studying society
> for the sake of increased understanding. Critical
> theorists set out to use research to critique society,
> raise consciousness, and change the balance of power
> in favor of the less powerful (548).

My epistemological stance [here] is mostly that of storyteller as this
is a study of my lived experiences with racial discrimination from early
childhood through the present day. I have endeavored to depict event,
time, and place "authentically in all its complexity while being self-
analytical, politically aware, and reflexive in consciousness" (Patton, 41).
Smith's (2010) definition of reflexivity resonates with me most

when I reflect on how I am learning and changing as a result of this study when she says,

> Personal reflexivity involves reflecting upon the ways in which our own values, experiences, interests, beliefs, political commitments, wider aims in life and social identities have shaped the research. It also involves thinking about how the teaching/research may have affected and possibly changed us, as people and as researchers (Smith, 2010 NLU, PowerPoint Slide #43).

I have concluded that I am continuously reflecting and continuously changing with each story I tell and with every paragraph I write. Chang (2008) explains storytelling in autoethnography in these terms:

> Stemming from the field of anthropology, autoethnography shares the storytelling feature with other genres of self-narrative but transcends mere narration of self to engage in cultural analysis and interpretation. It is this analytical and interpretive nature that ... distinguish [es] ... autoethnography from other self-narratives (43).

My research included documents such as newspapers from the Charleston, Missouri public library which were published in October of 1962, and I sought out television documentaries from the Civil Rights Era as well as relevant court cases such as *Brown v. Board of Education I and II*, and the actual court documents from the integration case against the Charleston, Missouri Board of Education of which I was a part. I also asked my [hard to call it my] high school to send copies of my permanent record and transcript so that I could examine those. I had questions about how the law suit came about and why there were only14 students who were involved in the case. I wondered how the Charleston High experience impacted their lives. These questions assisted me in analyzing and documenting my story of helping to integrate an all-White high school and its significance to the resegregation of schools today— many years later.

Through a critical theory lens I addressed how my high school experiences led me to attend Tuskegee Institute in Alabama, and how as a college student I became involved in the Civil Rights Movement. I have sought "not just to study and understand society but rather to critique and change society" (Patton 2002, 130) by highlighting how the injustice of racism can not only harm one individual, but how it can destroy an entire country. I told the story of my traumatic experiences with racial discrimination and the influence they have had on every aspect of my personal and professional life. As a critical theorist it is my deepest desire that through my autoethnography, a way of life will be illuminated (Patton 2002), and that something will be learned by others who have never experienced racism, or perhaps those who have lived with it will be encouraged to let their voices be heard as well—to help eradicate the injustices of racism for ourselves, our children and grandchildren and those yet unborn.

Theoretical Framework

To analyze my research I used Critical Race Theory (CRT) with a strong element of Culturally Relevant Pedagogy (CRP) as a theoretical framework. I believe my lived experiences with racism before I became a teacher positioned my pedagogical practices in social justice. As before stated, CRT was developed in the 1970s by Bell, Freeman and Delgado, three educational researchers who were looking for a way to address the effects of race and racism on the law and social order while bringing about changes that would lead to social justice (Decuir & Dixson 2004). *In Critical Race Theory: An Introduction*, authors Delgado and Stefancic (2001) offer this explanation of CRT:

> The critical race theory (CRT) movement is a collection
> of activists and scholars interested in studying and

transforming the relationship among race, racism, and power. The movement considers many of the same issues that conventional civil rights and ethnic studies discourses take up, but places them in a broader perspective that includes economics, history, context, group-and self-interest, and even feelings and the unconscious. Unlike traditional civil rights, which embraces incrementalism and step-by step progress, critical race theory questions the very foundations of the liberal order, including equality theory, legal reasoning, Enlightenment rationalism, and neutral principles of constitutional law ... although CRT began as a movement in the law, it has rapidly spread beyond that discipline (3).

In "What's So Critical about Critical Race Theory?", Trevino, Harris and Wallace (2008) refer to W. E. B. DuBois' *The Souls of Black Folk*, when he says "the problem of the Twentieth Century is the problem of the color line" (7). More than a half century later Critical Race Theory came forward as a critical response to the issue of skin color. Again, the mandate of CRT is "treating the social construction of race as central to the way that people of color are ordered and constrained in the United States" (7). CRT is committed to advocating for justice for those who find themselves without influence or voice. Giving a voice to those who have been silenced by the "master narrative" is one of the fundamental components of Critical Race Theory (Ladson-Billings 1998). CRT calls attention to the ways in which society's "structural arrangements" restrains and inconveniences some more than others. CRT "spotlights the form and function of dispossession, disenfranchisement, and discrimination across a range of social institutions, and then seeks to give voice to those who are victimized and displaced" (Trevino, Harris and Wallace 2008, 8).

My work aligns specifically with the tenet (principle) introduced by Critical Race Theory called "counter stories." These stories convey personal "racialized" experiences and counter the "meta or master" narratives of the privileged. Metanarratives are the stories and myths that the dominant White culture has contrived as a way of maintaining racial inequality. Counter stories/narratives provide us with a "better understanding of the multidimensionality of racism in America" (Trevino, Harris, and Wallace 2008, 8) that was not available before CRT brought "racial discourse to the forefront of informed discussion on civil society" (8).

In answer to the question: What's so critical about critical race theory?—"Critical Race Theory is a tool for revealing the subtleness of inequity across a number of social areas" (Trevino, Harris, and Wallace 2008, 10). It articulates better the barriers and dangers of racism. It uses its tenets, such as "counter storytelling and the permanence of racism", to bring hidden racism and inequality to the surface to be exposed.

> Studies highlighting issues of race and racism in education that are informed by critical race theory (CRT) have been prominent in North America for the past decade or more ... Many more scholars have applied this approach to research on education and educational leadership than have used other critical stances ... Gloria Ladson Billings and William Tate (1995) published an article that first brought attention to the need for 'race-related critical analysis in education.' (Briggs and Coleman 2007, 42)

Ladson-Billings and Tate (1995) are cited by Briggs and Coleman as arguing that 'even though class and gender and their intersections with race are important categories contributing to our understanding of many school achievement issues, they still do not account for all inequalities between whites and students of colour' (43). In my autoethnography, class and gender are not the main characters—race and racism are. I have thought about whether or not my female gender has influenced my experiences with racial bigotry documented here and have determined that, for the most part, it has not—being Black, African American, Negro and "colored" has. "Many researchers of colour and others have begun to investigate educational issues through a CRT framework so as to question the dominant white causal conceptions and theories" (43).

Culturally Relevant Pedagogy Revisited

Gloria Ladson-Billings coined the phrase, "culturally relevant pedagogy" in 1995. Culturally Relevant Pedagogy (CRP) places emphasis on the needs of students from a variety of cultures. Brown-Jeffy and Cooper (2011) looked at Ladson-Billings' definition of culturally relevant pedagogy which states that Culturally Relevant Pedagogy is--

> ... not unlike critical [race] pedagogy but specifically committed to collective, not merely individual, empowerment. Culturally relevant pedagogy rests on three criteria or propositions: (a) students must experience academic success; (b) students must develop and/or maintain cultural competence; and (c) students must develop a critical consciousness through which they challenge the current status quo of the social order (Billings 1995, 160).

Although Ladson-Billings' definition emphasizes students from diverse backgrounds, all of my students were African American. Many of these students tested as "low-achievers" and needed to "experience academic success." They, like me, were influenced by the White world in which they live. Brown-Jeffy and Cooper (2011) state the following:

> Teachers should realize that students who are racial or ethnic minorities see, view, and perceive themselves and others differently than those who are of the

> majority group … race is visual and has all too often
> been viewed as the determinant of intelligence … (73).

By including what I recently discovered as "culturally relevant pedagogy"; I was able to integrate my students' home and community cultural experiences, values, and understandings into my teaching and their learning environment (Brown-Jeffy and Cooper 2011). I had no student teaching experience when I became a substitute teacher in the Chicago public schools. I was fresh out of college where I had been a civil rights' activist. In addition, Dr. M. L. King had just been murdered in August of 1968 and I began teaching in January of 1969. The only requirement for subbing at the time was a college degree and the ability to keep the students in line until the regular teacher returned. My personal elementary school experiences did little to inform my own practice—what I remember mostly is that in Missouri, my upper-grade teacher used corporal punishment when students failed to get passing grades on something he had not even taught—so I mostly relied on "mother wit" and the teachers next door and down the hall to determine how I would implement instruction. After two years as a new teacher, I passed the National Teachers Examination (NTE) and became a certified teacher. I also drew from my college days as a Civil Rights Movement participant. I taught my students "freedom songs" and told them how I had learned them on the freedom buses that traveled from Tuskegee's campus to Montgomery, Alabama where I was taught non-violent demonstration tactics. I educated them about Dr. King and the non-violent movement. I shared with them how I had picketed and sat on the lawn at the Capitol building in Montgomery to protest the mistreatment of Black citizens in America. We made our own picket signs and held a "sit-in" at the principal's office protesting the school lunches and homework—issues which the students chose as important to them. The principal was cooperative and understood the importance of what I was trying to teach my class about social justice and non-violence. Esposito and Swain (2009) make the following claim about culturally relevant and social justice pedagogy:

> Teachers committed to raising their students'
> sociopolitical consciousness, developing their sense of
> agency, and positively affecting their social and cultural
> identities must find creative ways to incorporate social
> justice awareness into the curriculum (41).

I had not heard of the term, "culturally relevant pedagogy" when I began my teaching career. All I knew was that these children needed to know their history and its importance to their future. I had to teach my students that they were smart, and descendents of a great African people. I told them about brilliant African American scientists, educators and inventors and that they too were capable of doing great things in life regardless of what they had seen or heard to the contrary, and that they deserved to be treated with dignity and respect and were expected to give respect to their teachers and classmates in return. I realized more and more that this was a place where I could have a positive influence on hundreds of lives and I stayed at that school where I began as a substitute teacher for nearly three decades. After two years as a new teacher, I returned to college to learn methods of teaching and passed the National Teachers Examination (NTE) in order to become a certified teacher. There was so much I wanted to share with these students with whom I had so much in common. I recognized that this was God's plan for my life—to teach. Esposito and Swain (2009) spoke to the importance of culturally relevant pedagogy for improved academic achievement when they said:

> Culturally relevant pedagogy and social justice
> pedagogy both aim to combat negative messages
> by instilling in students cultural pride and critical
> consciousness. Empowered by positive messages
> about themselves and their heritage, students are
> able to exceed academic expectations and overcome
> the obstacles of social injustice placed before them ...
> Teachers who promote the academic and social

> development of their students through culturally
> relevant and socially just pedagogies prepare them
> to make a tremendous impact on their communities
> and the world (46).

There were many days when the responsibility of teaching and caring for students was overwhelming, but I never thought of quitting—unlike working in the CPS central office where I thought of quitting often—a story told in a later chapter.

When standards-based instruction first arrived on the scene in the Chicago Public Schools I was one of the first in my school to sign up for the training. I was concerned about the academic achievement of the students not only in my classroom but also in the whole school. Not nearly enough of our students were achieving at expected levels in Reading and Math and other subjects. It was my mission to not only teach these students about their culture, but ultimately to raise their academic achievement scores. In Chicago, when you speak of high-poverty schools, unfortunately stories of the achievement gap are not far behind. This was one of those schools. I later challenged the status quo and the low achievement scores by running for the Local School Council, winning, and through Divine intervention leaving to work in the Teachers Academy at the central office.

Data Collection/Presentation

Most of the data I collected was from my memory of lived experiences. I found that as I wrote, some events I had forgotten returned to mind. Other information, for historical accuracy, was obtained from primary source documents, such as my high school diploma and transcript, to verify times, dates and places. In addition, the electronic media proved help in locating relevant sources. Following a lead I found on the Internet, I was fortunate to locate an attorney who worked on the case where the NAACP and a number of parents of African American students, who were being discriminated against, sued the Charleston Board of Education in 1962 because *Brown v. Board of Education* (1954) was being ignored. Through email correspondence I learned that he is currently a law professor who teaches Constitutional Law at Wayne State University, a large mid-west university. Professor Robert Sedler and I arranged to have lunch together at a restaurant on one of his trips to Chicago, where he has family members. It was hard to believe that he (in early eighties) was actually present in the court room when the court order was issued. He wanted to make sure that I knew he assisted in the case and that Attorney Clyde Cahill, who later became Judge Cahill, took the lead. He informed me that I should contact the District Courthouse in St. Louis, Missouri to obtain the documents from the court case of which I was a part. After some additional research I was able to uncover the court documents in the Kansas City, Missouri court archives. He is my only interviewee and has been a very valuable resource. Although he said he never knew what happened to the students once the case was won, he was able to help me understand the legalities of the court case.

As aforementioned, I contacted the local library in Charleston, Missouri and they found and mailed to me old newspaper articles which dated back to October, 1962. These articles basically talked about the desegregation plan the Missouri District Court had required in the school district. I have also included data from various other papers, projects, and my doctoral superintendent internship, which focused on racial equity and excellence for all students in a near-by high school, which I completed during my educational leadership coursework.

A great deal of the data for this autoethnographic study is presented in the form of vignettes. These short stories and my reflections on them have enabled me to not only share the happening, but also to delve into conscious and sub-conscious feelings and emotions associated with it. These accounts offer the reader opportunities to actually see how institutional racism shows up in various forms in my everyday life, sometimes personal, sometimes professional—and also in the life of the average African American living in the United States of America today. I have written eight vignettes which offer me the opportunity to use events, feelings, and dialogue to draw the reader into my experiences where he/she will be able to perceive and feel that I am in reality "a human being experiencing fear, laughter, [anger, joy, and pain] and perhaps most significant, uncertainty and ambivalence" (Humpheys 2005, 851). These vignettes help to develop the reflexivity of the stories told and serve as a vehicle for connecting the past to the present.

Ethical Considerations

I interviewed one person for this study through a lunch conversation. Ethical considerations were accounted for in the Letter of Consent which the interviewee (s) signed. The letter spelled out what my study is about, how much time would be needed and how the interview would proceed. The results of my research will be shared with the interviewee when this work is completed, and hopefully in the near future as a published work for students, educators, scholars and the general public, "lest we forget" how devastating racism can be.

I am appreciative of the information and time the interviewee shared with me toward completing this project, and committed to honoring the information he has provided. I take very seriously the responsibility of doing no harm to any subject mentioned in this dissertation. Pseudonyms have been used throughout to protect the privacy of certain places and individuals.

CHAPTER THREE

AUTOETHNOGRAPHIC REFLECTIONS

Everything that we see is a shadow cast by that which we do not see.
-Martin Luther King, Jr.

Growing Up in a Racist Environment

I was born a Black female on Groundhog's Day—late in my mother's childbearing years. From that moment and even at the moment I was conceived "race" has impacted my life. My mother and my father were both raised Black and poor in the United States of America, said to be the richest country in the world. I was raised as an only child in a Christian home mostly by my mother, Emma, who was widowed when I was three years old. Sadly, I have no memories of my father and my mother never married again so there was never a "father-figure" in my home. Sometimes I wonder if my life would have been different had I been raised by a father and a mother. At least I know my father didn't leave on his own accord, as so many fathers seem to do. One of the things I do remember is as a little girl my mom and I would go to church every Sunday. I can see it clearly; Rush Ridge Baptist Church, a few miles from where we lived and off the beaten path, if there is such a thing in a community where most of the roads are gravel and look like paths anyway. The church was located in a rural area, even more rural than the little town where we lived, Wyatt, Missouri, but Mama had a friend who drove us to church and I remember singing in the choir, my favorite thing to do, up until I left home for college. My mother's brother, uncle Henry, and his family went to church there too, so I saw my cousins often. There were seven kids in his crew and I always liked visiting them. I liked that it was always noisy, and in their house there were lots of people sitting around the dinner table. We would eat dinner in shifts—first shift and second shift. It was fun being with my cousins because at my house it was much quieter with just my mother and me. My only brother, Willie, born to my mom when she was a teenager, was for the most part, a stranger to me. We had different fathers and a world of other differences that never allowed us to become close. He was raised by his dad and was a grown man with a wife and kids when I was born; in addition he lived in another state so we seldom saw each other. When Mama and I would visit him in Mississippi, I always felt he behaved more like a father than a brother because he constantly tried to boss me around. It was probably hard for him to see me as his sister. He had a whole bunch of sisters and brothers on his father's side after his father remarried. His three children, my niece and nephews, are all older than I, and they say he was very mean when they were growing up—strict no doubt. I remember him visiting us once or twice in Chicago. He also came to see Mama when she was very ill, but he only stayed a short while. I thought it was because he couldn't stand to see her suffering. All of the caring for Mama in her illness was left up to me. Although I thought "why?" for a minute, but it was only a passing thought. She had taken care of me alone from the time I was three until I became an adult, so I was happy to take care of her. My brother passed away a few years after my mom. I loved him although I never really knew him. Mama said she had five pregnancies all together. Only Willie and I survived. He was her first child, I was her last. I have written the following vignette as a tribute to my mother and to point to characteristics that I see in myself which were hers first.

Vignette One
"I Remember Mama in a Special Way"

My mother was born in 1898 in Indianola, Mississippi. Mama was 85 years old when she died. She referred to her birthplace mostly as Sunflower County, perhaps because she lived on the outskirts of the city—in the rural area. I remember her talking about the dusty country road near where she lived. She told me my great-grandmother, Jane, had been a slave. I have very faded memories of my mother's mother, Sally, who lived for a while after I was born. I have one picture of her where she looks to be in her eighties or older. All I remember of her was one day when she stood up from the rocking chair where she had been sitting, I, probably three or four years old, pushed her back down in the chair. I don't why, perhaps it was my way of making her stay there—she was very fragile at the time. Mama had three brothers, Henry, Sam and Anderson. I got to know Uncle Henry and Uncle Sam but Mama said Anderson, had run away from home after getting into a fight and seriously injuring a White man. He knew he would be killed, maybe lynched if he stayed and so he left in the middle of the night, and when she passed away at age 85, she still didn't know what happened to her baby brother. Sometimes I think of trying to find out what happened to him. Perhaps that will be my next research project. Uncle Sam and his family lived in Mississippi and so we were never close.

Mama was an attractive, robust, woman with long, think, black hair that came down to her waist. We always talked about how she probably had an American Indian somewhere in her background. For many years I would comb her hair, part it down the middle, braid it, and then cross it on top of her head. That's how she wore it most of the time. She was totally surprised when she, at age 48, found out she was pregnant with me. She thought it was menopause at first. I surely was not planned, however, I never, at any time, felt anything other than special, spoiled and the baby of the family. My mother only had a fourth grade education. She told me that back then poor children would sometimes drop out of school to help their families with working the farm where they lived—probably sharecropping. I'm not sure when

Mama left Mississippi, but she was married when she was very young and became a mother for the first time when she was fifteen. She legally changed her name from Anna to Emma because she didn't like it. Even then she was a fighter, not willing to put up with something she didn't like. I must have gotten that from her. I remember an ex-boyfriend of mine telling me I didn't know how to "take no for an answer"; he meant it as a putdown, but he was absolutely right, and I consider that one of my strongest characteristics. I don't give up easily. I am willing to fight for what I believe in, and as a mother it is a trait I tried to instill in my son and as a teacher in my many students over the years.

My brother, Willie, was a product of Mama's first marriage and was raised in Mississippi by his father. I never really got to know him and I grew up feeling like an only child. When my father passed away I was very young and Mama kept us going. I was always fed and clothed. As a single mom she did all she could to raise me in a loving, nurturing, and safe environment. It seems I was in 2nd grade when we moved from Missouri, where I was born, to Ohio for a few years because Mama and some other people from our home town had found decent work there. In my home town the only jobs for Blacks was farm work—picking or chopping cotton. The "good" jobs were reserved for the White people in the community. In Ohio we lived with a family—husband, wife and two kids—where Mama rented a room and the adults became my baby-sitters until Mama came home from work. I recall that the husband had a sense of humor. Whenever people were kissing on television he would say to one of his kids, "Turn that television off—ain't gon' be no kissing on my television!" I thought he was kidding at first, but he wasn't. Maybe he was just trying to protect us kids from what he felt was inappropriate.

I remember some of the late night snacks Mama brought home from the restaurant where she worked. I always tried to save a space in my stomach just in case she brought me something. Sometimes it was ice cream; sometimes it was a foot-long hot dog with ketchup and onions on a bun which tasted like homemade. It was sooo good and my favorite! I think the best part was sharing it with her. That might have been the beginning of my plus-size figure. Mama was plus-size *too until she fell ill in her eighties, but she lived a long life and most of it in "pretty-good health", as she would say. It was just Mama and me for a long time. She remained a widow for the rest of her life. I think it was her way of protecting me from "outsiders." After living for several years in Ohio, we went back home. I couldn't understand why we were moving from Ashtabula (Ohio) back to the little hick town where I was born. I think I was in 5th grade then. It must have been a part of God's plan, which has led me to this autoethnographic study today.*

I'm not sure how it all rolled out, but without my mother's support I would not have been involved in a court case in 1962 against the Charleston, Missouri Board of Education so that I and other Black children who lived in the district, could attend the all-White Charleston High School (CHS), the best high school in the area at the time. I wonder how she must have felt knowing how I was being treated after enrolling in CHS. I'm sure I shared with her how terrible it felt to be belittled each time we walked in the door. She might have been afraid for me, but she stood firm and because of that I was able to stand firm as well. I'm glad she never knew all the "cussing" I did at that school. Man, would she have been surprised at the words that came out of her "baby's" mouth! Every time one of the White kids used a word which hurt me, I had some choice words for him/her in return. I'm not sure where I learned those words. My mom didn't use profanity, not really. The only "bad" word I ever heard her say was murmured under her breath, when she burned her hand on the stove or something like that and it was mild compared to the phrases I put together to fight back at that school. Using profanity was my defense mechanism. Some of the other kids that came to CHS with me got into actual physical fights almost daily, while I chose to fight with words. I hoped my words would hurt them the way their words hurt me. Fortunately, before long I found another way to fight through studying and receiving high marks in all my classes and being on the honor roll. "What you got to say now?"

Although we were considered poor, I never wanted for anything. My mother worked and we owned our home. When we first moved back to the farming community in Missouri, Mama even raised some chickens and planted a garden on the property. I hated chickens and was a little bit scared of them. After all, I thought of myself as a "city girl" after having lived in Ohio for a few years. I think I killed the neighbor's rooster which was actually a "fighting" rooster. I thought he was about to attack me one day because he followed me home and was right behind me as I stepped onto my front porch. I was so scared that I hit him on the head with the big stick I had with me, and watched as he wobbled home. I never told a soul what I did, but I never saw that rooster again … don't know why!

When it was time to go to college Mama borrowed a small amount of money from the local bank to help me get started. After that, I paid room and board and tuition by being in a five-year work-study program where I worked thirty hours a week and took only three classes (nine hours) per semester. All the tuition and fees that work-study didn't pay for, my student loan did. I even received a grant one semester. And three and a half years later when I returned home not yet a college graduate, Mama was nothing less than loving and supportive, although I knew she was disappointed that I had not finished the journey I began. My mother taught me what it means to love unconditionally. She never made me feel that I had failed and she believed me when I told her I would go back, finish and obtain a college degree. So when my son was about one month old, I left him with my mother and returned to school to complete the one semester I needed to graduate. Leaving him so soon was a really hard thing to do, but I did it for him, for me, and for my mother. Mama always encouraged me and never gave me the feeling that I was incapable of doing anything. I really didn't know what I was doing when I became pregnant in my senior year of college—senior year of college! Needless to say, I was naïve and could hardly believe it. Intimacy in relationships was not talked about openly in my household, or in classes at school. That's the way it was back then. Many of the teenage girls in my community were single moms very early, but I was determined to live a different life. I didn't know God then as I do today, yet I prayed for His help and He answered my prayers. After my son was born, I returned to school for the one semester that I lacked and graduated from college, the first person in my immediate family to do so. To finish I continued on the work-study program and took seven classes that semester, twenty-one hours. I earned 4 A's and 3 B's, my best semester academically because although I was disappointed in myself for having to leave school, I was determined to graduate that semester. Nothing was going to stop me. Mama helped me raise my beautiful, healthy son. God, in His mercy, worked it all out. I never had to hire a baby-sitter and Mama loved him so much that when I came to Chicago to find work, she sold our house in Missouri and moved to Illinois to be with us. My mom was a great cook and he was fed a home-cooked meal every day. He, like me, never wanted for anything. By Mama giving so selflessly and helping me as she did, I was able to work full-time and go back to school at night where I earned a Master's degree—still determined to live a better life than we had lived in Missouri. We were a family—Mama, my son and me. She would be so proud of the work I'm doing right now, and of her grandson who is an attorney, a kind and considerate man, and a great father to his two children, and yes I believe she is still watching over and supporting us every step of the way. Thank you Mama! And thank you God for Your loving kindness and second chances.

Reflection

I wrote this vignette about my mother to serve as a counter narrative (Delgado and Stefancic 2001) to the ones perpetuated by the powerful and privileged in American society who declare that Black parents do not take care of their children, are not involved in their education and are not good role models (Singleton and Linton 2006). My mother was always an involved parent, from elementary school throughout my college years and then some. Without her support years ago, I would not have been able to pursue an advanced degree today. Delgado and Stefancic in *Critical Race Theory* (2001) speak about the importance of counter narratives or "counterstorytelling" in the fight against racial discrimination:

> The hope is that well-told stories describing the reality
> of black and brown lives can help readers bridge

the gap between their worlds and those of others. Engaging stories can help us understand what life is like for others, and invite the reader into a new and unfamiliar world (41).

There is much in the educational literature regarding lack of parental involvement in the Black community, but less about those parents, who like my mom, often carried out noble and courageous acts such as seeking justice through the court system against segregated educational institutions to guarantee their children's rights to a quality education. President Barack Obama was raised mostly by his mom and grandparents after his father abandoned the family and returned to Kenya in East Africa. He spoke of his mother and other single moms as heroines in the *Audacity of Hope* (2006) when he said: "Many single moms—including the one who raised me—do a heroic job on behalf of their kids" (393). My mother was truly my hero and a role model.

I write this story also to "break the silence" (Delgado and Stafancic 2001) regarding the socially constructed myth that single parents, particularly in the Black community, raise children who are headed for a life of crime and are, in general, unproductive citizens. My mother was everything opposite of neglectful and even though she was not "educated" by societal standards due to circumstances beyond her control, she, like so many others in the Black community—valued education highly and did all she could to help me realize the education she had not been able to attain. She also understood in her infinite wisdom, that her power, her voice, rested in her ability to speak out politically through participating in the voting process. She and other Black people of her generation, through Jim Crow laws and other discriminatory actions, were often deprived of "their constitutional right to vote" (Appiah and Gates 2003) until the Voting Rights Act of 1965. Blacks, who lived in the South especially, were faced with illegal poll taxes and literacy tests and "risked harassment, intimidation, economic reprisals, and physical violence when they tried to register to vote" (983). Critical race theorists, Delgado and Stefancic (2001), offer an additional point of view concerning why "counterstories" are essential to eradicating bigotry in America:

> Critical writers use counterstories to challenge, displace, or mock … pernicious narratives … Powerfully written stories and narratives may begin a process of adjustment in our system of beliefs and categories by calling attention to neglected evidence and reminding readers of our common humanity (43).

One image of my mother that stays in my mind is when she was in her eighties and arthritis had taken its toll on her ability to walk unassisted, but she still got up, dressed, grabbed her walker or her cane and went to the polls to vote every time there was an election. Sometimes walking was difficult for her even with a walker, but it didn't stop her from fulfilling her civic duty. She had lived through a time when Blacks were not allowed to vote. Today I would never entertain the thought of not voting come hail or windstorm, because I know my mom would be so disappointed. Being able to vote came at too high a price for African Americans in this country not to take advantage of the privilege. President Lyndon Johnson declared on the day the Voting Rights Act of 1965 was signed, that the vote was "the most powerful instrument ever devised by man for breaking down injustice and destroying the terrible walls which imprison men because they are different from other men" (The Editors of *Black Issues in Higher Education* 2005, 24).

The Voting Rights Act was born out of three civil rights marches which protested the hindering of voters' registration for Black people in Selma, Alabama and other places in the South. Dr. Martin Luther King, Jr. and members on SNCC (Student Non-violent Coordinating Committee) and the SCLC (Southern Christian Leadership Conference) aimed to confront Alabama's Governor, George Wallace, for failing to provide protection for those who were attempting to register to vote. The first non-violent march which took place on March 7, 1965 has come to be known as "Bloody Sunday" because the marchers were met by state troopers who beat them bloody with nightsticks and turned tear gas on them refusing to let them cross the Edmund Pettus Bridge, which they had to cross in order to get to Montgomery, the state capital, from Selma, where the march began (nps.gov 2010). Of the three, only the third march, which began on March 21 and ended on March 25, succeeded after the marchers were granted a permit and President Johnson called out the National Guard to protect the protesters. By the time the marchers reached Montgomery they were 25,000 strong as protestors joined the march all along the way. Lives were lost during the protests at the hands of hateful White people. Jimmie Jackson, a Black man, was shot to death while trying to protect his mother and grandmother from being hurt during one of the voters' rights protests where the police were firing shots into the crowds. White minister, James Reeb, who had come from out-of-state to join the protest, died after being badly beaten and Viola Liuzzo, a White woman whose car was fired upon by the Klu Klux Klan died as she carried marchers to and from the march on the Alabama Capitol building. She had five children. Countless numbers of people were bloodied with injuries during the first two marches. My college friends and I joined the third march once the marchers reached the outskirts of Montgomery, Alabama and sat in at the Capitol building. I remember sitting on the lawn and listening to speeches made by various protest leaders including one by Dr. King. "On August 6, under pressure from President Lyndon B. Johnson's White House, Congress passed the Voting Rights Act of 1965 (VRA) ending the South's Gestapo-like control of the polls" (The Editors of *Black Issues in Higher Education* 2005, 2).

I'm not sure if Mama knew about all of that, but she knew she wanted to be involved, just as she had been in the integration of the schools in Charleston, Missouri, and she wanted to have a say in what was happening to Black people in her community and in America as a whole. Part of President Johnson's speech to Congress on March 15th, 1965 concerning why they should pass the Voting Rights Act was as follows:

I speak tonight for the dignity of man and the destiny of democracy. I urge every member of both parties, Americans of all religions and of all colors, from every section of this country, to join me in that cause. At times history and fate meet at a single time in a single place to shape a turning point in man's unending search for freedom. So it was at Lexington and Concord. So it was a century ago at Appomattox. So it was last week in Selma, Alabama ... There is no cause for pride in what has happened in Selma. There is no cause for self-satisfaction in the long denial of equal rights of millions of Americans. But there is cause for hope and for faith in our democracy in what is happening here tonight (Lawson and Payne 1998, 85).

Most of all I thank my mother for taking me to church when I was a little girl and introducing me to Jesus Christ. She was not only concerned with my physical and emotional well-being, but also my spiritual well-being. Without God I would not have been able to go through the experiences of dealing with racial hatred and come out not hating anyone—"not bitter, but better." I would not have had the strength and determination to go back and finish college after having to leave before I graduated, after all, obtaining a college education was my goal—the reason I had left Lincoln High School and endured isolation, indignation and verbal abuse for years at Charleston High School. And I would not have had the fortitude, some of my friends say "craziness", to enter a doctoral program as a retired teacher and administrator, and have the energy and resolve to finish what I started, refusing to "take no for an answer." I have renewed strength and a story that I need to tell to help bring a better, perhaps different, understanding to those who don't have a clue about the toll racism takes upon an individual and a country. I thank my mom for her courageousness and for passing it on to me.

"When I Think of Home": Cairo

Even though we lived in Missouri, the Missouri-Illinois border was just a few miles away. Cairo (KAY-ro), Illinois was just across the bridge. Growing up I heard about the xenophobic practices against Blacks in Cairo, and later how Cairo was destroyed by its own racist inhabitants—this was the environment where I spent most of my childhood, and it was only a ten-minute drive away. Wyatt, my home town, is a small, farming community in the "boot hill" of Missouri. As a young child, I was always uneasy when my mother spoke about the bridge leading from Wyatt into Cairo. I remember Mama and me sitting in the back seat and her showing me out of the car window where the "muddy" Mississippi and the Ohio rivers came together. I was afraid to look, so I mostly scrunched up my face, squeezed my eyes shut and waited to open them when I thought we were on the other side of the bridge on dry land again. Occasionally we would go to Cairo to shop for clothes. All of the stores were White-owned. Because of Jim Crow laws, Blacks weren't allowed to try on clothes in those days (1960s). Store owners claimed it would prevent Whites who might want the same item from buying it because a shirt or blouse had been on a Black person's body (hooks 1994). Sometimes I think hatred makes you crazy—encumbers your ability to think clearly, as in this case. The mentality of the privileged, even the not so rich, continues to amaze me even today. Bernice King (1997) in *Hard Questions, Heart Answers* says: "The Jim Crow era signs are gone, but they are etched in the hearts and minds of men and women" (47). Black women cooked and cleaned for White women and their families, handled their food and diapered their babies, yet always stood a chance of being humiliated because of their skin color at any time on any given day. Everyone knows the unspoken rule is to be kind to those who handle your food. The arrogant privileged, however, may think such a rule does not apply to them. I've heard stories about happenings in kitchens that suggest they would be surprised to know it does. In *Teaching to Transgress*, bell hooks (1994) states:

> In those days a poor white woman who might never be in a position to hire a black woman servant would still in all of her encounters with black women, assert a dominating presence, ensuring that the contact between the two groups should always place white in a position of power over black (94).

Cairo, once a thriving city with a population of over 15,000, today has a population of nearly 3,500—the majority of whom are poor and Black. Cairo had been the site of racial turmoil dating back to the late 19th century. *The Legends of America* website (http://www.legendsofamerica.com/il-cairo.html) has a nearly ten-page story on Cairo entitled, "Death by Racism", which tells the history of murder and racial prejudice and how it led to the town's demise. In the early 1900s an angry mob of Whites lynched Will James, a Black resident, who had been accused (no trial, no guilty verdict) of murdering a White girl. In 1910 another White mob killed a deputy sheriff while attempting to lynch a Black man accused of snatching the purse of a White woman. The National Guard was called in to restore order (5). This was Cairo; a few minutes from where I was born and raised— where the atmosphere of hate and bigotry was constantly in the air.

Black children and White children attended separate schools in Cairo until 1967, more than ten years after *Brown v. Board of Education* made segregated schooling illegal. With every act of bigotry the city of Cairo was dying. The public swimming pool was closed to keep Blacks out. The State of Illinois closed Cairo's banks because they would not hire Blacks. Whites from the surrounding states of Kentucky and Missouri were hired to work in local businesses rather than hire Cairo's Black residents. To keep Black children from playing baseball with White children, Little League baseball was cancelled. An anti-picketing law was passed and Blacks could not gather in parks or sporting events. Blacks were not allowed in the city's one bowling alley, and as expected, racial tension was high in Cairo and growing higher. That same year the Illinois National Guard was called in once again when Blacks rioted following the death of a Black soldier on leave, who died while in police custody. Police claimed it was suicide, but after so many acts of violence against the African American community, the Black population didn't believe them. Racism and only racism caused the death and destruction of a city that had once flourished. Unthinkable events like these make me reflect on hate and how it comes about:

Hate
2011

Where does hate come from?
Is it with us from birth? I think not!
Hate destroys us—
Eats away at our core from the inside out!
Do we even understand why we hate?
Hate turns us into something less human …
When we hate
Is it ourselves we loathe?
And what about the children? Will we teach the children to hate?
Will we ever understand that hate can only lead to our own demise?
Are you willing to give your life over to hate?
And what then have you accomplished?

In 1969, Cairo was the site of an intense civil rights fight to end racial segregation and create jobs for its Black citizens. The National Guard was called in to prevent violence and restore order as it had been several times before in the history of Cairo's racial relations. As a result of this continuing racial conflict, Blacks formed the Cairo United Front, a civil rights organization. It led a boycott against White-owned businesses which lasted for more than a decade. Practically all the businesses in the town were owned by Whites and so Cairo was economically crippled as White businessmen still refused to hire Blacks and allowed their businesses to close or moved out of town. Between 1986 and 1988, the city's one hospital closed and bus and train service was discontinued. Although Cairo was originally built for a population of 20, 000 it has not totally recovered from the years of racial violence and today is described as a "ghost town." *The Legends of America* website describes Cairo this way:

> Doors stand wide open on commercial buildings that display rubble filled interiors, windows are broken or boarded up, Kadzu crawls up brick walls, streets signs are faded and rusty – the streets and sidewalks cracked and choked with weeds. On a side street, the lovely Gem Theatre stands silent next to the Chamber of Commerce. In other parts of the city, the large brick hospital is overgrown with vegetation, churches are boarded up, and restored mansions sit next to abandoned and crumbling large homes (Weiser 2011).

It's amazing that White residents were willing to give up everything—their homes, their businesses, their recreation, their town, to keep from integrating with Blacks. President Barack Obama (2006) mentioned Cairo in *The Audacity of Hope* as one of the Illinois towns he visited while campaigning for the US Senate and called it "a town made famous during the late sixties and early seventies as the site of some of the worst racial conflict anywhere outside of the Deep South" (281). Unfortunately, when I think of home, I think of Cairo.

I spent a portion of my high school life working as a Candy Striper in a hospital in Cairo. I was a student at Charleston High School by then, so it must have been a program connected with the school that allowed students to volunteer at the hospital on the weekends. For one day every weekend a friend of mine and I would dress up in our Candy Striper uniforms—red and white stripes resembling a candy cane, and go to work in St. Mary's hospital in Cairo. I loved that uniform! It made me feel special, like I was doing something really helpful for someone else. After dealing with hostile students and teachers all week at the high school, it was good to feel appreciated, even for a little while. I don't recall if the wards were divided into Black and White, but I remember that I worked in Pediatrics and that I fell in love with this one little Black baby boy, who was probably about 18 months old. I was assigned to care for him on several weekends when I went to volunteer. He had the whooping cough and was very sick when I first saw him. I would hold him and feed him as best I could. He was such a cute and bouncy little lad when he was feeling better, and he would smile when he saw me coming. Every week I could see he was getting better and then one weekend when I ran to his bed to see him, he was gone. The nurse said he had gone home because he was well again. I was very sad—happy for him, but broken-hearted that I wouldn't see him anymore. Even in the midst of all the racial hatred and conflict, I had found something to love about Cairo.

"Hatred paralyzes life; love releases it. Hatred confuses life; love harmonizes it. Hatred darkens life; love illuminates it."
-Martin Luther King, Jr.

Vignette Two
"It Makes You Crazy Sometimes"

Sometimes I think it's my duty as a Black person to dislike White people because of the injustices I and my people have suffered at their hands. Intellectually I know that not all White people are responsible for slavery or racial discrimination, neither for the lynching of Black men and boys solely because of the skin they were in, or for the senseless bombing that killed four innocent Black girls in a Birmingham, Alabama church one Sunday morning during the Civil Rights era, or for any of the terrible, dreadful things that have happened to my people, both here and in Mother Africa, but it always seems to come back to the same "privileged, powerful" group of people. I realize also that some of the people who have given their lives for the cause of racial justice have been White people— people who could have avoided the whole situation in which they placed themselves, but became involved because they believed they were doing the right thing. They gave up their "White privilege and power" for the cause of someone else's right to racial equality. Then I recognize that what I know and what I feel, my head and my heart, sometimes don't agree. The residual emotions and the remembrance of the humiliation I felt as a young girl, even as I write this account, bring back feelings of resentment and sadness, and heaviness of spirit. Then my heart takes me right back to what I was taught by my mother and my Christian faith, that we should love one another. I never learned to love one group of people and hate the other, and so I let the hurt go—most of the time. I am, however, always aware that I am Black in America, a place where there is a history of discrimination and treating people badly simply because they are Black or poor or both. Occasionally it's the microagressions (Lindsey 2009), subtle racism, such as being "overlooked" at a store counter where you've been waiting patiently and the White person who arrived after you is offered helped first, or the arrogance of a White person who speaks to you in a condescending manner in any situation, as if you must lack the ability to understand as they do. That's when I ask myself am I being treated this way because this person has bought into the stereotype that I must be less intelligent than they. I wonder if the time will ever come in America when I won't have to be aware of the "race" to which I have been assigned and how it impacts my life twenty-four hours a day, seven days a week. I agree with what Leonard Pitts, Jr. (2002) says in his essay, "Crazy Sometimes." He says, "...this thing makes you crazy sometimes. Race I mean" (21). He goes on further to say,

> The result is that to be black in modern America is to feel the touch of hidden hands pressing down upon you. ... Their effect is clear in government and university statistics documenting that, in terms of education, employment, housing, justice, health, and other quality-of-life indicators ... You know the hands are there, but when you turn around to catch them in the act of pushing you down, you encounter only white people with 'Who me?' expressions on their faces (23).

From time to time I am baffled by a few things. I am amazed at White people who lay in the sun to get darker skin, even in some cases risking sun damage and skin cancer, yet desiring to be "tanned", while skin color in America has caused so much pain to some who were born with the "tan" skin they seek and are discriminated against, treated unfairly, and abused because of it. It makes you crazy! And what about those White women who were born with thin lips and go through medical procedures to make them bigger, thicker, and plumper. Special lipsticks have been created just to make thin lips look "pouty" and "more attractive." Big lips have historically been a "so-called" characteristic of the African American "race", the most denigrated group in this country, yet White Americans, who have poked fun at and drawn derogatory pictures of Blacks with big noses and thick lips for decades, now want them for themselves. Today, make-up companies and tanning salons are big business. Again I say, "...this thing makes you crazy sometimes. Race, I mean."

There was a time, not too long ago in America, when Black women *finally thought we had something to brag about—now it's "all the craze" and women of other races and nationalities known for being lesser endowed, want large ones too and sometimes undergo expensive surgical procedures to obtain a bigger gluteus maximus. It has always been a discussion among the women in the Black community ever since I can remember that White girls had flat bottoms--for once they didn't have something we had. Now large ones are claimed and celebrated by the White movie industry seemingly as "their discovery" and a few celebrities may even have theirs insured. "...this thing [really does] makes you crazy sometimes. Race, I mean." So make up your mind White America! You borrow our vernacular and use it incorrectly, but once you make it yours it's accepted as brilliant ... things of which television commercials and late night talk shows are made. Rapping is even acceptable now that some non-Black artists are doing it. You want to dance like us, and look tan like us. Some of your women even want a man Black like us. So make up your mind is all I ask. Do you really hate our blackness—or envy it? Isn't the whole thing making you crazy too?*

Blackness
2011
Would I change my blackness
to be accepted by you?
Then would you love me?
One drop of Black blood and you are me!
How powerful
It must be—red blood
that makes White Black.
Do you fear I am stronger
braver, wiser, more beautiful?
Is that why you lock me away
so deliberately?
To keep me held down,
Held back

Un-educated?

Don't you know
that when we are all
free to rise ... to claim our place,
Free!
Like a flood
hate will be washed away
and a new day will begin.
Or is it just me—
dreaming again?
Would I change my blackness
to be accepted by you?
I am as God intended
And so are you.
And I can love you ...
I do love you—
Just the way you are!

Reflection

Looking back, I don't recall my mother and I having a sit-down conversation about race or racism. She was more a woman of action than of talk. It must have been in the late 1950s, early 60s, when the National Association for the Advancement of Colored People (NAACP) and the Student Non-violent Coordinating Committee (SNCC) began having civil rights' meetings in Charleston, Missouri, a few miles from my home. After attending a few of those meetings I began to understand, for the first time, how Blacks were being mistreated in the South and discriminated against right there in my own community. It must have been then when I began to think like an activist, and when I decided that someone had to stand up for what was right. I'm sure the experiences I had as an African American growing up pre-and-during the Civil Rights era have been the biggest influence towards career choices, academic interests, parenting and other significant decisions in my life. More than a half-century later, I still live in a nation where institutional racism exists. Even the country's election of the first Black president has not changed the hearts of many. The trauma of helping to integrate a high school in Missouri will never be erased from my memory. The name-calling, the tomato-throwing, the writing on our lockers, "go home" and the taping to them pictures of old, ugly, homeless Black people or anything degrading about Black people that the students could find. It was October and classes had already started, but everybody knew we were coming. Some of the newspaper articles I located from Charleston, Missouri, September 1962, told the story of the court case and that Black students would be coming to CHS. It's hard to understand at sixteen, or any other age for that matter, why human beings treat other humans in such an inhumane manner because we differ in skin color. And I realize that there have been other world events where people spewed racial hatred that was not Black/White and put others to death for ridiculous and preposterous reasons. The phrase "man's inhumanity to man" comes to mind here. President Obama said in a (2008) senatorial speech—

> For most of this country's history, we in the African American community have been at the receiving end of man's inhumanity to man. And all of us understand intimately the insidious role that race still sometimes plays – on the job, in the schools, in our health care system, and in our criminal justice system.

Robert Burns, Scottish poet (1759-1796), is credited with coining the phrase "man's inhumanity to man" which he used in his poem entitled *From Man Was Made to Mourn: a Dirge*, in 1785 (http//:forum. wordreference.com). This is a verse from that poem:

Many and sharp the num'rous ills
Inwoven with our frame!
More pointed still we make ourselves
Regret, remorse, and shame!
And Man, whose heav'n-erected face
The smiles of love adorn, -
Man's inhumanity to man
Makes countless thousands mourn!

And what does it mean to be White in America? Evidently the students at Charleston High School must have learned it at an early age. Black kids and White kids had been separated by where we lived, where we went to school, and what jobs our parents held for as long as we, as children, could remember. It was a farming community where most people were poor or middle class so there were few rich kids at the school. Their rejection of us was strictly race-driven, probably passed on to them by their parents from an early age. We know that not all White Americans are middle or upper class. There are poor Whites in America, but what makes Black poor and White poor significantly different is a phenomenon called "White privilege." White privilege is defined by Sue (2003) as—

> the unearned advantages and benefits that accrue to White folks by virtue of a system normed on the experiences, value, and perceptions of their group. White privilege automatically confers dominance to one group, while subordinating groups of color in a descending relational hierarchy; it owes its existence to White supremacy; it is premised on the mistaken notion of individual meritocracy and deservedness ... rather than favoritism ..." (137).

Being White in America, even if poor, comes with certain advantages. Tema Okun (2010), in *The Emperor Has No Clothes:*

Teaching about Race and Racism to People Who Don't Want to Know makes this point:

> When race is the focus, all those who are white belong to the dominant or mainstream group (although individual white people do not have the same level of power; other identity markers such as class, gender, sexuality, able-bodiness, will [only] modify [not take away] white privilege) (xii).

Whites, no matter their socioeconomic status, are still considered first-class citizens in American society, more likely to be seated first in a busy restaurant or waited on first in a department store. Ask a Black man as late as the year, 2010, trying to catch a cab in New York City (NYC) if White privilege matters. In a recent trip to New York I learned that laws regarding cabbies in NYC have recently been instituted which assess fines to cab drivers who have been reported for failure to pick up minority passengers. Beverly Daniel Tatum (2002) points out in "Choosing to Be Black: The Ultimate White Privilege?", that benefits come to Whites simply by virtue of skin color. In every day situations such as dealing with the police or a clerk in a store, Whiteness gives "the benefit of the doubt." Blackness, however, gives a greater possibility of guilt (216-218). I further agree with Okun (2010) when she states that "We live in a culture where racism, all oppressions, operate to keep us separated from each other and ourselves" (139), and that racism and bigotry in our culture "infects" us all (142). The history of racism in America is not just African American history but is the history of everyone who calls themselves American (Barton 2004). And so we all share in the crazy that is racial bigotry in this country.

Racial Identity Development: Family

I thank God for my family. My son is the only child I will ever give birth to seeing as I am no longer of child-bearing age or ability. A necessary emergency surgical procedure ended that possibility before its time. He has been the sunshine of my life and for some reason which I still have not figured out, after he left home for college, every time I would see him I would start to cry. When he became a lawyer and beginning to live on his own, he always looked and sounded so professional. We would occasionally have dinner together just to stay connected, and I was so proud of him. I still am. Of course I was always happy to see him, but I think the tears disturbed him a little. I just couldn't hold them back. He'd say "Mom, why are you crying"? And I would respond, "I don't know." My mother told me when she found out she was pregnant with me at forty-eight years old, she cried a lot, so perhaps crying easily has been handed down to me. I believe God gave us tears to help us express emotions we can't put into words; a way to wash away the hurt and begin anew, and a way to express happiness when it spills over. Perhaps I couldn't believe that I was the mother of a walking, talking, breathing human being, or maybe it was residual hurt over his father's seemingly lack of interest in the most wonderful gift one can ever receive—a child. Perhaps it was the guilt I felt for not bringing him up in a home with a mother and a father, to love and care for him. I don't cry anymore when I see him. I'm much too busy thanking God for how He has blessed us. I never expected the turns my life has taken, but I believe it was all in God's plan and He is certainly wiser than I. My son has helped to shape my racial identity and who I am today because I've tried to be an example for him, culturally, academically, and spiritually. I raised him as a single mom, but looking back I believe it was better that way because I was able to chart the course for my son without anyone else's interference. I was, however, careful not to "bad mouth" his father because I didn't see the benefit of doing so, and I didn't want to make him feel his father's actions were a predictor of who he was or what he could become. I remember reading *The Little Engine That Could* (Piper 1930) to him many times when he was very young. The Little Engine's mantra, as he tried to reach the top of the hill, "I think I can, I think I can, I think I can", was motivation for both of us to keep trying, keep striving and to not give up even when reaching a goal seems impossible. I wanted him to know that growing up a

Black male in America would be a challenge, but that his race had nothing to do with what he could achieve in life if he trusted God, worked hard and kept a positive attitude. In a November 2002 article in *Essence* magazine, "Single Moms, Strong Sons", Ylonda Gault Caviness said,

> Rearing a Black boy is a formidable task even for two-parent households. Like no other citizens, Black males are forced to wage a daily battle against a racist society that presumes them guilty–of criminal intent, of ignorance, of just plain worthlessness (216).

I am happy that I was able to place and keep my son on the right track by seeing to it that he received the best education I could afford. I first enrolled him in an excellent Catholic elementary school which was only a short distance from our residence and at the time had the reputation of being one of the best grade schools in the nation. Then when I could not meet the expense of sending him to a private high school, God provided a way for him to attend one of the best high schools in Chicago virtually free of charge to me. A academic scholarship program, LINK, which was connected to his elementary school, provided sponsors for high-achieving students to attend Catholic high schools which they otherwise may not have been able to, and that sponsor, a White man who was a successful businessman in real estate, provided my son, with a connection to the business community and paid the majority of his tuition for the four years that he was a high school student. Through that connection, my son worked after school in a downtown lawyer's office which I'm sure was influential in his decision to become an attorney himself.

In elementary and high school my son and I would compete to see who could get the most achievement certificates on one of our living room walls. I would put my certificates and awards on display on one side of the wall and his on the other. We had certificates on that wall for everything: perfect attendance, participating in a workshop, being on the honor roll, or for anything academic, as well as diplomas from elementary school, high school, and college. It was my way of motivating him to succeed in school. I wanted to teach him that we were both intellectually bright people who could be and do whatever we chose, and that we would both succeed against the odds, regardless of what the statistics said about Black single mothers' abilities to raise respectful, law-abiding sons. That is not to say I did everything right when it came to parenting, but I prayed for God's guidance continuously for myself and my son as I still do today. In a 2005 July/August issue of *Health* magazine, Alexis Jetter, author of *Raising Boys without Men: How Maverick Moms Are Creating the Next Generation of Exceptional Men,* states—

> … even without live-in dads, boys are boys. They're hardwired with an innate capacity to become a man, and good parenting by mothers or fathers can nurture that. If a son is supported, encouraged, and loved, he's going to go out there with confidence and find the additional support he requires. No family can provide it all … The fact that women can and do raise healthy sons should be reassuring and affirming. The human heart doesn't have a gender (119).

I also motivated him monetarily, although some say you shouldn't, but I did and I think it was all a part of the picture I had for his success. I rewarded him for each A or B on his report card, C's or anything below that got nothing. I don't recall him ever receiving less than a B on any of his report cards. He spent most of his money buying books because he loved to read, so it was a win-win for both of us. Because of his high ACT scores, he won a *full scholarship* to the University of Illinois. He was considered a Presidential Scholar and his scholarship covered room, board, tuition and books—everything! Everything! He has never seen the inside of a jail, he doesn't do drugs, and he takes care of his wife and children. I am so very proud of the man he has become, and I thank God for His protection from the time my son was born to when he was just a little lad, to when he was growing into manhood and even now in this day and time.

After majoring in Economics in college my son went to law school and now serves as vice president and legal counsel to a company which does business with other companies globally. He just returned from India, his third business trip abroad. My daughter-in-law earned her doctorate degree in education in 2009. My granddaughter is a very beautiful and talkative little girl. At every opportunity I talk to her about Africa. She knows where it is on the world map and told me a few days ago that she had put together a puzzle I sent her of the continent, and she has decided she wants to go to the Ivory Coast. I asked her why she wants to go to that particular country and she said in her little girl voice, "Because that's where I'm from." Hmmm ... I have no idea why she said that, but one day, God willing, we might be able to take that trip together. My grandson, a little younger than his sister, wants to be an artist. He's always saying "good job" because his mom and dad say it to him and his sister whenever they accomplish something they have tried hard to do. My grandchildren will know that education is so very important in their family, and we will each serve as a role model for what they too can achieve. My family continues to help shape my racial, academic, and spiritual identity daily.

Of all the civil rights for which the world has struggled and fought for 5000 years, the right to learn is undoubtedly the most fundamental.
—W. E. B. Dubois

Developing Images of Self: Personal and Professional

Immediately after graduating from college I began looking for work. I felt the responsibility of having a child to nurture and care for, and so I needed a job! After a few weeks of looking, I found work in the Chicago public schools, and after a few months was assigned to Baker (pseudonym) Elementary School. At first it was just work, and then I discovered that teaching offered me an opportunity to change someone else's life the way mine had been changed by the three Black teachers at Lincoln High School who saw potential in me and pointed me in an alternative direction from that of most of my peers—to a college education. There was little employment to be found for someone with a Bachelor's degree in Political Science, so I decided to become a substitute teacher until I could find other employment. To my surprise, I really liked teaching. It was fulfilling, so I went back to college to take a few methods courses which I needed to become a certified teacher. Somewhere around my 25th year of teaching, Local School Councils (LSC) were created and I, along with one other teacher, was elected by my fellow teachers to represent them on the LSC. That was a real challenge because the principal and his supporters didn't like it that I pointed out that most of our students were not achieving at the level they should be, and that we needed to re-evaluate our practices, or do something, so that we wouldn't keep "getting what we were getting." Even though they elected me, I think I represented change and everyone knows change is hard. Some said, "Don't rock the boat", "What are you so worried about?" It was a volatile time. For the students the boat was not only rocking, but sinking. I saw Black children not being educated and some blamed the parents or the students' lack of ability when the academic achievement scores showed the majority of our students were two, three, or even four years behind in reading, math and other subjects. By the time I received students in eighth grade, the grade I taught most of my teaching life, it was pretty much too late to get them where they needed to be to attend the high school of their choice. Many of our students ended up going to the feeder school which most did not want to attend because of its reputation as being for "low achieving" students.

Both principals I worked with were White men. The first one was there for approximately ten years after I arrived. We mostly saw him at the end of the day when he came out to talk with the staff as we signed out. The assistant principal, a White woman, was all over the school, working very hard. Had it not been for her, I believe students would have been further behind than they were.

The second principal was a younger version of the first, although he did move around the school more. By that time CPS had Local School Councils which were responsible for rehiring principals when their 2-year contracts came up for renewal. My concern was that students were not receiving the education they needed to successfully compete in high school. I thought teachers needed ongoing professional development training in how to teach reading, math and other subjects, but there was no big push to put that in place. Most seemed satisfied with the status quo. The staff never discussed, to my remembrance, how we could improve as a school.

Somewhere before being elected to the LSC, I took and successfully completed the Chicago Principal's Examination which was given in those days (1988) to determine who was qualified to serve as principal. It was an incredibly hard exam—a written part and an oral part. Newspaper reports said 5,000 people took the test and only 1,500 passed. I saw it as a challenge and with God's help I passed the examination and received a Principal's Certificate. I think part of the problem at my school was that I was seen as a threat. Some thought I wanted the principal's job. I didn't. Even if I had seriously considered a principalship it would not have been at my own school. After passing the exam, anyone wanting to become a principal still had to interview for it, and so I went to one interview at another school to see what it was all about. The first clue that this may not be the job for me was that the people who interviewed me: the area superintendent, several parents from the Parent Teachers Association and a few other stakeholders--about ten people sitting around a table in what felt like a criminal inquisition, wanted a principal to not only solve the problems of the school, but the problems of the world! A few years later, after leaving my school to work in the main office, in the midst of a few health challenges, and after a year in the Leadership Academy and Urban Network of Chicago (LAUNCH) principal preparation program, I realized that the principalship was just not a part of my destiny. I knew there were other ways I could influence student achievement, and so I returned to my position as professional development facilitator at the CPS Central Office.

Interestingly enough, in the midst of infighting and personal discouragements, one day while in my eighth grade classroom, I received a telephone call from "God" in the form of the Deputy Officer of Teacher Development under former CPS Chief Executive Officer, Paul Vallas. She asked me if I wanted to come to the Central Office to work with teachers in a trainer-of-trainers program model for implementing the Chicago Academic Standards (CAS) in the classroom. I had been recommended by the Director of the Chicago Teachers Union Quest Center because of the training in implementing the standards I had received and the leadership role I had taken to work with a few teachers at my school to write instructional units aligned to the standards. With all of the confusion that was going on at my school, I said "Yes!" and left my eighth graders, with their blessing, to work at the Central Office. I was placed in the Teacher Development Office. At first the director was not very friendly; I thought it was because of my affiliation with the Teachers' Union. I think she thought I was an "undercover agent" of sorts, but after getting to know me and seeing the quality of my work, she gave me a huge project. The project was to coordinate the development of a *Standards-Based Instruction* manual for teachers (27,000) throughout the system to use as a guide for implementing the standards in their classrooms. She assigned me to supervise fourteen teachers who would work with me after school to provide input for that project. At the time I thought she was too particular—everything had to be in perfect order if it was coming from her office. There were several other projects in the office that I had an opportunity to be a part of and I could see that everyone knew not to "drop the ball", as she would say, or you would feel her wrath. Needless to say I was anxious, but she gave me a chance to prove myself and I remember her saying, "Always do your best so that you can be proud of whatever you put your name on." As the result of the success of that project I was given another gigantic project, the Goals 2000 Standards Implementation Project, in which I worked with principals and teams of teachers from over 100 schools. Today I thank that director for expecting and accepting nothing but excellence. I still hold many of the skills she taught me about working with people and earning their respect. I have discovered that those we demand little of are not the ones who come back to say thank you (Reeves 2002).

The last position I held at CPS before retiring was as Manager in the Teachers Academy for Professional Development. I managed the School Teams Achieving Results for Student (S.T.A.R.S) program consisting of a four-member capacity-building team (coordinators) and a five-member team (four teachers and the principal) from each of 135 schools. I also managed the Professional Development Catalog of Classes which was distributed systemwide. My biggest challenge was working with one member of the office staff who was known to be "hard to get along with." It was rough at first, but I was able to win her over by showing her how much I appreciated her and valued the excellent work she did. In addition, I also supervised one staff member who had a health crisis which could have been terminal. When she returned to work she was very delicate and spent a lot of time talking to co-workers rather than doing the work she had been assigned. Even though I was very concerned about her situation, there was still work to be done and deadlines to meet so I had to insist that she complete her work. To show her I cared and to brighten her day, every week I bought flowers and before she arrived, put them in a vase on her desk. I also bought her books and cards to encourage her to stay positive. Others thought I was being too demanding of her by insisting that she complete her work, but every year for seven years, she and her husband have sent me a dozen beautiful roses at Christmas time. I'm not sure exactly why. Perhaps she remembers how she felt when I brought flowers to her. We now share a special relationship.

One of my most cherished memories of the Teachers Academy is working with a friend and colleague, Carolynn, to sponsor several Black History Month celebrations at the Professional Development Center where we worked. We felt it was important to share our culture with the diverse group of people in the building. And even though I was no longer a classroom teacher at that point, what I had learned about my African heritage when teaching about Africa to my students was now very influential in my life, and I wanted to share it with others. We planned a program which included an African fashion show, African music, African proverb storytelling, and of course, food. I was in charge of decorations and the program and Carolynn was in charge of the food which consisted of all of the comfort foods, some of which she prepared herself. We collected money to serve a traditional soul-food lunch and several hundred of our co-workers came, during their lunch hour, to celebrate the African American culture.

The folks at the Center started to look forward to our celebration, but Carolynn became ill after our 3rd year of holding the Black History month celebration. After a time which seemed like a very short period, six months to a year, Carolynn passed away from breast cancer. I think about her now because she was studying for her doctorate degree during that time. God had other plans for her, but I will always treasure Carolynn's memory and will never forget the special bond we shared.

As before mentioned, after teaching in the same public school for many years, I decided to leave my eighth-grade classroom in an inner-city school to accept a position in the Chicago Public Schools central office. My identity as an educated Black professional woman was being developed as I was able to experience working with a more diversified group of staff members. As a central office professional development facilitator and manager, I worked with principals and teachers of many races and nationalities. I learned that we all have more in common than we think, and I discovered that I was able to deal fairly with individuals no matter what their ethnic background. I ran a successful teacher-training program in an educational system which had nearly thirty thousand teachers at the time. There was a lot of responsibility on my shoulders and I did my job well. Being blessed to travel to places like the West Indies, South and West Africa, London, Paris, Dublin, Rome, Denmark, Sweden, and Prague in the Czech Republic, has given me a greater understanding and appreciation for the peoples of the world and has helped me to become more accepting of those from other cultures and nations. The world is a much smaller place now that I am a "world traveler."

Only God's favor has allowed me these traveling experiences and to have seen His array of children of many colors from various parts of the globe.

In her book, *A Return to Love,* Marianne Williamson (1992) writes words which touch me deeply and best sum up my thoughts and feelings about my life's journey and my character development. In 1994, Nelson Mandela used a line from this quote in his inaugural address when sworn in as President of South Africa and many incorrectly attribute it to him. Williamson writes:

> Our deepest fear is not that we are inadequate. Our deepest fear is that we are powerful beyond measure. It is our light, not our darkness that most frightens us. We ask ourselves, who am I to be brilliant, gorgeous, talented, fabulous? Actually, who are you *not* to be? You are a child of God. Your playing small does not serve the world. There's nothing enlightened about shrinking so that other people won't feel insecure around you. We are all meant to shine, as children do. We were born to make manifest the glory of God that is within us. It's not just in some of us; it's in everyone. And as we let our own light shine, we unconsciously give other people permission to do the same. As we're liberated from our own fear, our presence automatically liberates others (190-191).

I am truly grateful to my mother for enrolling me in the all-White Charleston High School back in 1962, and even though it was tough, the people and situations there taught me that I have the strength to endure difficult situations, and that I am smart and can accomplish whatever task is before me. The more than 800 students I have taught over the duration of my teaching career also helped shape my personal and professional identity. I felt I owed them my best self, and so I went back to college after a few years of teaching to become a better teacher. I attended every workshop and seminar offered through my school whenever a learning opportunity became available. I had to learn many things that I did not learn in college as a Political Science major, such as new math and standards-based instruction, because I needed to know them in order to teach my students what they needed to know in order to succeed academically. Through studying ancient African history we learned to appreciate our African cultural heritage together. I thought I was doing it for my students, but as it turned out I needed to feel the same pride in my heritage that they did. I am grateful to my students for influencing me to make that connection with Mother Africa which I have visited twice over the past ten years. And although I had never thought of myself as political, I ran for teacher-representative in the first Local School Council election in 1989 and won. I thought I could make a positive difference in our school for teachers and students. I stood up against low test scores and the status quo and stuck to my guns even in the light of being ostracized in my own school by colleagues of many years who thought we should "just let well enough alone." In *So Much Reform, So Little Change*, Charles Payne (2008) explains local school councils this way—

> ... in 1988 the Illinois legislature sharply reduced the size and authority of the Chicago central office and gave individual schools expanded autonomy. The law created local school councils at each school and gave a majority of votes to parents. The councils were given some real powers, including most importantly, the power to hire principals, in addition to substantial authority over the discretionary budget, curriculum, and school-improvement planning (11).

Nearly fifteen years later, the same school had a Level 3-low academic level standing for school year 2009-2010 (latest report) and is on the State's probation list for failure to make Annual Yearly Progress (cps.edu). The student population is still 100% African American and 98% live in poverty. After nearly half-dozen administrative changes since I taught there, some improvements have been made, but I can't help but wonder what kind of school it would be today had we tackled our problems of low achievement so many years ago, instead of ignoring our failures and burying our heads in the sand?

It's hard to believe now, but I spent a quarter of a century teaching at one school. The following vignette is about two students, one in one of my eighth grade classes, and one student in one of my sixth grade classes—all boys coincidently. The girls had their share of challenges as well—pregnancy, child abuse. Those who dare to say that teachers "have it easy" because they may have a shorter work day and weeks off during summer vacation know nothing about a dedicated teacher's daily struggle to teach "other people's children" (Delpit 2006) and care for them, their safety and welfare, as if they were your own. Becoming a teacher doesn't happen in a university classroom; it happens day-by-day when you make a commitment to high expectations for your students and yourself. It causes you to spend extra hours after the school day ends, striving to be the very best teacher you can be each and every day realizing that as a teacher you help to shape another human being's future. What an awesome responsibility.

Vignette Three
"Matters of Life and Death"

One particular morning is forever etched in my memory because one of my students was shot by another student and had to be rushed into surgery to save his life. Thank you Jesus, he survived. Shortly after his release from the hospital, his mother transferred him out of the school, and I never saw him again after our short visit in the hospital. He wasn't talking much that day and so I only stayed long enough for him to know I had come to see how he was feeling after what he had been through. It was the first time anything that serious had happened in my twenty-five years of teaching. The student who was shot was not physically in my room at the time because the first period of our departmental schedule had begun and my class was in another classroom. It was a double period of sorts. But it dawned on me later and cringed at the thought that a loaded weapon had first been brought into my classroom that morning. It was the makings of a tragedy.

The upper-grade teachers were experimenting to see if we could cover more of the academic standards the students were supposed to master by using a departmental model. I believe this was the first year of our self-imposed pilot. As the story unfolded, it seems this shooting was an accident. These boys were good friends—one showing the other what he had brought to school. The whole scenario was traumatic. Ironically, both of these young men were good students and well-behaved. Both students had parents who were concerned about their successes in school. I could not believe what happened! I know it was selfish, but I was happy they were not in my classroom when it occurred because I didn't know if I would have handled it as calmly as the other teacher did. I was saddened because two young, Black boys, full of potential, were stopped in their tracks that day. Thankfully, no life was lost. Neither of them returned to our school.

And then there was this: Some details are a little fuzzy, but it seems to me this incident happened in the late 80s. It was also a matter of life and death. I believe the student was in sixth grade. He was a nice, quiet boy—kind of hefty. I've heard it said that coincidences are God's way of remaining anonymous. Well, some might say what happened was a coincidence; I say it was Divine Intervention.

It was the weekend and I decided to clean up my apartment so I turned on the radio to listen to music while I cleaned. Music seemed to make the time go by quicker and the cleaning smoother. Sometimes I finished cleaning before I even realized it because I was so focused on the music that I wasn't aware of the dust or the disorderly room until I was done. This particular day for "some reason" I decided to listen to talk radio as I occasionally did. The host was talking about what to do if you ever encountered someone choking on food in a restaurant or anyplace else for that matter. They talked about what the medical books call the Heimlich maneuver (HM). This procedure was described and discussed at length on the show and by the host and the person he was interviewing. Medterms.com, http://www.medterms.com, an online medical dictionary, defines the HM as "an emergency treatment for obstruction of the airway ... It may be needed when someone chokes on a piece of food that has 'gone down the wrong way.'" This online medical dictionary also describes how the procedure should be done:

> *To perform the Heimlich maneuver, stand behind the victim, wrap your arms around their waist, make a fist with one hand and hold the fist with the thumb side just below the breast bone. Place your other hand over this first and use it to pull sharply into the top of the choking person's stomach and forcefully press up into the victim's diaphragm to expel the obstruction (most commonly food). Repeat as necessary.*

The Heimlich maneuver was named for Dr. Henry Heimlich, an American surgeon, who noted that food and other objects that obstructed airways were not being expelled by giving quick blows to the back, which had been the procedure before his discovery. In 1974 he developed a new method which he called "the new manual thrust method"—the Heimlich Maneuver which is in wide scale use today. If the HM doesn't work a tracheotomy would need to be performed in order to keep the victim from suffocating from lack of oxygen (medterms.com).

As I continued to clean my apartment, I pictured everything I heard in my mind and hoped I would never have the occasion to use it. I was wrong. Shortly after that weekend, a few days at most, one of my students, was choking on a piece of chicken from his lunch. I was sitting at the next table in the lunchroom when one of the kids shouted, "He's choking!" I looked around and I could see that one of the students was in distress. He wasn't making a sound, but holding his throat and looking panicked. I told another student to run and get the gym teacher who was the school's designated first aid person, and then I remembered what I had heard on the radio. He was sitting and somehow I lifted him up a little so that I could get my hands around this diaphragm area, and I did what had been described on the radio. The first thrust didn't work, but the second one did and out popped that piece of chicken. I had not had any training and I wasn't sure it would work, but I had to do something! After it was all over I was shaking, weak in the knees, and had to sit down, but the student was fine. By the time the gym teacher arrived it was over. We gave the student some water and everyone gave a sigh of relief. (People in general, don't know all that teachers go through on a daily basis). I called his parents and told them what happened and asked if I should send him home. His mother said "No." She said since he was okay to let him stay at school. A few weeks later, the Teachers' Union representative had a photographer come to my room to take pictures. The story was published in the national teachers' union newsletter. Coincidence? I was so glad I had listened to the radio and quite possibly saved a child's life.

Reflection

I wrote this reflection to explore how I became a teacher and remained a teacher in an inner-city elementary classroom for almost thirty years, and also to highlight some of the unbelievable experiences a teacher may have on any given day. When I went to college I had being anything but a teacher on my mind. I just knew

I wanted a college education and had not thought far beyond that. Had Black students not been exiled to the all-Black, inadequately equipped, Lincoln High School, I probably would have taken the science classes I would need to carry out my life's work in the sciences. I liked Biology a lot and when I first declared a college major that was it, but I soon discovered that without a strong background in math and the sciences, my chances of passing classes like Calculus and Chemistry were pretty much nil. I got through botany and zoology because they were mostly reading and memorizing, but I knew the other required courses would be over my head. At Lincoln I had only taken Biology I (One) and never took Chemistry, Physics, Geometry, or anything above Algebra I because those courses were not offered, but a few blocks away at the all-White high school, Charleston High (CHS), all of those classes and more were being taught. In addition, at Lincoln there were just two years of English. I suppose the people running the schools in Charleston, Missouri didn't think Black kids might want to go to college or just didn't care. Even after entering CHS by court order in my junior year, I had missed a lot of the classes a successful college career required. So, I soon changed my major to Social Science. I was thinking that with a major like Social Science I wouldn't have to take any science or math classes and perhaps that would be the best route for me to earn a degree. I still had to take a remedial math class which I barely survived, and by the time I graduated from college, after changing majors several times, I ended up a Political Science major. At that point I was thinking about going to law school when I graduated. Someone told me later that the best course of study for law school is to major in English because lawyers must do enormous amounts of reading and writing, but it was too late to do anything else but graduate. Although I was absent for one semester, I worked hard to make up for lost time because I knew then that my path was leading to finding a job so that I could take care of my son. And so I graduated from Tuskegee Institute with a Bachelor of Science in Political Science, and had no idea what I was going to do with it, but I had kept my promise to my mother and myself to finish college, and I did.

I really believe teaching chose me, I didn't choose it. Perhaps I was born to be a teacher. I was a good teacher and I strived each day to be better one. I know it's far "out there", but I used to think that God planned for me to be there when that child was choking, to save his life—maybe that was why I became a teacher. After all, it was very mysterious how I came to know how to perform the Heimlich maneuver the weekend before it was needed, while listening to the radio in my apartment. I've heard in church services all my life: "God works in mysterious ways, His wonders to perform." Although these words are not found exactly that same way in Scripture, Isaiah 55:8-9 (KJV) does say "For my thoughts are not your thoughts, neither are your ways my ways, saith the LORD. For as the heavens are higher than the earth, so are my ways higher than your ways, and my thoughts than your thoughts." So, in my mind and heart, all things are possible—some are natural, some are supernatural. When my student was shot, miraculously I was shielded from dealing with the trauma of having a child killed for whom I was responsible. The whole thing was mind-boggling.

Sometimes I also think I was deliberately placed in the lives of the children I taught to help them reach higher goals academically and to aid in their understanding of the beauty of their own cultural heritage. Ladson-Billings (1994) in *The Dreamkeepers* makes reference to "good teachers ... who can help African American students choose academic excellence and yet not compromise their cultural identities" (127). That was my goal. Even when I tried to stand up for what I believed about why our students were not achieving at the rate they should have and got virtually "shot down" by colleagues whom I had worked with for many years, I knew I had been chosen to be right where I was. No one else spoke out regarding the fact that *only* about 20% of our students were and had been for years, at or above grade level in reading and math, 80% were not, and some members of the staff seemingly wanted me to just be quiet. I wasn't.

Fresh out of college, I was on the face of it, "forced" into the teaching environment because after looking for several months, it was the only job I could find. Even though my first position was that of substitute teacher, I quickly learned that teaching can be the most tiring, the most frustrating, as well as the most fulfilling and the most important work one can do. After I realized the enormity of the task I had been given, I acquired a Masters degree, took the necessary tests and became a certified teacher.

As an experienced elementary school teacher, I learned to expect the unexpected. I never knew when an irate parent might show up unannounced and upset my day. And I didn't know if some child would pull the fire alarm on the coldest day of the year and everyone made to go outside, or the principal would hand out some new, asinine report from the central office. On the other hand, it could be a day when a former student would come back to visit and say "thank you for what you did for me when I was your student" or it could be an exhilarating day when students finally grasped a concept I'd been trying to teach all week. Most of the years I spent as an elementary school teacher were good ones. The children I described in this vignette were just a few of many whose lives I touched and who touched my life as a classroom teacher. There were countless days of happy times with the children in my classroom over the years; however the events involving threats to life are the kind you lose sleep over and are impossible to forget.

I had finally found my niche as an upper-grade teacher after about five years of teaching. I taught every grade from second through eighth and discovered I really liked the older students and could communicate well with them, so most of my teaching life was spent with seventh and eight graders. Several years before I unexpectedly left the school to take on a new job, we decided to departmentalize the upper grades. I taught 7th and 8th grade language arts and social studies. The upper graders were all on the same floor so it was fairly easy to have my students go to other upper-grade teacher, for math and science and have his students come to me. My students were seventh graders and his eight graders. We changed classes every 60-90 minutes in the morning and worked on projects aligned to the academic standards in the afternoon or the students would go to music, art, or physical education. By that time most of the teachers were getting acquainted with standards-based instruction. Charles Payne (2008) explains the 1990s' standards-based instruction (SBI) movement this way—

> The idea behind standards-based reform is that if states or localities set high standards for curricular; develop assessments that measure student performance against the standards; give schools the flexibility they need to change curriculum, instruction, and school organization to enable their students to meet the standards; and hold schools strictly accountable for the outcomes, then student achievement should rise (169).

I had taken standards-based instruction training a few years before we departmentalized, and did what I could to pass what I'd learned on to other teachers. I would invite parents and other classes to my room to see students make presentations aligned to the standards. Prior to our implementation of the departmental model, I had taught my students how to work in cooperative groups on standards-based projects and to write and use rubrics. I also taught a group of teachers who met with me after school, to write instructional units aligned to the standards and higher-order thinking. I was the first teacher in our school to use SBI. Because of my training, I was asked to help write standards for the Chicago public schools (Chicago Academic Standards) and became an instructor for the Chicago Teachers Union Quest Center which dealt with teachers' professional development. My after-school or summer classes were composed of teachers from all over the city who wanted to learn more about how to teach to the standards.

I remember when I left my teaching job to work at the CPS Central Office. It was 1996, and I had the honor of being asked to work with the Standards Project. Although it meant leaving my students, I took the job because it was a great opportunity and because when I asked the students what they thought, they said I should go. I was a no-nonsense teacher so I thought they were probably happy to get rid of me. I found that wasn't true by the overwhelming response I received when I returned to the school to retrieve some of my personal items after being gone for a few weeks. My students literally jumped on me, hugged me, and told me how much they missed me. It was good to know they weren't really happy I had left, but I considered it serendipity because as a Local School Council member for two years, I had grown weary of fighting with the administration about the low academic achievement of our students. I felt a sense of accomplishment and thought taking the job was a good way to let the naysayers at my school see that someone else appreciated my ability and achievements. (I believe because of the implementation of standards-based instruction, performance-based assessments, and using rubrics in my classroom the year before I left, my students' reading scores increased more than any other classroom in the upper grades). And besides, I was beginning to feel isolated, perhaps even unsafe, at work. The timeline is fuzzy, but someone keyed my car on the parking lot. The few friends I still had were almost afraid to be seen with me.

Local School Councils (LSC) had many problems back then. It was new to everyone and no one really knew exactly how it was supposed to work. The LSC was responsible for renewing the principal's contract or they could hire a new principal. As an LSC member I thought it my duty to say we should look at other candidates for the principalship before renewing the sitting principal's contract. I soon learned that there was a lot of underlying distrust amongst staff members and that as Payne (2008) indicated some considered my saying we needed to improve as a school, a personal attack. It was truly a "political spectacle." Smith (2004) submits that the theory of political spectacle "holds that contemporary politics resemble theater, with directors, stages, cast of actors, narrative plots, and (most importantly) a curtain that separates the action onstage—what the audience has access to—from the backstage, where the real 'allocation of values' takes place (11)."

What I experienced was all of that. And so, for my physical and mental well being and to escape the "drama", I took the job at the CPS central office, which just happened to be offered to me at the very moment I needed it, and I left my life as a classroom teacher behind. Was it another Divine Intervention? "Surely goodness and mercy… all the days of my life."

Another reason I believe I was "chosen" to be a teacher is regardless of how hard it got, and even under adverse circumstances, I never thought about quitting my job, unlike the many times I thought about it seriously as an administrator at the Central Office. Never thought about it even through years of struggling to improve students' test scores, one child being shot by a classmate, one almost choking to death in the school cafeteria, and one of my other students who left school on Friday and never returned because her house caught fire over the weekend and tragically she was killed. I don't remember her name now because it was early in the school year and I didn't know her well, but she was there and then she wasn't. It was rough on her classmates and on me, and there were no Crisis Intervention teams back then to help us through it. I never thought to myself, "This is just too hard." Instead, I thought my students needed me and I wanted to be there for them. Although as their teacher you try to keep it together for your students, sometimes the tears will come and they get to see your "humanness." At the end of the day I would go home, refresh and renew and return the next day. I don't remember either incident interfering with my ability to teach. Once you consider the needs of your students, there is seldom time within the day to focus on yourself or your feelings. I believe the worst possible scenario for a teacher is to have one of his/her students die, in or out of school.

There were many stressful days leading up to my departure from the school, and it was like Moses parting the Red Sea—without any prompting from me I was freed to pursue a new adventure. But after all those years in a classroom, I missed my students. At the Central Office there was no children's laughter or bells ringing. I wondered if the people who worked there at their desks and telephones ever thought about the children they served, or was it all just meetings and spreadsheets. At times I thought about leaving that job because it just didn't feel like important work. I heard a lot of "submit this report; attend that meeting, cancel that report ... we don't need it anymore." It was not at all what I expected. I felt disconnected from the schools and the students for whom we planned programs and wrote curriculum. I remember telling one of my colleagues, "We need a school in this building, just so people don't forget why we're all here." Little did I know that my days as a teacher were not over, my students were just different—they were teachers themselves, and sometimes, administrators. I was happy to be a teacher again, to be able to pass on the knowledge I had. Knowing it would be passed on to students in teachers' classrooms all over the city was a blessing I had not imagined. I am still a teacher at heart, and I pray that in the future more opportunities will come where I can continue to teach. It's what feels very natural to me, as if it were meant to be.

Racial Identity Development: Cultural Proficiency

I recall an occasion when after many years in the classroom, I felt the need to become more "culturally competent" (Lindsey 2009), even though all of the students in my class were Black like me. And when thinking about the "cultural proficiency" of teachers who teach students who are not like them, I believe teachers today have a lot of work to do to understand how important it is to "see" all of their students and to not be "colorblind" as teachers once thought was a good thing and politically correct. I realized that being culturally aware and sensitive also applies to students when their teacher has the same ancestral heritage, but a different culture, such as when one day six Haitian students arrived in my classroom. A few years before I left the classroom, a group of Haitian students transferred to my school. Some of them, because of their age, landed in my classroom. Lindsey (2009) defines cultural proficiency as "a paradigm shift from viewing cultural difference as problematic to learning how to interact effectively with other cultures ... cultural proficient leaders address issues that emerge when cultural differences are not valued in schools and other organizations"(4). We had a Haitian bilingual teacher at the school and so when Haitian students arrived in the district they were sent there. Needless to say, the Haitian students were "different" from the African American students. They didn't look different, but their first language was French. Some spoke English well enough to communicate, some spoke only French. The African American students didn't like it that the Haitian students spoke another language and seemed to think that they were "foreigners" and therefore not as "good" as they were. Also, the Haitian students were very polite and respectful to teachers. Some students didn't like the bar they were setting. They saw the difference and didn't like it. This just demonstrates that people who are of the same "race" can lack understanding of differences and show culturally destructive behaviors to those of their own heritage, but I decided we were all going to learn to get along and respect one another.

Working with the Haitian students at my school helped me to become more culturally proficient and I was determined to help my African American students become more accepting of their differences also. I was resolute in helping the African American students see that the Haitian students were not someone they needed to shy away from, talk badly about, or single out because they were different. In fact, I set out to prove we were a lot alike. The first thing I did was ask the Haitian bilingual teacher, if he could find some time to come into my room and teach a few French words and phrases to the rest of the class. He was happy to do it and the African American students loved it and felt empowered because they were learning a new language, and the Haitian students seemed to feel more accepted as members of the class. We talked about Haiti; where it was, how long the Haitian students had been in this country, and the how we were all a product of the African Diaspora, the spreading of Africans to other parts of the world through the slave trade. This situation truly made for many teachable moments. The next thing I did, a month or so later, was hire a Haitian caterer whom the bilingual teacher recommended, to bring some Haitian food to the school for a celebration with my students. He also invited a Haitian artist who brought some of her paintings and masks and other artifacts. We invited parents—a few came, and my original students, who at first turned up their noses and said they didn't want any of the food, eventually sucked up all of the chicken, beans and rice, vegetable salad, plantains and everything else on the table. Most of it was food they had eaten before, but this time prepared Haitian style and it was very tasty. We played Haitian music and danced together. Those two events went a long way towards getting the African American students to accept the Haitian students as equals and classmates. I believe we all felt better after the party where the students laughed and talked among themselves. I believe they discovered they were more alike than different, and from that time on we were able to operate as one class and appreciate each other's culture.

Vignette Four
"God Knows My Name"

God knows my name. He knows who I am and where I am every moment of every day and He knows just what I need even though sometimes it's not what I want. I've loved God for as long as I can remember—since I was a very little girl singing in church. Loving God doesn't mean you always do the right thing. What it means for me is that I am always aware of what the right thing is, and I can stray only so far from the way I was raised and the love for Christ that I carry in my heart, before something pulls me back to a place of faith. I believe God places people and allows circumstances in our lives to help us with our journey. Some of these people and events teach us lessons of love, faith and trust. Some teach us lessons of disloyalty, distrust, and betrayal. I've had great teachers on both sides.

I sent my son to Catholic School although I was a public school teacher. I can understand why some people frown on that, but I did what I thought best for him. Having grown up as what the US economic system defines as "poor", I wanted a better life for him and I believed that meant getting a quality education. It was also important to me to give him a spiritual foundation just as my mother had given me. Dare I say there was a public school about a block away from where we lived when my son was ready for kindergarten? In this school however, most of the students were reading below expected levels and I decided I had to choose another school for him. I put him in a private nursery school when he was three or four and in Head Start before going to Holy Angels Catholic School. Holy Angels had a reputation of being one of the best Catholic elementary schools in the city. The majority of students there achieved at high levels, plus it was a religious school, and I wanted my son to be in an environment where he would learn the Word of God so that he would love God too. So from kindergarten to eighth grade he attended Holy Angels School. Most of the students, if not all the students there were Black; most of his teachers were nuns. Nuns are mostly White Catholic women who have dedicated their lives to Christ and have taken a vow not to marry. They say they are married to Jesus Christ. Unfortunately, they also have a reputation of being some of the meanest teachers on earth. Most of my son's teachers were not, in my opinion, mean, but serious about their work. I was willing to accept a few challenges because I believed he was getting the best possible education that I could make available to him. Fortunately, I didn't have to submit him to the disgrace I went through by placing him in a majority White school just so he could receive an excellent education. Tuition was affordable and less expensive for us because we lived in the school community. The principal, Father Smith, and the first African American pastor of the church, Father Clements, were both Black so that balanced out the racial thing a bit. They were both very visible and outspoken, not only in the Black community, but also throughout the city. Occasionally there were teachers who weren't nuns, but that was rare. I think my son had one Black female teacher when he was in 7th or 8th grade who wasn't a nun. And because all students were required to attend Mass on Sundays, Holy Angles became my church so that I could attend Mass with my son.

A friend who was a member of Holy Angles Church and knew of my singing background, told me about the gospel choir that had just been started by the pastor, and said I should come and join. A gospel choir in a Catholic church sounded intriguing; it encouraged Black culture and that spoke to me. After all, I had been Baptist all of my life and gospel music was our specialty. Catholic churches had historically been mostly White and the music they sang was quite mundane and boring to someone of my "handclapping, shouting hallelujah" background. The congregation was almost one hundred percent African American, so it made sense. Music has always played a big part in the Black church and from childhood I have always sang in a church choir. I joined the gospel choir at Holy Angels Church, and stayed there even after my son graduated from 8th grade. One Sunday in every month the choir, small but with powerful voices, wore African garments. Increasingly, I had begun exploring Africa with the students in my classes; I was being touched, moved, by all-things-African. I felt as if I were part of something bigger and more beautiful than the average person that I came into contact with could comprehend. Front and center in the church is a floor-to-ceiling mural created by an African priest and given as a gift to Holy Angels Church. The mural is divided into ten scenes from the Bible with all of the characters depicted with brown skin and dressed in African clothing. Jesus, Mary, and Joseph are in a large diamond-shaped depiction in the center of the mural, each with certain "African" features and Jesus' "swaddling clothes" are a brightly colored African fabric. This church fed my soul, not only spiritually, but culturally. There is a saying in the Black community that there is "a church on every corner." A drive through some Black communities would prove that statement true. With the inhumane treatment—beatings and rape—the many disparities and discouragements that the African American community as a whole has experienced going back to slavery times, the church has offered a place of refuge, of freedom, even while in bondage because when you worship and praise God your spirit is free, free no matter what your physical body is going through. This is a freedom that no one can take away because it's a feeling on the inside that brings peace even in sorrow.

I became a lead vocalist and I loved singing in the choir. The people there were very accepting of my talent and had become my second family and so I, like my son, was baptized Catholic. Years later Father Smith, the school principal, died from complications associated with a terrible car crash. Father Clements left Holy Angels to pastor a church in the Bahamas and I left to become a member of a Pentecostal church in a nearby neighborhood. It was difficult leaving all of my friends, but I felt it was a call from God to do so. I had been a choir member at Holy Angels for nearly twenty years and some members still ask me, "When are you coming back?" It's not a question that I can answer.

I've used my God-given musical ability many times as a classroom teacher because when nothing else worked, music did. People tell me I have been blessed with a melodious voice—given a special gift. All of my life I have sang in a choir somewhere, first as a child in the Baptist Church, then in high school, in college, in the Catholic Church I joined to be near my son and at the church where I am currently a member. There have been times when I've seen someone moved to tears, touched by the Holy Spirit through a song I've sang. Before singing in church I *sang with several bands in nightclubs around Chicago. I gave up the bands and rock and roll, and now I sing only for the Lord. No more "my-baby-did-me-wrong-songs." Having a song in my heart and on my tongue has also helped me through some tough situations. It's pretty hard to sing songs about forgiveness and peace each Sunday and not stay grounded in love and compassion.*

On June 10ᵗʰ, 1986, Holy Angels African American Catholic Church burned down to the ground. I was awakened in the early morning by a phone call saying the church was on fire. It was devastating news. I joined Holy Angels after enrolling my son in the school and he had been a student there since kindergarten. Even after he was no longer a student I stayed there because I had grown to love the church and the people. A picture, which captured my utter sadness and disbelief that our church had burned down, appeared on the front page of the Sun-Times newspaper that day. I hadn't noticed the photographer when he shot the picture, but when I arrived at school later that morning there was the photograph on the office counter, beside the sing-in sheets, for all to see. Everyone was sad for me that day knowing how much I talked about and loved my church. Several months later I wondered what I could do to help rebuild the church, so I held a gospel concert. I rented a hall, hired a band and sold tickets. I then gave the proceeds—about $1500 to the church. Since that event was successful I did it again—this time I organized a fashion show, begged for clothing from a store where I was a frequent customer, convinced some of the men and women of my church, including the pastor, Fr. Clements, to model. I and some of my loyal friends, sold tickets, and gave the proceeds to the church. The Holy Angels Church Web site states:

> *For nearly 5 years, tireless efforts and campaigns were begun to rebuild the church. Contributions were made by great and small folk alike, and in June 1991 a beautiful new church was dedicated on the very site of the old worship site (http//:www.holyangles.com).*

Father George Clements, once my pastor, has been a mentor and is still a friend who I speak to occasionally by phone and visit periodically. He called just the other day and his voice sounded like he wasn't feeling his best. He's getting up in age now, but he is still traveling and has speaking engagements on occasion. Having been a vocal social justice advocate for civil rights, for the adoption of Black children, and for the church to play a role in the rehabilitation of prisoners and drug addicts for many years, he has his own place in the American history books, at least the Black ones. And although I didn't know him at the time, I later discovered we were both in the same place at that march from Selma to Montgomery with Dr. M.L. King in 1965. At 80, he has retired and returned to living in Chicago. At one point in his career, after leaving Holy Angels, Fr. Clements worked in Washington, D. C. for President Bill Clinton. He is very humble and doesn't talk much about what he's done or who he knows. He sent me a picture of himself, Pope John Paul II, and President Clinton (1999) that was taken when he was invited on a flight to St. Louis in Air Force One. I also have encouraging letters that he has written to me about how a song I sang in church moved him or the congregation. More than fifteen internet sites appeared when I goggled Fr. George Clements. The historymakers.com site yields this historical bio:

> *Clements began his ministry in 1957 in the archdiocese of Chicago. He aligned himself with various social causes, especially the Civil Rights Movement. In 1968, while Chicago's African American Catholics were calling for a black pastor, Clements was in the front runner for the position ... In 1969, he was named pastor of Holy Angels Church ... 1981, he became the first priest to adopt a child, and later adopted three more. His One Church-One Child program subsequently resulted in the adoption of more than 100,000 children nationwide. He has worked to help students from Africa secure higher education in the United States and has been active in the war on drugs ... Father Clements has been honored by numerous organizations ... A*

> *film ... "The Father Clements Story", was produced and broadcast by NBC in 1987. [It] starred Academy Award winner, Louis Gossett, Jr., as Fr. Clements, Malcolm-Jamal Warner, as his adopted son, Joey and Carroll O'Connor, as Cardinal John Cody, who was the Archbishop of Chicago and a source of aggravation to Fr. Clements at that time.*

The Holy Angels Gospel Choir can be heard on the soundtrack of the made for TV movie. I was fortunate enough to be heard as the lead singer on the song, "Jesus Is Alive." And although it never became a "big" hit, it was played for a while on AM 1390, gospel radio in Chicago. It was a blessing to hear myself singing over the airways. I am grateful to God for the voice He gave me to sing His praises. I pray He will continue to let me use it to touch the hearts of His people.

And then a strange thing happened one day in one of my eighth grade classes at Baker Elementary School (pseudonym). I had been teaching there for maybe ten years, enough time for students and staff to know I was a singer. I sometimes sang at assemblies, and numerous times I worked with eight grade graduations to help organize the music for the ceremony, even though I was not a music teacher. Sometimes I sang in my classroom get my students' attention or to teach them about jazz or gospel music or about the Civil Rights Movement. Although I never preached church to them, they knew I also sang in church. We were in the new church by then and I'm sure many people all over the city had heard about the church burning down and had possibly seen my grief-filled picture, taken without my knowledge, on the front page of the Sun-times newspaper the next day. So one day one of my students, who had been absent too much and caused more than a little trouble in the classroom, asked if he could go to church with me. I was shocked and intrigued at the same time. What was his motive for asking that question? Was it just to challenge me? Maybe he just wanted or needed some attention. Having spoken with his mother several times before, I had the feeling that she wasn't getting much cooperation from him at home either. Just going with the question to see where it would lead, I said "Yes", of course he could go to church with me, but it would have to be on his own time on a Sunday. To my surprise other students began to ask if they could come too. This was turning into something I had not expected. In all, there were about fifteen-sixteen students who signed up to go to church with me. I told them this was not a school field trip, and that they had to get their parents' permission. I let the principal know what our discussion was and told him I would rent a school bus, have it come to school on a Sunday morning and take my students to church with me. And so I did. They all came on time with their permission slips and we went to my church. I sang with the choir and the students were very quiet and well-behaved on their own. At the end of mass I had them stand up and I introduced about half of my eight grade class to the congregation. They were so proud and I was so proud of them. Although attending church is a large part of African American culture, I remember thinking that most of them had probably not ever been to church before. I didn't have problems with any of those students after that, including the student who initiated the trip. We had developed a special bond.

Reflection

Worshipping at Holy Angels Church for nearly twenty-five years enhanced my identity as an African American, and being aware of my pastor, Fr. Clements', willingness to fight for the causes he believed in, influenced me to do the same. We always heard stories and saw him on television defying the system such as by going into neighborhood stores asking the owners to take their drug paraphernalia, which encouraged the use of drugs in the Black community, off the shelves. We, as the congregation, were audience to his fight for the adoption of Black children and to his own controversial adoption of four sons, and to his plea to the Black church to become more involved in the elimination of drug addiction. So we were not only being fed spiritually, but we also saw a social activist at work on a daily basis striving for the betterment of his people and his community. I was proud of the African heritage the church displayed in its decorations and in the African attire the choir sang in once a month. Fr. Clements was given African garments and the status of "chief" by a tribe in Nigeria for his help and involvement with Nigerian students and priests who came to study in the US—particularly those who lived at the church's rectory while they were in Chicago. My church was a place where I could express my own African-ness in comfort. One of the songs I led in the choir that I loved was a Nigerian praise song. So when the original Holy Angels Church burned down it was very heartbreaking for me and I wondered what I could do to help. Through several fund-raisers which I conceived and coordinated, I was able to provide funds for the rebuilding of the church. Holy Angels Church and School had been a vital part of the Black community for many years when the fire occurred. My colleagues at work, both Black and White, lent their support to a successful gospel concert where I performed, as well as a fashion show where I had Father Clements dress up in a White suit and a "bee-bop" hat. My students too, were aware that my church was a huge part of my life outside of school. Perhaps that's why they were eager to attend church with me. I saw this "outside of school opportunity" as another way of connecting with my students. Heather Pleasants, in an article "Showing Students Who You Are", which appears in Everyday Anti-Racism: Getting Real about Race in School (2008) asks an important question gives her response:

> ... in your experience, what opportunities exist for teachers and students to understand one another beyond their school-defined identities? Schools offer few occasions for teachers and students to connect as complex individuals outside their prescribed roles. While conceptions of culturally relevant teaching and learning emphasize the need for teachers to increase their knowledge of students' multifaceted identities, space for this kind of knowledge-building is often limited. Occasions for teachers to present themselves to their students as whole people is also limited (70).

Culturally relevant pedagogy speaks to teachers about connecting with students and the lives they live outside of school, and about sharing information about themselves with their students whenever possible. Teachers can't always reveal personal information about themselves, but they can share their interests and passions to let students know they are real people. Pleasants, a professor of qualitative research, goes on to say—

> By bringing what is meaningful to us in our out-of-school lives into the classroom and finding appropriate ways to include our interests in our instruction, we can grow our own spaces for connection to students who may feel that their own out-of-school lives are irrelevant to formal learning activities. By integrating what excites you beyond your work as a teacher into your pedagogy, questions ... can be framed by 'what can I do to help the kids better understand me?' as well as 'What can I do to understand these kids' (73)?

When thinking about the teachers I had growing up, unfortunately the memorable connections I made in elementary school are few, possibly because I wasn't in one school long enough. In one of my high schools, the connections I made with three of my Black high school teachers were life-changing, and in the other there were no connections with my White teachers other than that of a student occupying a seat in a hostile classroom environment.

Developing Images of Self: Charleston High School

In October of 1962, fourteen African American students integrated Charleston High School (CHS) in Charleston, Missouri; seven by court order. I was one of the seven. The National Association for the Advancement of Colored People (NAACP) supported a group of parents in suing the Charleston, Missouri Board of Education to allow Black high school students entrance into the town's best high school. We were following in the path of six-year old Ruby Nell

Bridges, who in New Orleans, Louisiana, November 1960, became one of the first Black students to attend an all-White school, escorted by federal marshals (https://www.britannica.com/biography/Ruby-Bridges). I was sixteen years old when I entered CHS and I believe that is where my desires for social change and social justice were born. I was in my junior year when I entered CHS because my first two years of high school was spent at Lincoln High School, where the Black high school students were traditionally required to attend. Lincoln was a fun place—all of my friends were there. My boyfriend was there. The problem was that it was inadequate—separate but definitely not equal. I had always dreamed of going to college. Even though I knew my mom couldn't afford to send me to college, I never thought of myself as poor. I knew Mama would find a way. As Walker (1996) posits in *Their Highest Potential*, "In this community, many parents were not silent victims of an oppressive system; instead, through a variety of roles they actively participated in providing resources for their children" (200).

A few blocks from Lincoln there was another high school with every class any college-bound student would want or need, but it was basically just for the White kids. I mentioned before that one Black girl was permitted to attend in her junior year. I never knew her, I suppose because she was in the senior class when I got there. She was the school board's way of "integrating without integrating", but that was unacceptable in court. At Lincoln we had the bare minimum as far as the curriculum was concerned: two years of English, one year of math, no chemistry or calculus or geometry and maybe a hundred old books in the so-called library. Even as a freshman in high school I knew I wanted more than most of my peers who just wanted to get out of high school and get a job, any job. My mother was always encouraging and had high expectations for me, so she allowed me to go to Charleston High School-even if it was by court order. A fitting quote from Dr. M. L. King, Jr. declares, "Faith is taking the first step, even when you don't see the whole staircase." And that is just what we did … we took that first step.

The interesting thing about being one of fourteen Black students to integrate a White high school is that even though we were there in the school and in the classrooms, we were still not really a part of the school. We were treated like outsiders. A court order got us in, but what we suffered on the inside could only be understood if you were there. Hooks (1994) recalls her similar experience when first attending a previously all-White school, " …we were always having to counter white racist assumptions that we were genetically inferior, never as capable as white peers, even unable to learn" (4). That's how it was at Charleston High. And I guess part of the punishment for our coming to "their" school is that the White students seldom if ever spoke to us or interacted with us in any way other than to call us some other derogatory name and sneer. They wanted us to know that we were not welcome there, and sadly neither we nor they ever broke through the racist walls that had been built generations before we were born—"the legacy of race and racism" (Tatum 2007). They never got to know us and we never got to know them. We were isolated even in the midst of four hundred other students. The teachers, who were all White as well, mostly ignored us. They were rather cold and didn't seem to want us there any more than the kids. Student-teacher relationships were basically non-existent. I remember one teacher, who said she had never taught "Negroes before." It was like we were a different species of human being and she had to figure out what to do with us. What an emotional toll on the psyche of adolescents just beginning to develop a racial identity! "We had to give up the familiar and enter a world that seemed cold and strange, not our world, not our school. We were certainly on the margin … and it hurt. It was such an unhappy time" (hooks, 24). Relationships there were just the opposite of what Howard describes in his book, We Can't Teach What We Don't Know (2006):

> An authentic professional relationship is one that communicates clearly to my students through my words, my actions and my attitudes the following sense of connection: I see you. I acknowledge your presence in this classroom. I know your name and

I can pronounce it correctly. I respect your life experiences and your intelligence. I believe in you and I will hold both you and myself accountable to honor your capacity to learn. I enjoy being in this work with you (129).

On the contrary, many minority students even today don't enjoy the kind of relationship Howard speaks of with their more than likely, White teachers. In a July 2010 article in, *Teacher Magazine* online, "Teaching Secrets: When the Kids Don't Share your Culture", by Elena Aguila, it was stated that:

- Nine out of 10 teachers in the United States are White.
- Four out of every 10 students are *not* White.
- Forty per cent of public schools have no teachers of color.

Living in the kind of racist environment that I was mostly raised in, it is not surprising that we were not welcomed at our new school. In fact, the first day we arrived at our new school some students showed their hostility and rage by throwing tomatoes at us. They let us know for certain that we were not wanted there. Imagine the humiliation of having to weave and bob and jump out of the way for fear of getting the inside of a tomato all over your clothing. That was the first time I knew what it felt like to be hated, and by people who didn't even know me. I didn't understand why we were being treated that way. I don't believe any of us were prepared for it. It still brings tears to my eyes and sadness to my heart more than fifty years later, when I think about the name calling, the fights, and the students writing "the N-word" in black shoe polish on our lockers and taping pictures of old, ugly Black people or anything they thought would make us look or feel bad. From that first day forward I did my very best to show the teachers and the students that they were wrong about Black people—that we were neither stupid nor lazy. I made the honor roll that first marking period. In fact, I had the highest average in the junior class. I recall covering up test papers so that the White kids sitting near me couldn't see what I was writing. After some of them discovered I was making high grades on everything, they had the nerve to try to look on my papers. I felt I was representing every Black person in the world and set out to prove all the "haters" wrong. And although the whole situation was something a teenager should not have had to go through, I did it because I felt I had a right to the same education the White kids were getting. I have since learned that trials and challenges come to make us strong, and this was definitely a character-strengthening, life-changing experience. But I decided that day, as Booker T. Washington, African American educator and founder of Tuskegee Institute said, "I shall allow no man to belittle my soul by making me hate him" (http:www.brainyquotes.com). Today I am proud that as a sixteen-year old I had the courage to do something that was very difficult and not cave in or run away, and I know I am a stronger person today because of it.

I remember it well—the oratory contest at my new school. I decided to enter it as a challenge to all the White folks who thought Blacks were inferior to them. It was called a Declamatory Contest. I had never even heard the word before! Each student had to memorize a monologue to perform for an audience made up of the student body. I don't know how I had the nerve to do it. The good thing about my monologue, "Gossiping Gertie", is that it was humorous. The main character, Gertie, a housewife, was having a conversation with her imaginary children while they were getting into all kinds of mischief as she was gossiping with her girlfriend on the imaginary telephone. Every few minutes she would yell something like, "Stop dumping that flour on your brother's head! Young lady you are going to be in major trouble in the next hour or two when I get off this phone!" Her kids practically burned the house down, but she wouldn't stop gossiping. I don't remember all the words exactly, but it was funny. I remember that the students laughed—a lot. I wasn't sure they would. What the White students didn't know was I entered the contest because I was still trying to prove to myself and to them that I was just as good, just as smart, and just as creative as any of them.

I've noticed an interesting phenomenon in the television media today where several popular shows have African American talk-show hosts. I don't recall there ever being so many Black hosts in my life time, and every one of them is a comedian. The "View" on ABC has two African American women whose claim to fame is comedy; the "Talk" on CBS, which is a clone of the "View", has two hosts who are African American women comedians; "Let's Make a Deal" and "Family Feud" both have Black male hosts who are also comedians. Is it that we are more accepted by the White establishment when we are humorous rather than serious? Since the exit of the Oprah Winfrey Show, the only Black successful television shows in the mainstream media are comedies. Observing through a Critical Race Theory lens, there seems to be a trend where Blacks are appreciated for our ability to be "funny" and make people laugh, more so than in positions where we seriously challenge the status quo as I did at Charleston High so many years ago.

I won second place in the Declamatory contest, although I should have won first place. It was the first time a Black student had been in the contest so "naturally" they couldn't actually let me win first place, but still they knew I was excellent. Anyway, I was proud that I opened the door for other Black students who may have been thinking of participating and that in itself was a good thing—worth all of the time and effort I put into learning the monologue and performing it.

I persuaded my best friend Betty to join the Glee Club with me. According to my mom I'd been singing since I was a tiny tot, so it was only natural that I would want to join. There was no Glee Club to even consider at Lincoln High School. Betty was a soprano and I an alto, so we "Blackened" up the Glee Club. I remember learning songs from *West Side Story*, especially "I Feel Pretty", ironic considering what we were going through at CHS. Nothing about it was pretty. And we sang "There's a Place for Us", paradoxical, considering where we were and what we were experiencing. Imagine singing these words in a racially antagonistic environment:

There's a place for us,
Somewhere a place for us.
Peace and quiet and open air
Wait for us
Somewhere.
(http://www.westsidestory.com) ©Bernstein and
Sondheim 1956, 1957)

It's hard to explain the hurt and indignation I experienced as a teen-ager who wanted only to be given an opportunity to receive the best education available to me at the time. Merely saying we experienced racism doesn't explain how hate played out for fourteen Black students in a school of four hundred White students and teachers who never failed to let us know how they felt about us each and every day by their cruel treatment. Why?—because of our race. They knew nothing else about us except that we were Black.

My story took place more than a half-century ago, yet Black and Brown students are still experiencing racial segregation in schools across America at this present time. In my moments of reflection, sometimes I ask myself, "Will we ever see Dr. King's dream fulfilled— that all people will be judged by the content of their character and not by the color of their skin?" Or are we just *not* the America we profess to be? Are we hypocrites when we say that "all men are created equal?" Even though I know the answers to the questions I ponder, I continue to have "the audacity of hope" (Obama 2006) that one day the nation where I was born and raised will be all it claims to be. Lisa Delpit (2006) in *Other People's Children* talks about America as a source of discouragement to her following the tragic events that occurred in New Orleans after Hurricane Katrina in 2005. She says,

> ... perhaps one of the changes that carries the most weight for all of us is the realization that we are not the country we once believed ourselves to be. The great putrid underbelly of racism and classism in our

nation has been exposed through the tragedy of New Orleans. The horror of nature's attack on a major U.S. city has been overshadowed by the distorted attitudes toward those who are darker and poorer (1).

Vignette Five

Junior Prom: "God Has a Sense of Humor"

High school doesn't hold many pleasant memories for me after entering Charleston High School (CHS). However, something unexpected happened that gave me and the other Black students involved one of the biggest laughs I have ever had. It was the end of my junior year and we had been there since October. I never made one friend at that school. There was this one boy named Dennis who would smile in passing and say hello every once in a while. He may have wanted to be a friend, but his White friends and perhaps his family, would have found that unacceptable. Sometimes I wish I knew how to find him just to say "thank you" for reaching out in a time when it was unpopular, perhaps even dangerous, for him to do so (hooks 1994).

It was the end of the school year in 1963 and some of us wondered what we would do about the Junior Prom. Should we go? Would there be trouble? Would all the music be "White" music that none of us liked? We only had one radio station in my home town and the kind of music they played was definitely not what most Black high school students wanted to hear. Because I have always loved singing no matter who's performing, I listened to their songs and sang along with Patti Page, Pasty Klein, and Rosemary Clooney, popular White women singers of that day. It wasn't until we began to be able to tune in to WDIA, a Black radio station in Memphis, Tennessee, that we began to hear Black artists like Jackie Wilson and James Brown. And then there was Motown Records out of Detroit which made R &B (rhythm and blues) and "soul" music popular and has since become an American icon. They had artists such as the Supremes, Smokey Robinson and the Miracles, and the Temptations. WDIA didn't come on until the evening hours, so until then it was basically country music, unless you had a television and could see American Bandstand. Bandstand was a rock-and-roll television dance show which became popular in the early '60s. In my neighborhood just having a television in your house meant you were "well-to-do." Television wasn't readily affordable for most people in my community. I remember going to my friend's house a short distance from mine, to watch television before we had one of our own. Her dad and mom were the only people I knew who had "professional jobs." They owned several school buses and provided transportation for the Black kids in the district who were bussed to the Black high school in Charleston. They had everything before everyone else—like a telephone and indoor plumbing. They were the "Joneses" in the neighborhood. The other families worked hard toward obtaining whatever they had.

There were few if any Black kids dancing on Bandstand until after it had been on the air for a few years. Everything in my life up until the time I enrolled into Charleston High School had been separated by race. Jackson (1997), author of <u>American Bandstand: Dick Clark and the Making of a Rock 'n' Roll Empire</u>, is cited in an August, 1997 edition of the Seattle Times newspaper as saying:

> *In the '50s, there were very, very few blacks on Bandstand … As a white teenager, you could turn on Bandstand and it looked like there were no blacks in Philadelphia. To see two blacks or maybe none is just about segregation. Bandstand didn't have its first black regulars until 1965.*

My first real boyfriend, who I dreaded leaving, was still at Lincoln, the all-Black high school. I went to Charleston High because I wanted to be in the best school academically; he was concerned about playing basketball, but why shouldn't the Black kids experience the fun part of high school just like the White kids? It certainly wasn't fun where I was and having to cut through racial hostility on a daily basis. So I asked him to take me to my Junior Prom. At least at CHS we had one prom for all the juniors. I have heard that in some school districts in years past, schools held two proms—one for the Black kids and one for the White kids. Separate but equal never seems to work, because as it turns out, Whites receive the "best" of whatever there is and Blacks receive whatever if left. That has been the means by which institutionalized racism has worked in this country for hundreds of years. It's the reason was why my mother enrolled me in Charleston High, so that I too could experience the best. "The White folks never seemed to understand that our parents were no more eager for us to socialize with them than they were to socialize with us" (hooks 1994, 24). Our parents just wanted us to be treated fairly and equitably, and being in the same space, at the same time as the White kids, seemed the best way to assure that occurrence.

Those of us who were juniors decided that we were not going to let anyone tell us that we could not attend our own Junior Prom. Even though we were sure we wouldn't enjoy their sad music, it was the principle of the thing that mattered. So my boyfriend and I, and about 3 or 4 other Black couples—although we were a little anxious and uncertain about what would happen—went to the prom. Would they throw tomatoes at us the way they did the first day we arrived and ruin our prom dresses? Would someone start a fight or use some hurtful words towards us, the way they had before? Would we spend the night listening to the music most of us found dull and boring that we heard from our hometown radio station? No, we were going no matter what! Our determination overcame our fear and then the funniest thing happened! As soon as we stepped in the door we noticed that the band was Black! ... Black! ... Unbelievable! They didn't want us at the school, but I guess it was ok in their minds to hire a Black band—typical! Everyone knows how Blacks love to entertain White folks! I remember seeing a film about Marvin Gaye, a popular Motown artist in the early '70s, singing to an all-White audience. They were really enjoying his song, dancing and singing along, yet he probably had to leave by the back door. And in a film that I recently saw about the Temptations, a popular Grammy-winning Motown singing group, there was a rope down the center of the room where they were performing which separated the Black kids from the White kids. There were uniformed policemen present to make sure everyone only danced on their side of the rope. The ridiculousness of it all reminds me of words from "Inner City Blues" (1971), one of Marvin Gaye's hit songs, when he says, "Makes me wanna holler, throw up both my hands!"

After looking at each other in awe and shaking our heads in disbelief, we laughed so hard that we held our stomachs as we got on the dance floor. The music was rhythm and blues—our kind of music— the Supremes, the Four Tops, the Miracles. The band was cool! We were surprised to see that the White kids liked the music as much as we did. Luckily, we didn't have any trouble that night, but we still kept to ourselves and did our very best to show them up on the dance floor! We always joked about Whites having "no rhythm." I suppose we were happy to find a stereotype we could buy into. We even talked to some of the band members who were probably surprised to see Black kids there. Needless to say, we danced our butts off! It was like God was saying we deserved to finally have some fun!

Reflection

Nelson Mandela said and I believe, *"Education is the most powerful weapon which you can use to change the world."* Most adults look back on their high school days as a time when they had a lot of fun with friends, going to the football or basketball games, cheering for the team—that was not my experience. Attending a high school reunion is out of the question for me. To my classmates at CHS I was just another Black face invading their school. I never got to know anyone and no one knew me, not really. So in order to attend Charleston High, those of us who went there gave up the fun part of high school. Sometimes I wonder if the White kids really hated us or did they just fear the unknown. We had been separated by race for so many years while growing up in southeast Missouri. Howard (2006) suggests that "fear is the classic White American reaction to any intrusion into our culture capsule" (14). There was very little social life at Charleston High except for the other Black kids, few in number, and the students we knew and would see every now and then who were still at Lincoln High School. And it was just as bell hooks (1994) explains her own experience after entering a previously all-White high school, "We had to give up the familiar and enter a world that seemed cold and strange, not our world, not our school. We were certainly on the margin, no longer at the center, and it hurt"

(24). The prom is one of the few enjoyable experiences I can recall at Charleston High and even though we were under the same roof with the White students, we were still separated into our own corners of the gymnasium. Howard (2006) speaks of his senior year in high school as the year when he first discovered his "Whiteness." He and his friend, also White, "afraid" and "curious" went on a date with two African American female students (interestingly) from another school. He reports, "The one connection I made in high school with a person outside my own race symbolizes an essential step for any dominant culture person who wishes to grow beyond the limits of encapsulation" (Howard, 15). Unlike my experience, he was able to connect with another person across a racial barrier that had been created around their lives by a society which had decided, for them, that their lives would never touch (14). Most of the students at CHS seemed to want to be encapsulated, so the ones who didn't call us names pretty much ignored us, pushed past us, as if we weren't visible.

The court order letting me and the six other Black students into the school also required the district to consolidate all the schools. When the schools were combined a year later, all of the Black teachers left town because they no longer had jobs. I'm sure White parents in those days would have balked at the thought of a Black teacher teaching their child. But these teachers were never given that chance. Shortly after the consolidation, Lincoln High School was closed. And so I have no high school to return to—one was a place where I started as a high school student and had fun for a while, but which lacked the college essentials, and the other from which I graduated, was a place where I wasn't welcomed or wanted. bell hooks (1994), who today is a writer, teacher and "insurgent Black intellectual" speaks of her similar lived experience and says " ...we were always having to counter white racist assumptions that we were genetically inferior, never as capable as white peers, even unable to learn ... We were always and only responding and reacting to white folks" (4).

We were proud of ourselves at the prom that night. Proud that we had been courageous enough to face the unknown and come out victorious. We were setting an example and carving a path for those who would come after us, and even though CHS was not fun most of the time, it was necessary and I would do it again. We didn't know it then, but we were making history and in spite of the negative experiences, we graduated and I went on to college believing that getting an education was the best thing I could do to improve myself and make a positive contribution to society. Now in the Charleston R-1 School District, and for many years, there has been one high school, one middle school and one elementary school. All races of children in the district go to the same schools. In 2011, there are only a handful of Black teachers at Charleston High School. In 2010 Charleston High School was reported to have had 318 students—52% Black and 47% White students and did not make AYP (Adequate Yearly Progress). Sixty-one percent of students were eligible for free lunch (http://www.education.com). It would be interesting to know what happens in classrooms on the inside of these schools. Is there tracking? Are the classrooms still segregated? Perhaps that is a topic for additional research.

Attending Charleston High School was a challenge, but we stuck it out. We as a country have made some progress in the area of race relations and educational equity since that time, but Blacks and other minorities in America still live their lives in a racist society. African Americans are a people stolen from their homeland, stripped of their culture, and forced into slavery. We helped to build this country, but still, 500 years later, are enslaved politically, economically, and educationally. I believe the inequities still exist because the privileged and powerful want to maintain their hegemony at all cost. I'm reminded of the recent "debt ceiling" fiasco where members of the mostly White US Congress nearly caused the entire country to default on its loans, and did cause a lowered credit rating, because the President's opponents' say their number one goal is to make sure that President Barack Obama, the first Black president of the United States of America, "is a one-term president." Even those who appear in public to be supportive of the President may not be with him behind closed doors. What better way to sabotage his re-election than to blame him for all of America's economic problems. It seems that some Americans have forgotten that we live in a democracy with three branches of government, not one. Each branch is responsible for representing all the people. Some accuse the President of not being a leader, but in order to lead there must be those who are willing to follow. Thinking back on critical race theory which treats race as "central to the laws and policies" of American society (Delgado and Stefancic, 2001), it is very hard to see these events in the nation's capital as anything but racist. Congressmen and women, who voted numerous times to raise the debt-ceiling when President George Bush was in office, refused to do so for President Obama until the last hour. Again, *"It makes me wanna holler and throw up both my hands!"* to think that this country could go down like a sinking ship because there are those who still can't get pass race. Jennifer Steinhauer, journalist for the New York Times, said in "G.O. P. vs. Obama: Disrespect or Just Politics", a September 1, 2011 online article regarding the President's relationship with certain members of the Republican Party in Congress,

> There is the persistent and deeply uncomfortable question of race. Many African Americans, including black lawmakers, and even white Democrats, have complained that some of the disrespect for Mr. Obama stems from distaste among some whites at the idea of seeing a black man in the Oval Office.

Steinhauer quotes Representative Raúl M. Grijalva, Democrat from Arizona, when he said, 'I think people want to not deal with that issue, but I think, like it or not, some of the disrespect—and I stress some, not all—stems from the discomfort of having a person of color be president of the United States.' And I ask again, will we ever get pass this notion of White supremacy? Steinhauer also relates that President Obama has been adamant and has stressed his objections to the staff about playing the proverbial "race card", and that he would like to think its just politics. " ...critical theory reminds us that there is always more than one story if we look for it; there is always more than one reality in any human experience" (Hinchey, 81). But just as it happened at my Junior Prom in 1963, God is the final dispenser of justice. What is meant to harm, He can turn around for good. I am relentlessly hopeful for my country to—as Dr. M.L. King, Jr. said in his famous "I Have a Dream" speech, ironically in 1963 as well—" … rise up and live out the true meaning of its creed: We hold these truths to be self-evident: that all men are created equal" (usconstitution.net). The question is, how many of those serving in Congress and other government positions, actually believe those words written over 200 years ago in the Declaration of Independence and in the pledge of allegiance to the flag of the United States of America, "…and to the republic for which it stands, one nation, under God, indivisible, with liberty and justice for all." There are millions of children of color who say this pledge in their classrooms everyday, they too see the news and watch the hateful political wrangling between our national leaders. How do we explain this hypocrisy to them? hooks (1994) offers this insight:

> … I have encountered many folks who say they are committed to freedom and justice for all even though they way they live, the values and habits of being they institutionalize daily, in public and private rituals, help maintain the culture of domination (27).

If I could have a conversation with President Obama I would remind him that he has already secured a place in history of which African Americans can be proud. Although it seems he has been forced to deny half of his ancestry because he is the son of a White mother and an African father, in America he has been declared Black. African Americans embrace him as one of our own regardless of the fact that he is bi-racial. I would tell him that he is from a strong and great people who experienced and survived the Middle Passage, who lived in and survived chattel slavery in this country, who have the courage of Harriet Tubman, Frederick Douglass, Booker T. Washington, and W. E. B. DuBois, the beauty of Cleopatra and

Queen Nefertiti, the talent of Paul Robeson and Mahalia Jackson, the intellect of Thurgood Marshall and Whitney Young, the creativity of Dr. George Washington Carver, the faith and compassion of Dr. Martin Luther King, Jr., and the conviction of Nelson Mandela (King 1997); and that the strength he needs to continue to be the leader of the "free world" is already in him, put there by God through every one of his ancestors who were "tried by the fire", but came out triumphant, just as I did at Charleston High so many years ago.

It has been a challenging first four years for President Obama, but I believe as one of the songs sung regularly in the Black church says, "What God Has for You, It Is for You." So it doesn't matter how many obstacles are placed in his way, he will remain in office if that is God's plan for him. So many of the problems America has faced since 2008 when President Obama was elected were inherited. Still there have been successes that those who oppose him would rather forget. For instance, a few that resonate with me are listed below:

- The Lilly Ledbetter Fair Pay Act that ensured women can get paid the same as men for the same work was signed into law.
- Thirty-two million more Americans are able to afford health insurance for the first time and nearly all Americans—95% of those under age 65—will have insurance.
- The nearly ten-year War in Iraq was brought to an end and US troops came home.
- Osama Bin Laden was captured and killed under President Obama's watch allowing the nation to breathe a sigh of relief from one of the nation's greatest threats (http://www.BarackObama.com).

Success is to be measured not so much by the position that one has
reached in life as by
the obstacles which he has overcome
—Booker T. Washington

Racial Identity Development: Tuskegee Institute

Tuskegee Institute (University since 1986) in Tuskegee, Alabama is one of America's historically Black colleges and universities (HBCUs). Its motto is "Tuskegee, the Pride of the Swift-Growing South." Anyone who has heard of Booker T. Washington or Dr. George Washington Carver probably knows they were both instrumental in the establishment of Tuskegee as a respected educational institution. Booker T. Washington was the first principal of Tuskegee in 1881 which began with 30 students who were teachers themselves, wanting to further their own education.

In *Africana: the Encyclopedia of the African and African American Experience,* Appiah and Gates (2003) had this to say about Washington:

> Washington's most significant contribution was his belief in industrial training as the key to success for African Americans ... Tuskegee was incorporated as a private institution in 1892. Because social conventions would have prohibited white instructors from serving under a black principal, Tuskegee became the first black institution of higher learning with a black faculty. In 1896 the school hired a young teacher who would become famous—George Washington Carver, whose groundbreaking agricultural research received international recognition (931).

I'd always wanted to go to college, even though most of the kids who lived in my small hometown in Missouri seemed to be satisfied with just finishing high school. After graduation most of them would move away to find employment in Chicago, Cleveland, Detroit or some other big city. I, on the other hand, just knew I would go to college. That dream came true, as before mentioned, with the assistance and persistence of three of my Black high school teachers from Lincoln High School who had graduated from Tuskegee before coming to teach at Lincoln. Mr. and Mrs. Campbell and Mr. Allen (I don't remember first names) were my guardian angels. They saw my potential and told me about a five-year work-study program Tuskegee had to help needy students earn their college degrees. Even after I left Lincoln and they stayed, (Black teachers were not allowed to teach at Charleston High School), they kept up with me and helped me submit all of the papers I needed for admission to Tuskegee and put me in touch with the right people. I have them to thank today for pointing me in that direction and for being a significant part of my education journey. Walker (1996) talks about the many roles Black teachers have played in the Black community—

> Traditionally the black teacher has played multiple roles in schools. Among these have been teacher, parent surrogate figure, counselor, disciplinarian, and modeling figure. These roles have been anchored in a collective black identity where these teachers perceive the success or failure of their pupils as gains or losses to the black community. That is, the teacher and pupil share a common interest and mission. The teachers view themselves as ethnically responsible for preparing these youth for future leadership and for making contributions to this unique mission, namely the liberation and enhancement of the quality of life for black people (206).

Work-study first led me to work as a receptionist in the Registrar's Office and then for the last two years of my college life I was a dormitory counselor. In my senior year I was the overnight "dorm mother." The job of keeping the young women who lived there safe was on my shoulders. Any emergency that arrived, I handled. Some nights I barely slept at all. What an awesome responsibility that was!

I felt safe at Tuskegee. I knew the racial trauma I had suffered in high school would not be repeated there. Unlike Charleston High, my environment was saturated with people who looked just like me and understood racial heritage. It was a time of healing for me. For once in my lifetime I didn't have to be aware that my skin was Black twenty-four hours a day. I remember some of my friends and I, on several occasions, going home with two of the women's dormitory advisors for church service and Sunday dinner. They lived in the neighborhoods surrounding the college and were like our mothers while we were away from home. They made us feel welcome and cared for, not only as students, but as a part of their family.

While at Tuskegee I joined the Civil Rights Movement by participating in picketing segregated public facilities and marching in protest rallies. What stands out mostly in my mind is the time when students from Tuskegee rode the "freedom buses" to Montgomery to protest the prejudice policies of Governor George Wallace. My mother was always fearful that I was going to be thrown in jail or dogs or water hoses would be turned on me like they had been on so many others, but none of that happened. I was felt it was where I was supposed to be at the time and I didn't have any fear. God was watching over me even then.

I remember when Sammy Younge, a student at Tuskegee, was murdered senselessly in downtown Tuskegee in 1966 for trying to use a "Whites-only" bathroom at the Standard Oil gas station, or so the man who shot him claimed. An eerie sadness fell over the whole campus that night. We couldn't believe what had happened right under our noses. Sammy was only twenty-two years old and had been in the Navy before enrolling in Tuskegee. I didn't know him well, but I do remember seeing him around campus. The White man who murdered Sammy was tried by a jury of his White peers and found not guilty. He alleged that Sammy had confronted him with a golf club. None of us believed that story, but of course the all-White jury did. He shot Sammy twice—once in the head, presumably over the use of a public facility—a toilet!

Many of the students from the college marched the streets of Tuskegee the next day to show their anger and mistrust of the city's White community. Had it been a more violent protest, more students would probably have been killed. The major destruction was of a Confederate statue that someone threw black paint on. I don't remember being in that crowd, but I do remember seeing the statue, possibly the following day, with the words "Black Power" scrawled across it. An online source: (http://www.encyclopediaofalabama.org), said this about Sammy—

> Samuel Younge, Jr. was the first black college student to be killed as a result of his involvement in the American civil rights movement ... Samuel Younge, in life and in death, represented the struggle for black freedom in Alabama in the 1960s. In his short life, he worked to break down barriers of inequality by registering black voters and pushing for the desegregation of public facilities. It was this work that ultimately cost him his life and made him a martyr for the civil rights movement in Alabama and the rest of the nation, inspiring countless others to take up the cause of racial equality in the United States.

On Veterans' Day 2011, as I listened to a morning Christian radio program, I was reminded of the celebrated Tuskegee Airmen. The White host of the show called out various wars and aircraft that had been used in those wars and particular squadrons which are typically remembered on Veterans' Day, but he did not mention the Tuskegee Airmen. I'm not sure he even knew they existed. He has, in the past, by some of his opinions about President Obama and various governmental operations, let the audience know he is a staunch conservative in his political views. I however, listen to this station for a Biblical perspective, not for a political one, which I can find on a plethora of television stations on any given day. In my role as a social activist, upon several occasions I have emailed this talk-show host to tell him of comments over the airways that were offensive to me as an African American. He has responded by denying the possibility that he could have said anything that sounded vaguely racist. I continue only to listen to this station because there are a limited number of Christian radio stations available to me, and for the most part the Christian programming meets my needs through music and sermons. There are three Black ministers that I am aware of, out of a total of ten or twelve, associated with this station. Two provide daily sermons and one (perhaps a token representative of the Black community) is the station manager. I have become increasingly more aware that listening to Christian radio does not guarantee an anti-racist agenda. This particular station has programming which mostly caters to conservative Whites. And just as guilty of segregated programming, the Black gospel radio station that I sometimes listen to caters to African Americans through its music and topics that mostly affect the Black community. They have no White ministers preaching sermons and they play no "Christian" music sung by White folks. Even though we claim to serve the same God who made us all, race is still a thorn in the side of Black as well as White "so-called" Christians. I wonder what some Christians will do when they discover that heaven is not separated by race, or nationality, or denomination for that matter. Time will tell.

To continue my initial focus, the Tuskegee Airmen were a group of more than 900 Black pilots who wanted to serve their country as aviators and were trained at Tuskegee Institute during World War II (WWII) by the US Air Force (Appiah and Gates, 2003). Nearly half of those who were trained served in combat in WWII or the Korean War. "The all-Black squadrons of Tuskegee Airmen were highly decorated World War II combat veterans and forerunners of the modern day Civil Rights Movement" (http://www.Tuskegee. edu). In a November 11, 2011, Veterans' Day article in the Pittsburg Tribune, "Sewickley Memorial to Honor Tuskegee Airmen", writer Craig Smith states, "Before 1940, the then-segregated military did not accept blacks as airmen. The Tuskegee Institute in Alabama was chosen to train the pilots, navigators, bombardiers, maintenance and support staff, whose achievements paved the way for full integration of the "armed forces" (http://www.pittsburghlive.com). Smith goes on to mention monuments that have been dedicated to the Tuskegee Airmen which are located at the Air Force Academy in Colorado Springs, the Air Force Museum at Wright-Patterson Air Base near

Dayton, Ohio, and various other locations. Memorials such as these have tried to right the wrong of non-recognition which the Tuskegee Airmen have endured for so many years.

Along those same lines, in 2007 Congress and President George W. Bush awarded a Congressional Gold Medal to the Tuskegee Airmen, collectively, including the Black men and women serving as support personnel, "in recognition of their unique record, which inspired revolutionary reform in the Armed Forces" (Gropman 2007, 48). The Tuskegee Airmen suffered racial prejudice and bigotry in the US Armed Forces pre-and post-WWII, yet they had many successes along the way. The Congressional Bill of 2006 states—

> The 99th Fighter Squadron, after having distinguished itself over North Africa, Sicily and Italy, joined 3 other Black squadrons, the 100th, 301st and the 302d, designated as the 332d Fighter Group … From Italian Bases, they destroyed many enemy targets on the ground and at sea … and they destroyed numerous enemy aircraft in the air and on the ground. Not without cost—66 of these pilots were killed in combat, while another 32 were … captured and became 'prisoners of war'. The pilots came home with 150 Distinguished Flying Crosses, Bronze Stars, Silver Stars, and Legions of Merit, a Presidential Unit Citation, and the Red Star of Yugoslavia. The Bill noted the racial pioneers 'overcame the enormous challenges of prejudice and discrimination, succeeding, despite obstacles that threatened failure' (49).

Some of those obstacles were reports like the ones by the Army War College, in the 1920s and late 1930s, which said Blacks were "unfit for leadership roles and incapable of aviation … blacks were a 'mentally inferior subspecies', low in the scale of 'human evolution' with a smaller cranium than whites and a brain that weighed only 35 ounces contrasted with 45 ounces for the whites" (Gropman, 48).

In addition, recommendations said that Blacks were liars, thieves, "immoral and inherently cowardly." Despite all of this ridiculous, racist rhetoric, in 1941 President Franklin D. Roosevelt ordered the creation of an all Black flight training program in keeping with his promise to Blacks who would vote for him in the 1940 Presidential election. Critical race theorists (CRT) would understand that "Roosevelt did not order the Army to begin training blacks because he thought they deserved the opportunity, but he did it because he desired re-election" (Gropman, 48). Looking through the telescopic lens of Critical Race Theory it is effortless to see how the "interest convergence" tenet plays out in this scenario. "The interests of whites and blacks, for a brief moment, converge ... and Whites tolerate advances for racial justice because it suits their own self-interests" (Delgado and Stefancic 2001, 19 and 149).

Discrimination is a hellhound that gnaws at [African Americans]
in every waking moment of their lives to remind them
that the lie of their inferiority is accepted as
truth in the society dominating them.
*-**Martin L. King, Jr.***

Vignette Six
"Trials Come to Make Us Strong"

All of my life I have been a singer—in church, in high school glee club, in the Tuskegee Institute Choir, in a girls' R & B singing group in college, and as a solo jazz and blues vocalist. I sang at my mother's funeral. Some of my friends said they could not understand how I could do it. She would have expected no less. Singing helps me through difficult situations. When I became a teacher, at times I would sing in my classroom to entertain my students and especially to draw them back in whenever I felt I had somehow "lost" them. Sometimes I would teach a few of the "freedom songs" I learned as a college student while riding the "freedom buses" from the campus at Tuskegee to wherever we planned to protest. Songs with lyrics like—

> *Ain't gonna let nobody turn me 'round, turn me 'round,*
> *turn me 'round*
> *Ain't gonna let nobody,y turn me 'round*
> *Keep on a walkin', (Yeah!) Keep on a talkin' (Yeah!)*
> *Marching up to Freedom Land.*

And one song which I especially liked was principally directed at Governor Wallace of Alabama—

> *Oh-o Wallace!*
> *You know you can't jail us all----*
> *Oh Wallace!*
> *Segregation's bound to fall.*

"Freedom" songs many times were spiritual and gospel songs the protesters sang in churches on Sunday with a few words changed here and there to fit the purpose of the Civil Rights Movement (CRM). These songs were very important because of the uncertainty in the atmosphere the protests created. Singing songs of hope gave everyone renewed energy. Singing was an integral part of the mass meetings

where marches were planned or where speakers like Dr. King would speak of what was to come. The people participating in the marches and sit-ins needed encouragement and hope. Many times they did not know whether a demonstration would lead to attack dogs, or beatings, or a night in jail or worse. Some of the CRM leaders were ministers, some nuns, some priests, and some rabbis. Mary C. Turck (2009) in Freedom Song: Young Voices and the Struggle for Civil Rights *says—*

> *Many religious people defended the human rights of all people. They brought their stories and their beliefs into the civil rights movement. The Bible's story of the Jews' exodus from slavery was familiar to both Christian and Jewish Americans. The prophets of Jewish scripture cried out for justice. The Christian Gospels preached about loving your enemies and embracing nonviolence. And religious songs expressed this longing for freedom, justice, and peace. So it is not surprising that many religious songs became movement songs (45).*

As a result of my high school experiences with racism I became a social justice advocate. I found I had the courage and the tenacity to stand firm on my beliefs. I joined a public service sorority while in college and ran for a student government office. My continuing pursuit of social change and social justice caused me to become involved in the Civil Rights demonstrations that were so prevalent at that time. Those who wanted to "sit-in" on or picket an establishment were required to attend workshops on "demonstration tactics" which focused on how to remain non-violent even if someone spat on you, or attacked you in any way while picketing. I prayed, "Lord, please don't let anyone spit on me." Thankfully it never happened because I wasn't sure how I would respond. Spitting on someone, in my mind, crosses every line imaginable. We were told to fight back would destroy the non-violent movement. Thank God, I never had to make that decision. I never went to jail or had any of the terrible things happen to me that was happening to others, but I was ready for anything. People all over the world watched via television the cruelty of police that was happening in Alabama's capital at that time. *On the third day of the Selma to Montgomery March in 1965, when the marchers finally reached their destination, my friends and I, along with thousands of others who had joined the march, listened to Dr. King and others speak (while we sat on the lawn of the capital building) mainly about voters' rights and the illegal tactics which White politicians used to keep Blacks from voting. Some of the protesters were White, and like us were putting themselves in serious peril, not knowing what to expect, but being willing to sacrifice whatever was necessary for the cause. "On August 6, under pressure from Lyndon Johnson's White House, Congress passed the Voting Rights Act of 1965 (VRA) ending the South's Gestapo-like control of the polls" (The Editors of Black Issues in Higher Education 2005, 2). I am proud to be a part of that historical march, how in the history books. "The route the marchers took is now memorialized as the Selma-Montgomery Voting Rights Trail, and is a US National Historic Trail" (http://www.nps.gov./nr/trave;/civilrights/al4.htm).*

I was beginning to think of myself as "militant", not in the sense of violent, but in the sense of defiant, willing to go to jail or have water hoses or dogs turned on me just as it had been done to other demonstrators. I could feel myself becoming stronger. I was fighting for the civil rights of all Black Americans to be treated with the same dignity and respect as any other human being regardless of skin color. So I understand what Dr. King meant when he said that night in Memphis in 1968, before his assassination, "It doesn't matter what happens to me now" ... I changed my hair and wore it "natural" as opposed to straightened by a chemical as I had done previously, in an attempt to connect with my African heritage and break away from the "White dominance" that determined how most Black women wore their hair in those days, and as it still does for many African American women today.

Reflection

One of the songs which most people have identified with the Civil Rights Movement is "We Shall Overcome." According to Bernice King (1996), it "has been sung in Berlin, Soweto, Bosnia, Johannesburg, India and Russia" (7) for the cause of social justice since it was first introduced in the US in the 1960s. King says about her father, Dr. Martin L. King's influence worldwide, "They were able to kill the dreamer, but they will never kill the dream" (8). Some time ago, on a television segment of the nightly news, I heard participants in the Occupy Wall Street Movement singing, "We Shall Not Be Moved", another one of the songs that protestors sang in the 1960s. Although I can relate to non-violent protests because of my experience as a participant in the Civil Rights Movement, I could not truly connect with the Occupy Movement. In an October 24, 2011 issue of *Time* magazine, an article, "Taking It to the Streets", by Michael Scherer, reported Occupy as "A small protest on Wall Street [which] has exploded into a nationwide phenomenon." And then he asked "Will populist demands for jobs, fair taxes and corporate oversight shape the political landscape?" (21). I believe the journalist was biased in referring to the first people to show up in protest a "collection of punks, anarchists, socialists, hackers, liberals and artists" who were protesting what they called "the disproportionate power of the U.S. corporate elite" (23). They "occupied" and spent the night in a New York City park near the New York Stock Exchange and the Federal Reserve. Unlike the writer in *Time,* what I have noticed on television news reports are groups of mostly young, college-age, common people and some veteran social activists who had found a voice in a peaceful, non-violent way to express their frustrations with the US economy, unemployment and the unfair taxation of the poor while the rich receive more and more tax breaks. The Occupy Movement "opposes the economic greed and corruption of the wealthiest one percent" (*Essence,* January 2012, 48). Protests spread from New York City to other US cities and averaged in size "from a few dozen to a few thousand." Unlike my experience in the Civil Rights Movement, most participants in this movement are Whites who perhaps identify with large-scale demonstrations and protests in the past—against the Vietnam War, for women's rights, for civil rights. It seems to me as an outside observer that this movement lacks organization and that there is no one specific leader whose name everyone knows, as in the 60s Civil Rights Movement. Occupy has, however, called attention to the divide between the rich (the 1%) and the middle class/poor in America (the 99%), and is a call for the majority to get involved. These protests have been more against the wealthy than against the government. Perhaps when the 99% realizes that the power lies with us, that's when the power of living in a democracy will shift and the 99% can begin to make demands.

I have also recently noticed the resurgence of one African American woman who went through public trials, literally and figuratively, because she stood up for what she believed to be right and just. Anita Hill is the woman of whom I speak. I identify and admire her because she is a Black, educated, woman who faced challenges, could not be moved, and triumphed in their wake. Anita Hill, author of *Reimagining Equality: Stories of Gender, Race, and Finding Home* (2011) received her law degree from Yale Law School in 1980, and is currently a professor of "social policy, law, and women's studies at Brandeis University" (book cover). In 1991 she spoke out against her boss, Clarence Thomas, for sexual harassment during his confirmation hearings for Justice of the highest court in the land, the Supreme Court. She testified before the US Senate Judiciary Committee that Judge Thomas had "talked about pornography in the office; described X-rated material … badgered her about why she wouldn't go out with him; bragged about his physical endowment and sexual prowess; and taunted her with lewd remarks …" (Bennetts 2011), behavior certainly unacceptable for a potential Justice of the Supreme Court, but the Senate (all White men) apparently did not believe her and Clarence Thomas was confirmed and is now one of the Chief Justices of the United States.

These hearings occurred twenty years ago, but Miss Hill, says she still remembers the experience as being traumatic. It damaged her personally and her career suffered, causing her to leave her job and her community, which hurt her deeply. In an October 2011 interview by *Newsweek Magazine*, entitled "Surviving Clarence", Anita Hill told the reporter, Leslie Bennetts, what hurt her most was the fact that she was treated by the Senate Committee as if she had done something wrong. Instead of just being victimized by Thomas, she was also victimized by the Committee whose goal seemed to be discrediting her. Bennetts describes the hearings this way—

> The Senate Judiciary Committee interrogated Hill with a ferocity that shocked even political veterans, impugning everything from her competence to her sanity to her sexuality. Like a horrifying mismatched gladiatorial contest pitting a powerful gang of well-armed men against a woman with no defense save her own account of what someone had done to her against her will, the televised hearings mesmerized the nation. Many female observers were aghast at the way Hill was bullied and demeaned by the committee, whose members seemed both hostile and clueless about the pervasiveness of sexual harassment in the workplace (51).

Although Justice Thomas denied each of the allegations, I remember watching the hearings on television, and I believed Ms. Hill then and I believe her now. It's unfortunate that Justice Thomas is one of my least favorite people, when he should be someone I can look up to as the second Black Chief Justice of the United States; instead I would rather not mention him at all.

The trial by fire that Anita Hill went through, though it did not prevent the confirmation of Clarence Thomas, had another outcome that she did not expect— "it transformed the national debate over sexual harassment ... and sexual-harassment complaints filed with the EEOC [Equal Employment Opportunity Commission] increased by 50 percent in the year following the hearings ... sexual-harassment complaints doubled in the five years after that ..." (52). She counts what she suffered worth the sacrifice to give other women the strength to speak out as well. She says her number one goal now is to continue to work towards gender and racial equality and to "have a good life ... a life that's worthwhile and meaningful" (50).

I have had my own trials, so have most adults, of one kind or another. Character is built upon the backs of disappointment, discouragement, and discontent. But the Holy Bible says-- *Weeping may endure for a night, but joy cometh in the morning*—Psalm 30: 5. It also says in Romans 8:28 (KJV)—*And we know that all things work together for good to them that love God, to them who are the called according to His purpose.* Sometimes, even as a Christian, I have found these statements really hard to believe. In those times I trust that what God says is true for *God is not a man that He should lie* Numbers 23:19 (KJV). I am also in agreement with what author Melissa Harris-Perry offers on this subject in, *Sister Citizen* (2011) when she says: "For many women, faith in God and in Christ in particular, is part of their identity. Being Christian feels to some like no more of a choice than being black or female" (233). What keeps me grounded is hope. It bridges the gap between the trial and the strength gained from it. In *Resonant Leadership* Boyatzis and McKee (2005) describe hope as an ingredient which "enables us to believe that the future we envision is attainable ..." (9). So whenever I am experiencing what I consider a trial, I vision my self on the other side of it, having gone through it and having learned something from it.

> Hope engages and raises our spirit and mobilizes energy. It causes us to want to act and enables us to draw on personal resources in the service of moving toward our goal. Beyond this, hope and the visions that come with it, are contagious ... Hope is an emotional magnet—it keeps people going even in the midst of challenges (75).

Hope is the subject of many of the freedom songs we sang while protesting the unfair treatment of Blacks in America during the days of the Civil Rights Movement. As before mentioned, the best known protest song was "We Shall Overcome", which spoke to what our hopes were then and still are now and for the future. There are several different versions of this song. This is the one I remember singing as a participant in the Movement:

> *We shall overcome, someday*
> *Deep in my heart, I do believe*
> *We shall overcome, someday.*
> *Black and White together*
> *Black and White together, now*
> *Deep in my heart, I do believe ...*

Other verses began with: "God is on our side", "We shall live in peace", "We are not afraid" and "We shall all be free." Turck, in *Freedom Song ...* (2009) wrote this statement about the song:

> Part of the melody of 'We Shall Overcome' may date back to slavery days. Some believe that it came from the spiritual 'No More Auction Block for Me'. The auction block was the place where slaves were bought and sold ... 'No More Auction Block for Me' expressed hope. Parents hoped that their children would not be sold away to another state, a faraway plantation, a cruel master. They hoped that they themselves would not be sold away from their children. They hoped for an end to the buying and selling of human beings, an end to slavery (54).

The fight for racial equality and equity is far from over. I don't know if it will ever be completely over, but the people who continue to labor for social justice today, stand ready to face every new trial. Every day, every year, brings with it a new challenge. One of the newest public debates that threaten racial equality is the new Voters Right Act.

Voters' rights were the reason why I and thousands of other people marched to the capital building in Montgomery, Alabama in 1965. In 2011, there is a move by some state governments to block poor and minority people from voting in the 2012 presidential election. The proponents of new legislation to require every person who votes to have a government-issued picture identification card sounds like the illegal poll tax and the literacy tests that Blacks had to endure prior to the Civil Rights Movement in the 1960s. They say they are interested in preventing voter fraud, but Critical Race Theory tells me to look at political maneuvers such as these through a race lens. It seems the determination of some privileged and powerful White men to unseat the first Black president of the United States is the driving force behind this movement.

In "New State Rules Raising Hurdles at Voting Booth" an October 3, 2011 article in the *New York Times*, Michael Cooper reported that nearly five million voters could be affected by the mostly Republican efforts to change voter identification requirements in some states. Democrats call these efforts "voter-suppression" tactics aimed at skewing the 2012 elections. Many of the states affected traditionally vote Democratic—Ohio, Florida, Wisconsin, Nevada, Virginia and California. Democrats worry that the new rules may discourage some previous voters—senior citizens, students, the disabled and African Americans in particular—from voting in future elections. Cooper points to a new study just released by the Brennan Center for Justice at New York University School of Law which has tried to determine just how many voters stand to be affected. In the study entitled "Voting Changes in 2012" by Weiser and Norden at http://www.brennancenterforjustice.org, it is reported that the number of people affected by the new rules recently put in place may be larger than the "margin of victory in two of the last three presidential elections." Based on the Brennan Center's analysis of the 19 laws and two executive actions that passed in 14 states, it is clear that:

- These laws could make it significantly harder for more than five million eligible voters to cast ballots in 2012.
- The states that have already cut back on voting rights will provide 171 electoral votes in 2012–63 percent of the 270 needed to win the presidency.
- Of the 12 likely battleground states ... five have already cut back on voting rights (and may pass additional restrictive legislation), and two more are currently considering new restrictions.

This is the first study to consider how the voting process might be impacted by new voter registration laws.

> States have changed their laws so rapidly that no single analysis has assessed the overall impact of such moves. Although it is too early to quantify how the changes will impact voter turnout, they will be a hindrance to many voters at a time when the United States continues to turn out less than two thirds of its eligible citizens in presidential elections and less than half in midterm elections.

Democrats have called these "voter-suppression" tactics to the attention of the Department of Justice in hopes of stopping further impediments to the voting which will mostly affect the Democratic Party of which most minority people are members. Is that coincidence? Observing through a critical race theory framework, I think not. Brown and Moffett's (1999) *Hero's Journey* speaks of the wisdom of modern-day educational researchers such as Louis and Miles (1990) who say "problems [tests and trials] are our friends" and should be viewed as opportunities for organizational as well as personal growth (127). The Apostle Paul states in Romans 5: 3-5 (NIV), *"Not only so, but we also rejoice in our sufferings, because we know that suffering produces perseverance; perseverance, character; and character, hope. And hope does not disappoint us ..."*

Before reading or knowing of author, bell hooks, I too believed in "education as a practice of freedom." Drawing on my own personal experiences with schooling and the Civil Rights Movement up until that time, in 1987 when Chicago teachers went on strike for 19 days, I started a "freedom school" for the students who were enrolled at the school where I taught. Although I believed in the strike, and I took my turn on the picket line in front of the school, I felt students had been out of school too long and we didn't know when the strike would end. I spoke with the pastor at a neighborhood church about holding classes there for students who wanted to come. He agreed and I convinced a few of my colleagues to join me, and we held classes in the church basement until the strike ended. I believed then and now, as Hinchey related in her work, *Finding Freedom in the Classroom*, "However cynical many Americans have become … it is still reasonable to work towards a more just, ethical, and moral world" (1998, 140). I am proud that my efforts to give back to the community paid off.

Vignette Seven
"The Content of Their Character"

Jim (pseudonym) was a little younger than I, humorous and energetic. He wore jeans pretty much all the time. He was easy-going and good-looking. He always walked as if he had some place to go and needed to get there quickly. At that time I had no particular romantic feelings towards him, he was a White man after all, and given my history with racism and picket signs, my relationship with White people in general was guarded to say the least, but on a dare we went out on a date. We met in one of the many classes I took. He was easy to talk to and a good listener. He drove a supped-up Chevy and he would remind you of actor, James Dean, a little, by the way he wore his hair. If he was afraid or felt uneasy coming into my neighborhood, he never let on. We didn't see many White people in my neighborhood on any given day, unless they were delivering some goods or service to someone. Not that it was a bad neighborhood. I always felt safe there and my son grew up there without any major problems. Both the elementary and high school he attended was within walking distance from our apartment. The area has changed tremendously since that time several decades ago—especially in the face of racial diversity. With McCormick Place Convention Center and White Sox Park being close, and the Illinois Institute of Technology (IIT) being within walking distance as well, "other" people have begun to "invade" the neighborhood. Most of the newcomers are Asian and Indian college students attending IIT and looking for an affordable place to live, and this neighborhood is a hop, skip and jump from Lake Michigan, the beach and two major expressways. Who wouldn't want to live in this vicinity—especially now that the low income projects have been torn down, White flight has subsided, and Whites are moving back into the city? It's interesting that White people are seldom afraid to move into a Black neighborhood—unless it's a Cabrini Green, inner-city type project, or some other gang-infested place, but the opposite is true when it comes to Blacks moving into a White neighborhood. I've heard stories of how Black people in the past, have been "run out" of the nearby Bridgeport community, the childhood home of once mayor, Richard M. Daley, and that Black boys and men have been beaten up just for walking through the neighborhood, let alone trying to move there. When I first moved to Chicago years ago, I was told that Black folks stayed away from Bridgeport at night. Things may look different on the outside now, but I believe it takes a long, long time and many "courageous conversations" and actions concerning race to change the hearts of men—and women.

It was a surprise to me, but Jim and I started spending a lot of time together. I had never thought further than that one time meeting, however before anything really got off the ground I asked my teenaged son how he would feel if I dated a White man. All of his life he had heard my stories of dealing with racism and being involved in the Civil Rights Movement, so I wasn't sure of what kind of message it would send. I knew it would mean bringing someone new into his life as well. I had never taught him to dislike White people or any other people for that matter. Most of his elementary teachers were White nuns at the Catholic school where he spent his elementary school years. Interracial couples just weren't something we saw often, and it was still pretty taboo at that time—in the early 1980s. We discussed it and he said it wouldn't bother him and so to my surprise I allowed a White man to come into my Black world. I don't know why, but Jim and I never discussed race, and I still wore my African clothing sometimes when we went out—that probably messed with some people's heads. There especially weren't many Black woman/White man couples then. I was always aware however, that we had a relationship which was "uncommon." As boyfriends go he was caring, dependable, sensitive and supportive. I learned to trust him.

My mother got really sick and passed away while Jim and I were seeing each other. He was always there when I needed him. My son was in high school then and we were both pretty devastated when Mama left us to be with the Lord. I was consoled by the fact that she was not in pain anymore, and that God had allowed her to stay with me for a very long time. She would have been eighty-six in a few months when she passed away. Jim drove me and my son to my home town in Missouri to bury my mother. She had asked to be taken back home. Even in the midst of all of those Black people—family members and friends, Jim didn't seem to feel out of place and he never left my side. It didn't seem to make a difference to them that he was White and by that time, it didn't make a difference to me. He was what I needed at that time, and I was thankful he was there.

I remember one weekend before Mama's passing when Jim and I had decided to take a short trip just for relaxation's sake. Her illness had really taken a toll on me and this was to be a mental break. I hired a nurse to care for Mama and my son was a teenager, so I felt secure about taking a short trip to a place right outside the city. What happened next really shook me up, probably Jim too, but he didn't show it. We were driving along the expressway talking, laughing and enjoying each other's company when a Black couple drove up right beside us and started to look at us disapprovingly. All the time the man was sneering as they drove along side us long enough to let us know they didn't like the fact that we were together. We were used to people looking at us strangely by that time—a Black woman with a White man who seemed to be in a love relationship. The man, who was driving, stuck his tongue out at us and I did the same thing to him in return. That made him angry! Had I known it would cause such a reaction, I never would have done that! I would have ignored him. Although his window was up, we could tell he was enraged and cursing. It's remarkable how someone who didn't know either of us could get so upset about whom we had chosen to spend our time with. It had nothing to do with anyone else—at least not some strange man on the highway.

At the risk of sounding like a hypocrite, even today I can't help but take a second look when I see a Black man with a White woman who I think are romantically entangled. Even today I think about the history of America when Black men were not allowed to even look at a White woman without the threat of being beaten or lynched, or both. I do not deny that I have my own prejudices as I believe everyone does. None of them however have hate as the driving force, and none would ever lead to disrespect or violence. From a feminine perspective, I hope these men truly care about the women they are with and are not just trying to make a "look how far Black men have come" statement.

I suppose the longer the man on the highway looked at us the more agitated he became and so he pulled ahead of us. We thought it was over and then he stopped his car ... STOPPED HIS CAR! ... on the expressway ... right in front of us ... and got out of the car ... and headed in our direction! Cars were pulling around us and we could not believe what was happening. The woman in the car seemed indifferent to the whole thing. Jim said something like, "This fool might have a gun", and so he quickly put his car in reverse ... and began to drive backwards ... to try to get us out of harm's way. Luckily there weren't any cars close behind us. There was an expressway entrance ramp not far away and so Jim backed all the way down the entrance ramp ... exiting on the entrance ramp!! I was terrified, but his quick thinking got us out of that situation. We didn't know where we were once got off that ramp, but we drove up and down a few streets until he figured it out and we continued on our journey—safe but not the same in any way. It had to be a race thing. We didn't know this Black man and he didn't know us. I learned that day that racial hatred, coming from anyone of any race or color is a sad and scary thing. We had no idea that we would be faced with a situation like that when we left home. It could have ended tragically. It was probably just my paranoia, but I thought I saw that same man about 3 weeks later in the lobby of my apartment building. I nearly panicked! I wouldn't look directly at him for fear that it could actually be him, and he would recognize me. I never told Jim and nothing ever came of it, thank God.

I'm not sure how long Jim and I stayed together after Mama's passing. Our relationship just sort of fizzled out. I'm sure I wasn't very good company for a long time while I grieved for her. I had no room in my head or my heart for anyone except my son, who was sixteen at the time. It was a big loss for him as well. Mama had helped to raise him from the time he was born. I remember as a grown woman, sleeping while hugging one of my teddy bears (I had always loved stuffed-animal teddy bears and had a collection of them) for nearly a month after she died. It seemed to comfort me somehow. I felt like a little child again.

She had been my mother and father for so many years and had raised me as a single parent from the age of three. She had helped me to raise my son, and for a while I felt lost without her. I knew I had a teenage son to care for, and so I had to keep it altogether. Perhaps Jim was just meant to come into my life for a while to help me through this difficult situation. I know I was more secure in myself as an attractive, desirable woman who didn't have to settle for men who thought only of themselves; before he left he taught me that. Neither of us ever said the "L" word, but what we shared was something special that I won't forget. Someone has said that "love is an action word"—it's something you demonstrate, not just talk about. Jim did that. I believe that God allows some situations to manifest in our lives to teach us a lesson and certain people come to teach us as well. Jim was loving, respectful, and thoughtful, the friend and companion I needed. Looking back, we should have had the race discussion—many race discussions. Because we didn't address it, I don't think we ever "truly" knew each other and perhaps I could have helped to change his mind about some of the stereotypes I'm sure he was raised to believe regarding people of color. Perhaps our relationship would have lasted had we "put race out there." His family lived in the Whitest part of town, and I see that as some indication of how his parents raised him. I never met them in the time that we were together—he pretty much didn't talk about his family in any detail. All in all, I believe experiencing Jim's loving kindness towards our family taught my son that there are good people of all races, a lesson for me as well.

Reflection

Occasionally I question if I was trying to prove something by dating a White man and if so, what? When the relationship with Jim began my track record with dating had not been such a good one, and they were all Black men before him. The one I most thought I could trust had been a great disappointment. So perhaps I thought I would try something different. I was not attracted to Jim at first. I knew him as a friend first so it wasn't as if he was a stranger that I was just meeting for the first time. The history of Black/White interracial relationships is mostly that of African American men and White women and the literature is plentiful on that topic, however I found studies on the White man/Black woman relationship to be scarcer in the educational literature. In my exploration, White man/Black woman relationships seem to be more the subject of novels written by women who have had the experience than by any other source. bell hooks, writer of *Teaching to Transgress: Education as the Practice of Freedom* (1994) speaks about helping to integrate an all-White high school when she was sixteen, eerily similar to my own personal story. One major difference in hooks' story was that one of her "best buddies" was White and male (23) while I had no White friends in high school, male or female. She talks about how she valued his friendship and riding home from school in his car sometimes when she missed the bus. It "angered and disturbed" some who saw them, and may have thought they were in a "forbidden" relationship, and upon one occasion she writes that White men tried to run them off the road. Jim and I had our haters as well, but the person who tried to harm us was Black not White. I wondered if he thought I was betraying the Black race by being with a White man.

I've heard the word "miscegenation" once or twice before, but until writing this vignette it has not really been a focus of my thinking for more than a few seconds. While researching studies of interracial dating and marriage, the word appeared often. Miscegenation, according to the Merriam-Webster online dictionary, is "a mixture of races; *especially*: marriage, cohabitation, or sexual intercourse between a white person and a member of another race." The Internet site, http://www.WordIQ.com, defines it as:

> an archaic term invented in 1863 to describe people of different human races (usually one European and one African) producing offspring; the use of this term is invariably restricted to those who believe that the category race is meaningful when applied to human beings. In modern usage, the term is common only

153

among those who believe that such 'race mixing' is inherently bad.

I also learned it was at this point in history when the "one drop theory" was used to intimidate couples and discourage intimate relationships between Blacks and Whites by declaring that any person having so much as one drop of African (Black) blood must be considered Black. Miscegenation, also referred to as "race-mixing" was illegal in various states in the US until 1967 (Banks, 2011) when the Supreme Court, in *Loving v. Virginia*, "a landmark case", declared the law violated the 14th Amendment of the Constitution denying the plaintiffs due process and equal protection under the law. Virginia's anti-miscegenation laws had been on the books since 1691 and had been revised several times until their final version in 1924 (http:www. encyclopediavirginia.org/loving v Virginia 1967). This is the wording of the Supreme Court's opinion:

> In June 1958, two residents of Virginia, Mildred Jeter, a Negro woman, and Richard Loving, a white man, were married in the District of Columbia pursuant to its laws. Shortly after their marriage, the Lovings returned to Virginia and established their marital abode in Caroline County. At the October Term, 1958, of the Circuit Court of Caroline County, a grand jury issued an indictment charging the Lovings with violating Virginia's ban on interracial marriages. On January 6, 1959, the Lovings pleaded guilty to the charge and were sentenced to one year in jail; however, the trial judge suspended the sentence for a period of 25 years on the condition that the Lovings leave the State and not return to Virginia together for 25 years. He stated in an opinion that: 'Almighty God created the races white, black, yellow, malay and red, and he placed them on separate continents. And but for the interference with his arrangement there

would be no cause for such marriages. The fact that
he separated the races shows that he did not intend
for the races to mix'.

The lower court's opinion in Virginia was overturned and the
Lovings' sentences suspended. It's ironic that such a law would deem
racial-mixing illegal since it has existed since slavery times. Foeman
and Nance (1999) speak of this matter in "From Miscegenation to
Multiculturalism: Perceptions and Stages of Interracial Relationship
Development" when they quote Smith (1966) who reported:

The hostile history of Black-White intermixing in
this country stems primarily from White plantation
owners forcing themselves onto Black women without
the benefit or marriage, romance or any status that
might be associated with an affair ... this practice
became so widespread ... that laws were enacted
against the social association between the two races
(170).

These anti-miscegenation laws kept Black woman from marrying
White men and never allowed their offspring to become "legal" or
have access to their White father's wealth or influence. According
to the authors of the aforementioned article, who quote Porterfield
(1982), "No other mixture touches off such widespread condemnation
as black-white mixing" (17). Perhaps all of this negative history and
attempts to keep Blacks and Whites from sharing a love relationship
is the reason behind the rage displayed by the Black man who
threatened Jim and me on the expressway. Perhaps that event was a
determining factor in the dissolution of our relationship. I cringe to
think about what could have happened had we not gotten away from
this crazed man. I don't remember us ever talking about it again, so
I don't know how it affected the way he was feeling about dating a
Black woman at that point. We had never had any problems before.
My family and friends were accepting of him. I can't recall if Mama

and I ever talked about him. Her illness had taken a toll on her by the time we were deep into our relationship so I'm sure it was the furthest thing from her mind, yet still he was there—for me. It's doubtful that we would have ever married. I believe our relationship ended when and as it should have.

Today when I think about what Dr. King said about judging others by their character and not by the color of their skin. I don't think he meant we should not notice the color of a person's skin as in "colorblindness" to their particular culture—but that we should notice that a person's skin color is not the predictor of anything else: not of his character, his intellect, his ethics or his behaviors. Since Dr. King's famous speech in 1963, educational research has introduced the term, "cultural proficiency", defined as " …a way of being that enables people to engage successfully in new environments … ask questions without offending … and … create an environment that is open to diversity" (Lindsey 2009, 111). As mentioned in Vignette Three, those who are culturally proficient "believe that all children can learn, and they demonstrate that children from any neighborhood can learn well—if they are taught well" (11). Educators today are taught that the color of a child's skin, i.e. his/her heritage and ethnicity matter, should be valued and taken into consideration when planning and instruction are taking place, and that they should become "culturally proficient" in order "to respond effectively to people who differ from one another" (Lindsey 2009, 4). I did not, however, see Jim as a White man once we entered into a warm relationship. He was a man that I cared for who cared for me. We spent a lot of time together talking and walking on the beach, going out to dinner, going to parties and to church—and I did judge him by his character. He was an all-around good guy whose race I didn't see, perhaps didn't want to see. In hindsight, that was a disservice to him and to me because I don't think I ever really got to know what made him the person he truly was.

Vignette Eight
"My Brother's Keeper"—Cross-racial Friendships
(All names are pseudonyms.)

I woke up early one April morning, 2011, thinking about an occurrence which happened in my doctor's office a few days before during my bi-monthly visit. My usual nurse was absent that day, and I asked where she was. I was told by a substitute nurse that my usual nurse was out due to the death of her mother. I was saddened by the news. As someone whose mother passed away many years ago I understand the pain and emptiness it can bring. Cynthia is an African American woman who I estimate to be in her late forties or early fifties. I've known her as "my nurse" for nearly ten years and now she's like a family member to me. She always asks about my grandchildren and knows them by name. I take their latest pictures whenever I have an appointment with my primary care physician—Dr. Gohna—to show to her and to him. Cynthia is married and has one child—a teenaged son. I consider myself a special patient because I not only have my nurse's office phone number and e-mail address, but also her home phone number and home e-mail address. She tells me to get in touch with her if I ever need anything. Maybe she does that for all of her patients, but I don't think so. She's a direct line to my doctor so I can always get a message to him without going through the system set up for patients, which takes a longer time to get a message through to him. My doctor makes me feel very special as well. He always returns my phone calls and he encourages me to write down any health questions I have and bring them to the office so that we can discuss them. He's never in a hurry, and I know our discussions get long sometimes and other patients are waiting. Many times our discussions lead to stories about his family. We talk about his wife, his sons in college who plan to go to medical school and his deceased mother and father who lived in India, his homeland, all of their lives. He attended medical school in India. He has a good sense of humor, and I always tell him he owes me a fee for listening to his stories.

When he came into the room where I was waiting I had my list of health related topics to ask about. Sometimes he'll say, "How many *things do you have on that list? I don't have all day." And he laughs. I know he's just kidding because he seems eager to get to the next question and the next to see for himself just how smart he truly is. If it's something he can't answer or feels needs "checking out for completion" as he always says, he does not hesitate to refer me to a specialist. Unlike stories I hear from friends and family about their doctors and healthcare system, I am blessed to have a team like Nurse Cynthia and Dr. Gohna who have shown me time after time that they genuinely care about me, my family and my health. To show them how much I appreciate them both, every Christmas they are the first two people, after family, on my gift list.*

This particular day as Dr. Gohna and I were talking about the death of Cynthia's mom he began to speak about his mother. I asked how old Cynthia's mother was and he said she was in her late eighties. I told him my mom was in her eighties when she passed away also. He said he felt his mother died too soon. She was in her mid-sixties. He began to talk about some of the things he remembered about his mom and how he didn't treat her right when he was young. How he should have paid more attention to her. He said he regretted that he had not been kinder to her and had not been able to do more to help her with the extreme pain she experienced from arthritis. And then he began to cry—for a moment I didn't know what to do or say. I tried to console him by telling him we all do things when we are young that we regret later on in life. For a moment he was not my doctor, but a friend who was hurting. He must have felt safe enough to allow himself to be "human" with me, and I understood his vulnerability at that place and time. I believe his sensitivity is one of the things that make him a great physician.

I ask myself, "What if, in my ignorance, I decided I didn't want anything to do with anyone who was not Black like me?" Dr. Gohna was born and raised in India, on a different continent, into a different culture—a world away from where I was born and raised and yet we have a relationship that cannot be replaced. I thank God for placing people like my doctor—who is more that just my physician, in my life. We have not had the "race" discussion, but I believe as Tatum (2007) says, "In a society where residential segregation persists and school segregation is increasing, familiarity and contact across racial lines requires intentionality. We need to think about how we can structure meaningful dialogue opportunities" (102). I now see the relationship between my doctor and me as an opportunity to "stimulate cross-racial dialogue that has the potential of evolving into cross-racial connections deep enough to support community transformation" (103). I look forward to the opportunity to have future race discussions with my doctor to see what they yield. Hopefully it will be the first step in building one cross-racial friendship which will help in the fight toward racial equity and social justice.

And then there's Lei (pronounced Lee). Lei is a Filipino woman who I met at a neighborhood nail salon. She is very personable and cute, short with curly Black hair. She has been my nail technician for the past five or six years and so we get a chance to talk for the hour or sometimes two hour manicure-pedicure. She always takes her time with me and I don't rush her. I always look forward to my conversations with Lei. She has an accent when she speaks and has a great sense of humor. Sometimes she leaves words out or uses the wrong pronoun in her sentences, such as she might say "he" when talking about her sister or "she" when talking about her husband. However, I can usually follow what's she's saying. We talk about her children and grandchildren, and I talk about mine. We share secrets that no one else knows. She tells me stories about how her life was in the Philippines. Sometimes you can hear pain in her voice when she speaks. In spite of that, she has a real sense of humor and sometimes we laugh so loud that others look at us and wonder what could be so funny. I'm so happy that I got to know one of God's children from a place in the world unfamiliar to me.

Isaac I love. Isaac is probably thirty or so. Isaac is Hispanic and I tell him that he's my adopted son because my actual son lives so very far away. He tries to fulfill that role by letting me know I can call on him when I need help with anything. Isaac is a car salesman, but he's not just a salesman, he's my friend, as strange as that may sound considering the reputation car salesman have when it comes to women customers and car dealerships, in the Black community especially.

And I am not naïve, I realize selling cars is Isaac's job and his way to make a living and care for his family, but he goes way beyond the call of duty. He tells me of his great respect for teachers and that he sometimes thinks about going back to school, leaving the car business and becoming a teacher himself. I encourage him to follow his dream, and I tell him it's not too late.

Several years ago I decided I would purchase a new car. This time I would purchase only the car that had everything I wanted. I would not settle for less as I had done a few times in the past. One of the major features I wanted in my new car was OnStar and I also wanted a red car with beige interior. To my surprise there were no Pontiacs (which I preferred) fitting that description at the dealership or in the city at large. I was very disappointed when I left that day, and I told Isaac that I would see him in a year or so and that maybe by then Pontiac would have installed OnStar in all of its cars. We shook hands on that note and I left. Little did I know that Isaac hadn't given up. Later that day, Isaac called to tell me he had found the car I wanted in Michigan and that if I still wanted it he would go there and drive the car back to Chicago! He was as excited as I was because he had found a car which had everything on it that I had requested. Two days later I had the exact car I had described. Whenever there is something I can't figure out, one phone call to Isaac and the problem is solved. He tells me to always let him know what I need and he will take care of it for me, even if it's not car related. I have called him early and late and he always responds. So Isaac and I have developed a close relationship.

Several months ago when I would speak to Isaac over the phone for one reason or anther, I noticed that he sounded down and depressed, and so I asked him was something wrong. He told me that he was worried about his mom who had breast cancer. He shared her story with me and from that moment until his mother's death several months later, sometimes I called Isaac just to ask about his mother. He began to text me to give me a report. We talked about his mother's faith and I printed out verses from the Holy Bible for Isaac to share with his mom. Her condition worsened over the Christmas holidays and even while I was out of town celebrating with my family, my mind kept going back to

Isaac. I would send him a text message that I thought would encourage him and he would reply telling me how my messages were helping him to make it through the most trying time of his life. Even now when I think the monthly anniversary of his mother's passing is approaching, I call or text with something inspirational and he always responds. Sometimes when I'm not thinking of him I receive a text message from him, not to sell a car, but to say thank you for what you did for me. I tell him what a great mom he must have had to raise a son as kind and considerate as he. Yes, Isaac I love.

Recently, I asked Mr. Chen who operates the dry cleaner I have patronized for years, what country he's from and found out he is from Korea. This is a change in me that I welcome—to be interested in someone else's culture. I wonder how many customers actually know his name. His wife and I have conversations about her daughter who several years ago had a baby girl and since that time has been dealing with an illness. Mrs. Chen is a wonderful seamstress and makes alterations in my clothing for me whenever need be. She smiles and says she is always giving me a "discount." When she was missing from the cleaners for a while I asked about her. Mr. Chen said she was "in hospital." When she returned I gave her a rosary in hopes of giving her some encouragement. A few months later they closed the cleaners and said they had decided to retire. I wondered if it was because of her poor health, but I never saw them again. The old saying, "We are more alike than we are different" comes to mind when reflecting on the cultures of the various people who are a regular occurrence in my life.

I'm also reminded now of a college boyfriend who was from Nigeria, West Africa. He would comment that some "stupid" Americans would ask him if he knew "Joe", some other African they knew, not realizing that Africa is a vast continent consisting of more than fifty countries. There is so much that we don't know about people who have cultures different from ours. What would happen if each of us cared enough to listen to one another's stories? How much smarter and learn-ed we would be. It's a known fact that our world is getting smaller and smaller since the invention of the Internet. Our "friends" may no longer live in the same neighborhood or city or country, but may be someone of a different color and culture from the other side of the globe. So what can we do as individuals to help bring about social justice and racial equity in our own society and in the world? We can strive to make cross-racial/ cross-cultural connections. We can think of ourselves as our brother's keeper, and as the familiar quote from Mahatma Gandhi says, we can "Be the change we want to see in the world." In Genesis 4:9 of the Holy Bible (NIV) God asked Cain this question after Cain had murdered his brother: "Then the LORD said to Cain, 'Where is your brother Abel?' Cain's arrogant response was, "I don't know" ... "Am I my brother's keeper?" Cain was cursed by God from that moment on. My response to Cain's question would be "Yes", we are each responsible for caring for our "brother", looking out for him, treating him with dignity and respect and causing no harm to come to him.

Reflection

After reading Beverly Daniel Tatum's (2007) story about a cross-racial friendship, I began to think about some of the cross-racial/ cross-cultural relationships I have and how they could lead to what Singleton and Linton (2006) call "courageous conversations" about race. Tatum states:

> The opportunity for mutual relationships with someone who shares your life experiences is irreplaceable. But relationships across lines of difference are essential for the possibility of social transformation. Change is needed. None of us can make the change alone. Genuine friendship leads to caring concern. Caring concerns leads to action. And we need to take our action from the position of strength that comes from self-knowledge and social awareness. Cross-racial friendships can be a source of both (100).

Growing up in a home with Christian values has colored the way I view the world. I think I was in college when I first came to the realization that society's people had been divided into more than just Black and White. In my early experiences as a child no one ever talked about Mexican people or Polish people or Jewish people and the like. In the boot heel of southeast Missouri, where I spent most of my childhood, you were either White and lived in the bigger and prettier houses and owned the farms, or you were Black and lived in the smaller houses in all Black neighborhoods and supplied the farm labor. What a difference growing into adulthood and working with people from many backgrounds and cultures has made in my life. Even though some of my experiences dealing with racism were traumatic and life-altering, I still believe that we are all children of the same Father and I am accepting of and enriched by the diversity of cultures which the "brothers and sisters" who touch my life bring. Reverend Bernice King quotes her father, Martin Luther King, Jr., in *Hard Questions, Heart Answers* (1996) as having said "Racial understanding is not something that we find, but something that we must create. Our ability to work together, to understand each other, will not be found ready made; it must be created by the fact of contact" (122).

Since reading *Up Against Whiteness* (2005) by Stacy Lee, I have become more aware of the injustices suffered by people other than those who look like me and share my cultural heritage. Lee's book gave me the opportunity to think more deeply about others who have been discriminated against throughout history. I related closely to the Hmong students in her study because of my high school experiences and the "light bulb" went on that Black people are not the only ones in America who have been discriminated against and denied a quality education because of their cultural heritage. However, the lens I see through is based upon my own experiences as an African American. I'm not comfortable with colorblindness anymore, I want to see each person as an individual with his/her own rich culture.

In Chapter Four I continue to look at lessons learned from my educational internship experiences while observing a passionate White man who is responsible for more than 3,000 high school students. He is dedicated to achieving equity for all students in his school, and I value the friendship we have developed as a result of a common resolve—equity and excellence for every student--not determined by race, but by what is good and fair and right.

Dr. Martin L. King Jr. also said these words: "Darkness cannot drive out darkness; only light can do that. Hate cannot drive out hate; only love can do that" (brainyquote.com). Reflecting on his words, I write this prayer for the United States of America and the world.

A Prayer for Us
2011
Dear God,
Help us to see the light of love that shines
within ourselves and in others,
and make this world a place where
we can find our way out of the darkness,
to a place where we can love.
Please help your children
see the beauty inside another person
instead of looking for something to hate.
Help us to love one another,
value each other and know that you are
Father to us all.
Amen.

CHAPTER FOUR

LIVING WITH RACE

In this chapter I present my conclusions after having explored, through autoethnography, how my lived experiences with racism as a high school student, and as an active participant in the Civil Rights Movement in college, have impacted my life. I have surveyed racism's affect on my image of self as an African American living in the United States of America where I was born and raised and still treated as a second-class citizen, sometimes overtly and at other times covertly because racism has become an institution whose foundation was established hundred of years ago during slavery times and was never abolished. I have spoken of how my racial identity has been developed through simply living Black in America, which has included my spiritual development from childhood, and racism's impact on my personal and professional relationships. I speak of the lessons I have learned about courage, love, and forgiveness throughout this exploration, and my commitment to continuing the race and equity work I began as a sixteen-year old African American girl in high school, attending classes in a hostile environment ultimately for the purpose and cause of freedom (hooks 1994).

It is my hope and deepest desire that my story resonates with those who have experienced racism of any kind and lets them know there are countless numbers of people who are still, today, fighting against it, and that there are others who have lost the most precious gift—their lives—because of it. Battles have been won against racism, but the war is not over. I pray those who have not experienced racial hatred never do. To be degraded as a human being because of something over which you have no control, namely the color of your skin, your heritage, can be devastating and life-altering. Black/White racism is an institution first established when Black people, forcibly brought to this country in chains (Delgado and Stefancic, 2001) became the slaves of White people. The *American Heritage* online dictionary defines a slave as "One bound in servitude as the property of a person or household. One who is abjectly subservient to a specified person or influence." Erasing from the mind of a country the hegemonic thought that one human being can "own" another human being is no easy task. Critical race theorists hold fast to the idea that there are barriers and structures in place today specifically to control people of color. In their introductory remarks to *Critical Race Theory* Delgado and Stefancic (2006) state the following:

> Still by every social indicator, racism continues to blight the lives of people of color, including holders of high-echelon jobs, even judges. Studies show that blacks and Latinos who seek loans, apartments, or jobs are much more apt than similarly qualified whites to be rejected, often for vague or spurious reasons. The prison population is mostly black and brown; chief executive officers, surgeons and university presidents are almost all white (10).

Shirley Chisholm, the nation's first Black congresswoman and later first Black woman presidential candidate said, 'Racism is so universal in this country, so widespread and deep-seated, that it is invisible because it is so normal' (Singleton and Linton 2006, 41). But I say it isn't normal, perhaps to racists it is, but there are still victories to be won over racial prejudice and discrimination. Perhaps something I have said here will touch or move someone in a way which they have never been moved before, and will cause them to think about the role they too can play in the fight for racial equality and social justice. In that hope I rest.

The purpose of this research has been to conduct an autoethnographic study which would explore and tell the story of how my lived experiences with racial separation first as a small child, then as a high school student, and later as a participant in the non-violent, 1960s Civil Rights Movement as a college student, have impacted the whole of my life encounters—my image of self, my racial identity development, spiritual development, intra and inter-personal relationships, academic achievement, career choices, professional practices and daily life as an African American citizen of these United States of America. In my analysis of self I have come to the following conclusions, but change is constant and inevitable and these are my feelings at the time of this writing. Don't mind me if I change … for the better.

Discoveries

I have discovered that even though I have dealt with and lived in a racist society all of my life, it has not, thankfully, caused me to become bitter or skeptical of every White American I encounter in my personal and professional life. How sad it would be for me to harbor unforgiveness in my heart. "Forgiveness is freedom" is the tag line from a film entitled "Kinyarwanda." The film was written and directed by Jamaican-born, new independent filmmaker, Alrick Brown, and won an audience award at the prestigious Sundance Film Festival in 2011 (http://www.kinyarwandamovie.com).

"Kinyarwanda" tells the story of genocide in the African country of Rwanda in 1994 and how the senseless massacre of one ethnic group, the Tutsis (TUT-sees) by another ethnic group, the Hutus (HU-TUS), nearly destroyed the country. The war killed more than one million people and forced another two million to seek shelter in other countries (Appiah and Gates 2003). According to the film, Belgian colonization played a key role in the Rwandan Massacre. It seems different ethnic groups coexisted peacefully before the Belgians came to colonize Rwanda, but in order to better control the people, they physically measured each group and divided them according to who had longer noses and longer necks, believed to be an indication of White ancestry somewhere in their background. Those having more Caucasian characteristics were declared Tutsi and everyone else, Hutu. They were given separate identification cards and the Hutus became forced labor while the Tutsis were put in power over the forced labor. From this point forward, Hutus and Tutsis became mortal enemies which led to 100 days of killing and the awful massacre of thousands of people. Rwandans are now trying to rebuild their country through "education, reconciliation and forgiveness." The film continuously makes the point that "Forgiveness is freedom. Freedom is forgiveness." The Sundance Institute, a non-profit organization which "supports and advances" the work of autonomous film makers, provides the following synopsis of this important movie:

> Little is known about how the Mufti of Rwanda— the most respected Muslim leader in the country— forbade Muslims from participating in the killing of the Tutsi. As the country became a slaughterhouse, mosques became places of refuge where Muslims and Christians, Hutus and Tutsis came together to protect each other. 'Kinyarwanda' plumbs the shades of gray to find humanity in every perspective and offers a rich understanding of what it means to survive unimaginable terror, and the astounding resilience of the human spirit to find ways to heal and forgive (http://www.indiewire.com/kinyarwanda).

The tragedy of unforgiveness (failure to forgive), wherever it's found, is bondage, distrust, and looking back rather than forward. I've heard that unforgiveness eats away at the person who fails to forgive, rather than the one who needs to be forgiven. Still, knowing the history of the racial discrimination and degradation African Americans have experienced in this country can certainly be discouraging and even heart-breaking. On the other hand, every coin has two sides. Over the past fifteen-months, most of my graduate school professors have been White. The encouragement and support they have offered me has been phenomenal. Sometimes I wondered what it was like for them to read what I have written about situations that spoke about White privilege and power and the inequalities that minorities have suffered basically at the hands of White people. Two of my professors are responsible for my personal story about racial bigotry and racial hatred being told. Writing this autoethnography has allowed me to tell my story. I pray that they too have learned something from it that will keep them on the path toward social justice. I know that they, more than likely grew up privileged, but they reaffirmed my belief that good people come in all sizes, shapes, and colors. It is my dream to become a college professor after completing my doctoral studies and perhaps I will have the opportunity to work as a colleague with these people whom I highly respect, and be for my students what they have been for me.

I am an intelligent, courageous, educated, Black woman capable of navigating the prejudices that are still in existence. What I have learned throughout this study will give me the incentive to continue the fight for racial equity wherever and in whatever situation I find myself in the future. I especially would like to work with pre-service and new teachers to help provide them with a foundation for understanding why and how racial disparities and inequities exist for minority students, and encourage to them to resist buying into the stereotype that Black and Brown children are not as capable as White children. I would assist them in understanding that all students deserve the very best teacher they can experience, and by having high expectations for each student in a classroom, all students will benefit in reaching their highest potential. White teachers, especially, also need to understand that "colorblindness" is not a good thing as seasoned teachers may have been taught years ago. Every student needs to be "seen" and appreciated for his or her diversity. Students' cultures should be recognized and included in lessons that are culturally relevant to them.

Recently I have been appalled by reality television shows about Black women which present the worst scenarios of how Black women relate to each other. On these shows, which can be seen all over the world thanks to the Internet, Black, so called "well-to-do" women are constantly fighting, verbally and physically, while using profanity with an alcoholic drink in their hands, and I ask myself why are these women appearing to represent me, as a Black woman, on national television? I think of the impact television has on young people in general and in this situation, young, Black women and I cringe. I suppose it's about the fame and notoriety for these women whose "claim to fame" on one show is that they are wives or ex-wives of professional basketball players. Perhaps they have not thought about the message they are sending throughout the world to people who may never have had any personal contact with a Black woman —it is not an image of which the African American community can be proud. Oprah Winfrey, a Black woman who is known throughout the world because of her twenty-five years as a talk-show host and because of her integrity and generosity, serves as a counterstory for what these women portray. Unfortunately, Winfrey does not have a daily show and is not as prevalent in the television media as she once was. How easy it is to forget the "good" role models when the "bad" ones are in your face on a nightly basis!

I have visions of a program for African American girls in high school which would counter the unflattering "reality television" stories of Black women that so many young girls have access to in today's media culture. The program would be called Black Women in the Media (BWIM). There are many educated Black women who work in the local and national media who might sign-on to becoming role models for these young women if approached with the idea. The socialization experiences that young Black women encounter on a daily basis make the BWIM program a valuable and important one which would serve as a "counter narrative" to portrayals of Black women on reality television as uneducated, unprofessional, shallow, and unsophisticated. Black professional women, who work in the media in the Chicago area, for example, would serve as role models and share their educational backgrounds, work and personal experiences with these girls to offer an alternative to the negative conduct many Black women display as a trend on reality television. The program would also provide incentives for these young women to continue their education in college and to seek careers in the media or other areas of their choice. Black women who are currently working or have worked in a media environment such as radio, television, or print would be approached to volunteer. These women would provide information on the college course of study they followed for the positions they hold in the media, such as journalists, newscasters, reporters, or talk show hosts. They would discuss public speaking, professional attire and grooming, attitude, and interpersonal relationships.

One of God's early interventions was to make it possible for me to attend college—a college where my soul could heal from the trauma I experienced in high school. The thought has also crossed my mind recently that about teaching in a historically Black university or college akin to Tuskegee University where I first learned of my legacy of strong Black people who have done great and marvelous things for this country and the world. People such as Dr. M.L. King, Malcolm X, and Muhammad Ali came to speak to the students on Tuskegee's campus when I was a student there. Prominent Blacks such as Booker T. Washington, Dr. George Washington Carver, and the Tuskegee Airmen were a part of the culture at Tuskegee. Where else could I have been exposed to such notables but on a Black college campus? And so, my teaching at a HBCU would be an opportunity to "pay it forward." It is noticeable that there are no women on the aforementioned list of notables who visited Tuskegee, but that was many years ago and now there are many Black women who are currently in high-profile positions, such as Russlyn Ali, Assistant Secretary for the US Office of Civil Rights and Michelle Obama, First Lady of the United States of America, who could be added to that list.

Tracking and Re-segregation: A Closer Look

Continuing with a topic previously mentioned, for sixteen months I observed an unrelenting White superintendent and his high school administrators labor tirelessly to detrack their school for the sake of equity and excellence for all students. The school has a beautiful rainbow of racial diversity when it comes to students—White, Black, Hispanic, and Asian. It also has a reputation of being an "excellent" school. There are many excellent students who are mostly White. These students win awards and honors in every academic area and extra-curricular activity. A few White students last year had the nearly impossible, perfect ACT (American College Testing) scores. There are also many advanced-degreed teachers and numerous programs at the school which should assure that all students achieve at their highest level. The problem is that students are tracked by their seventh and eighth grade reading and math scores and whatever track they land on is the track most students stay on for the remainder of their high school careers. Even more telling of the inequalities that exist at this school, most of the Black and Hispanic students are, predictably, on the lower tracks making for classrooms which are segregated by race. These students seldom, if ever, experience those "excellent" teachers and the resources they use even though they are all students within the same school. Dr. Walker (pseudonym), whom I have such a high regard and respect for, wants to put a stop to tracking beginning with freshman Humanities and Biology in the 2011-2012 school year, but has experienced resistance from several members of the school board who want to "wait" until everyone is "ready" for this change. I believe what they are saying is actually code for "We don't want our high-achieving White kids in the classroom with these minority kids!" Research shows that when lower-track students only have exchanges with other lower-track students there is little growth (Oakes 2005). In addition, teacher expectations are lower for students on the lower tracks and students tend to live out the prophecy that has been given to them as less able to achieve. Dr. Walker has been very vocal about his desire to provide an equitable education for minority as well as White students. The question he has continuously asked the Middleton District High School Board (pseudonym) is "How can this school be an excellent school when so many of our minority students are failing?"

One of the most unfortunate things about tracking is that White students see that the majority of their fellow students in the lowest tracks are Black and Brown and they go away thinking that these students must be as the stereotype says—less intelligent and less capable, and they never learn about the disparities most of these students have dealt with throughout their school lives. They don't see or know that given the same opportunities and resources as White students, most of these Black and Hispanic students would do just as well in school as they, some better. And so the stereotype is perpetuated over and over again. I conclude that tracking should be eliminated in all high schools to level the playing field for minority students and offer them the same opportunities for success as their White counter-parts. Oakes (2005) said, after studying twenty-five secondary schools—

> Tracking seems to retard the academic progress of many students—those in average and low groups. Tracking seems to foster low self-esteem among these same students and promote school misbehavior and dropping out. Tracking also appears to lower the aspirations of students who are not in the top groups. And perhaps most important, in view of all the above, is that tracking separates students along socioeconomic lines, separating rich from poor, whites from nonwhites. The end result is that poor minority children are found far more often than others in the bottom tracks. And once there, they are likely to suffer far more negative consequences of schooling than are their more fortunate peers. This much we know (40).

Continuing the Race and Equity Work

Now, in thinking about opportunities by which I can continue the race and equity work I started so many years ago as a sixteen-year-old high school student, I think of the public service sorority, Delta Sigma Theta, which I joined while in college, and how through reconnecting with the organization, I can make a significant contribution to the programs they sponsor. Delta Sigma Theta Sorority (DST) was founded in 1913 at Howard University by a group of young women who wanted to use their combined strength to advance academic excellence and provide assistance to people in need. The sorority's focus is on "sustaining the growth and development of the African American community." Their first public act was participation in the Women's Suffrage March in Washington D.C. that same year. DST provides "assistance and support through established programs in local communities throughout the world." It has a membership of more than 250,000 predominantly Black college educated women with chapters in the United States, England, Japan and the Bahamas, to name a few. There are five major programs in which the sorority is invested globally:

- Economic Development
- Educational Development
- International Awareness and Involvement
- Physical and Mental Health
- Political Awareness and Involvement (http://www. deltasigmatheta.org).

As a life-time member of this public-service sorority, I think this is the right time to join in the quest for national progress in these five important areas. I would also like to see racial equity on the list as one of the major concerns. Perhaps I can be instrumental in bringing it to the forefront. In 2012 the sorority will hold its 2nd International Women's Conference in San Juan, Puerto Rico and will focus on topics relevant to women of all cultures: AIDS, homelessness, domestic violence; mental illness, health, self-image, anger management, and financial stability, to name a few. The title of the conference is "Secrets: Breaking the Culture of Silence." The main objective of this conference is to "develop strategies and an action plan" to combat secrets and the "culture of silence" which oppress women around the world.

Throughout my educational leadership course of study and conducting the research for this qualitative study, I have read numerous books and articles on transformative leadership, race relations, White privilege and power, racial disparities and discrimination, tracking and detracking, re-segregation, the global achievement gap, Critical Race Theory, and Culturally Relevant Pedagogy to name some. Now, I feel the need to share what I have learned with others to encourage them to also work towards transformation of heart and mind towards racial equity and harmony. In my study I have met with Beverly Daniel Tatum, Glenn Singleton, Lisa Delpit, bell hooks, Linda-Darling Hammond, Gloria Ladson-Billings, Gary Howard and Charles Payne to name a small number, and some of what they've had to say I have experienced. And so, I consider it a great opportunity to bring forth my own story to add to the educational literature on what it feels like to actually experience racial hatred and discrimination up close and personal.

A Matter of Gender?

As I conducted this study, from time to time I questioned whether or not my gender has influenced my racial discrimination experiences. I don't think it has to a great extent. I don't believe I would have had a much different experience had I been an African American male entering a school which had remained segregated years after *Brown v. Board of Education* (1954). Of the fourteen Black students enrolled in Charleston High School in 1962, only three were boys. They were in their junior year so I'm not sure what extracurricular activities they were eligible to participate in. We didn't spend much time together in or out of school, we were all trying to keep our heads above water and finish high school. Perhaps I would have tried to join the football team instead of the glee club, but other than those kinds of minor things, I believe my experience would have been nearly the same had I been a male.

As a participant in the Civil Rights Movement, it made no difference to hateful police if you were male or female—anyone who was in close proximity might have been hit in the head, dragged in the streets, or had ferocious dogs and powerful water hoses turned on them. I recently read a statement in Beverly Daniel Tatum's *Can We Talk about Race* (2007) which made me reflect on what next steps might be for me after completing this autoethnographic project. Tatum quoted a line from a 1984 speech Coretta Scott King gave at a Spellman College Commencement where she received an honorary degree. Mrs. King said to the women, "You have an awesome responsibility to pick up the burden of leadership which rightfully falls to the educated Black woman" (134). I am one of those to whom she was speaking. I ask myself, and considering what I have learned through this study, what my new accountability should be, first to the African American community and then to the world? I feel ready for whatever challenges await, and with God's guidance I will fulfill the destiny He has designed for me.

"The Courageous Stand Up"

My mind has been refreshed on how powerful words are, and that I can make a difference through the words I write and the stories I share. I am also further convinced of what Reverend Jesse Jackson, long-time civil rights activist, said in a recent Rainbow PUSH television program. He stated: "This is how change takes place. The courageous stand up—and more and more people come to their side." I witnessed this very occurrence as part of my superintendent of schools internship where Black teachers and White teachers and administrators were in the grip of a struggle with a few members of the school board who still don't understand how "institutional racism" has infiltrated their ranks. I was able to stand with this team of leaders whose meetings I attended for several months. I had seen the dedication and vigor with which they worked, and I was able to express in a public forum, in front of the Middleton District High School Board members, how my high school experience with racial separation and isolation negatively impacted my life, and how minority students deserve the same opportunities to succeed as other students, without facing the prediction of failure because of their race. The following is the three-minute speech I gave:

Good Evening,

First, I would like to say thank you to the members of the Board, Superintendent Walker and the faculty and staff of Middleton District High School (MDHS) for the hard work you have done and continue to do to insure equity for all the students. I wish someone in my high school years ago had cared enough to fight for me when I was a student in a segregated high school.

In 1962, fourteen African American students integrated Charleston High School in Charleston, Missouri. I was one of them. The NAACP and a group of parents sued the Charleston Board of Education to allow us entrance into the town's best high school. I was sixteen years old then and in my junior year. My first years of high school were spent at Lincoln High School, where all Black high school students were required to attend. Lincoln was a fun place—all of my friends were there. The problem was that it was inadequate—separate but definitely not equal. A few blocks away from Lincoln was another high school with every class and all the resources any college-bound student would want or need, but it was just for the White kids. At Lincoln we had the bare minimum as far as the curriculum was concerned— two years of English, one year of Math, limited supplies and a library that had maybe a hundred outdated books. Even as a freshman in high school I knew I was destined to do more with my life than just get out of high school and find a job.

The first day we arrived at our new school the students threw tomatoes at us, called us all kinds of derogatory names and let us know for certain that we were not wanted there. That was the first time I really understood racism and knew what it felt like to be disliked by people who didn't even know me. It still makes me sad today when I think about how we were traumatized by the name calling, the fights, and the students writing the "N-word" in black shoe polish on our lockers and posting pictures of old, ugly Black people or anything that would make us look or feel bad, all because we wanted the best education available to us.

In the November 2010 issue of Educational Leadership magazine (30), Beverly Daniel Tatum, renowned author, scholar and President of Spelman College in Atlanta, Georgia said:

When African American parents pressed for an end to legalized school segregation in the years leading up to the 1954 Brown v. Board of Education of Topeka decision, it was not the companionship of white children they were seeking for their children: It was access to educational resources. The schools white children attended had better equipment and supplies, and more curricular options than those serving black children. Black parents believed that equal access to those publicly funded resources was their children's birthright. Attending the same schools that white children attended seemed the most likely means to achieve it.

After years of struggling to integrate public schools, schools today are being "re-segregated"—many from the inside out. The struggle over how to educate minority students is not much different than it was nearly 50 years ago when I was a high school student; they just don't call you names "out loud" or throw tomatoes at you anymore. They use tracking. What does this have to do with students at MDHS you might ask? My answer to you would be—everything!! Thank you.

The issue was whether or not the school should continue to track students through ability grouping—which leads to re-segregation, or detrack so that all students would have the opportunity to succeed at high levels. I don't know if they really heard me or not, but after a long struggle, the Board voted to begin detracking with the freshman humanities class in the next school year. Members of the leadership team shared with me that by my just showing up at meetings where they felt a lot of negativity from disapproving parents and school board members, my presence let them know that someone was standing with them, on their side, and their fight was not for naught. I admire the tenacity of this group of people who continue to fight for the betterment of all students in their school. They have won a few battles now and the freshman year at MDHS has been restructured, more academic rigor has being added, and more minority students have the opportunity to begin on the same level as White students. In addition, a system of academic supports has been put in place to help students who need it. The superintendent, through his "mindfulness, hope, and compassion" (Boyatzis and McKee, 2005), while working with the school board members and his administrators for the betterment of minority as well as majority students, has shown himself to be a courageous model of a transformative leader. However, the equity work will not be complete until the entire school has been detracked in all subject areas. The superintendent knows and understands that the struggle has just begun.

"The New Jim Crow"

Just when progress is made in one area, another battle begins. Although there appear to be visible changes in many areas of discrimination in American society, could it be that institutional racism has just gone underground and is undercover? Michelle Alexander (2010) in *The New Jim Crow: Mass Incarceration in the Age of Colorblindness* argues that, "We have not ended racial caste in America: we have simply redesigned it" (2). The same could be said when schools which are thought to be integrated use the tracking system and minority students end up being re-segregated. Alexander reminds us that today it's not politically correct to openly discriminate as the Jim Crow laws did from the "late nineteenth century to the 1960s" (Appiah and Gates 2003) so now instead the White establishment uses the criminal justice system to profile and lock up four out of five Black men, label them as felons, have their right to vote taken away, and cause them to be *legally* discriminated against "in housing, education, public benefits, and jury service just as their parents, grandparents and great-grandparents once were" (2). The Critical Race Theory framework through which I have viewed my research causes me to ask: Has the mass incarceration of Black men become the new "slave plantation" and is it the "new system of control"? What does it mean for Black families and neighborhoods when so many of its men are incarcerated? What does it mean for the Black family—my son, grandson and grand daughter in the future?

In a February 2010 C-SPAN interview conducted by the *Washington Journal* newspaper, Michelle Alexander, civil rights activist, lawyer and legal scholar who teaches law at Ohio State University, talked about the research for her book which highlighted the alarming increase in the number of Black and Brown men in the US prison system over the past two decades. She stated that numbers have tripled and quadrupled in some states. "As of June 30, 2008, there are 846,000 black male inmates held in state or federal prisons or local jails in the United States. This represents 40.2% of all inmates for the same year. This data is based on the Prison Inmates at Midyear

2008 Statistical Tables of the U.S. Bureau of Justice Statistics. About 65% of black inmates are aged 20-39" (http://www.numberof.net). Alexander also stated that "most of that increase is due to the War on Drugs, waged almost exclusively in poor communities of color even though studies have shown that whites use and sell illegal drugs at rates equal to or above" that for Blacks. Many of these Black and Brown men receive long sentences for "low-level" drug crimes— even when caught with small quantities of marijuana. The United States has the largest prison population of any country on the globe. Currently there are more than two million people in the prison system and Black males make up a large percentage of that number. Many of these men, four out of five, who have no history of violence, are in prison for what "the privileged"—White men—do and get away with on a daily basis. Tim Wise (2002), anti-racist writer and lecturer, talks about White privilege in his essay, "White Like Me: Race and Identity" in Singley's (2002) compilation, *When Race Becomes Real.* Wise says this about White privilege—

- It had been there when one of my black classmates and I disrupted a reading class the first week of first grade, and only he was punished though I had been the primary instigator of the morning's chaos.
- It had been there in the repeated placements of me and virtually all the white students on the advanced track, and the parallel placement of most of the black kids on the remedial track: a placement that would follow us throughout our school years, no matter our promise or potential.
- It had been there when parties I attended in white neighborhoods were broken up by police because of noise complaints, and yet those same officers would overlook the flagrant underage drinking and drug use in ways they surely would not have done had we been black (230-231).

Also, in the C-SPAN interview Michelle Alexander spoke of the Sentencing Project, said to be "the voice of criminal justice reform" for the past 25 years. The Sentencing Project: Research and Advocacy for Reform web site (2011) reports:

> More than 60% of the people in prison are now racial and ethnic minorities. For Black males in their twenties, 1 in every 8 is in prison or jail on any given day. These trends have been intensified by the disproportionate impact of the 'war on drugs,' in which three-fourths of all persons in prison for drug offenses are people of color (http://www.thesentencingproject.org).

Benjamin Todd Jealous, current President and CEO of the National Association for the Advancement of Colored People (NAACP) stated the following when offering a critique of Alexander's book:

> For every century there is a crisis in our democracy, the response to which defines how future generations view those who were alive at the time. In the eighteenth century it was the transatlantic slave trade, in the nineteenth century it was slavery, in the twentieth century it was Jim Crow. Today it is mass incarceration (http://www.newjimcrow.com).

And another fight against Black/White racism—this one against the mass incarceration of Black men, has begun. In a story, "Prison v. College" (March, 2009) reported by Steve Rhodes for NBC news in Chicago, Phillip Jackson, executive director of the Black Star Project, a non-profit organization which targets excellence in education stated,

> What a cruel hoax to believe that if a black man can become president, then black men do not have problems that America is obligated to address ... Yet Black America cannot trade one black man in the White House for the million-plus black men languishing in American jail houses and millions

of black boys failing in American school houses (paragraph 8).

"Legacy"

As I near the completion of this study I find myself reflecting on places, people and things which have not stirred my interest before. Bearing in mind Critical Race Theory, I have opened up to new meanings and the significance of matters which were of prior insignificance. Case in point, as I consider all I have learned there is a twenty-six foot statue of actress, Marilyn Monroe, on Michigan Avenue in downtown Chicago which I walk pass on an almost weekly basis. As a woman I am embarrassed when I see young boys and adult men, sometimes women, standing beneath the statue which depicts a scene from the film, "The Seven Year Itch", where Marilyn is standing, legs apart, over a steamy, airy, open grate in the sidewalk and appears to be trying to hold her dress down to prevent it from flying up over her head. People standing underneath the statue are looking up, taking pictures of the movie icon's white underclothing, and I wondered what I would have to do to be immortalized in a "monument" nearly as tall as one of the buildings on the "Magnificent Mile", as the big-business, ritzy portion of Michigan Avenue is called. An August 9, 2011 report by Chris Bury and Julie Na for http://www. abcnews.com reads: "The sculpture, entitled 'Forever Marilyn' by artist J. Seward Johnson, leaves little to the imagination. The crowd at the plaza can go around to the side and at the back of the sculpture, and see Monroe's lace..." [underwear]. Bren Murphy, a professor of women's studies at Loyola University just a few blocks away said, "There's no getting around the fact that that's a sexual image … Of all the images that we could choose from, why do we keep coming up with that" (paragraph 6-8)?

Some would say that as a Black woman it's not an issue with which I need be concerned. It is very obvious that Marilyn Monroe was a White woman, but still there is a certain angst I feel when I think of all of the great men and women, Black and White, who have made great contributions to Chicago or to the world, whose statue could have been placed in the spot where Marilyn's statue is. Ironically, a few feet away from the statue is a less-than-life-sized bust of Haitian born, Jean-Baptiste Pointe DuSable, who in the 1770s was the first to establish a "permanent settlement" in what is present-day Chicago (http://www.dusableheritage.com). The founder's "small bust" is lost in the shadow of the statue of a woman whose dress is flying up exposing her white underwear. Little boys stand under Marilyn's skirt and look up. What they are hoping to see puzzles me. Other Chicagoans and tourists can occasionally be seen standing under the statue's billowing skirt for protection from the rain just as they would any other canopy. I question how Marilyn would feel if she knew how she is being portrayed. Is that her legacy to those who loved and admired her? I understand that it's art, so they say, but is this how she would want to be remembered? Visual artist, writer, and co-founder of the DuSable Museum of African American History (1961) in Chicago—Margaret Burroughs (2007), asks each of us in her poem, "What Will Your Legacy Be?", to think about what we will leave as our legacy to the world. The last few lines of the poem read this way—

> I ask you, what will your legacy be? Do you know? Have you thought about it? Do you have an answer? What will you leave as your legacy? If you have no answer, if at this point, you cannot say: Hearken! Listen to me! This is the moment. This is the prime moment for you to think and to get to work and identify what you will leave as your legacy for you to be remembered by. You are here. You are still here, alive and quick and you have time. You have time on your side. You have time to begin even now so get busy and do something to help somebody. To improve the conditions of life for people now and for those who come after. To build institutions to educate and broaden the minds for people now and for those who

come after and to make your life a contribution that will be your legacy … To insure that your legacy will be a positive contribution to humanity and you will be remembered, yes you will be remembered, on and on and in eternity as God wills it (http://peoplesworld. org/dr-margaret-burroughs).

In Likeness of Sankofa

In one of my educational leadership classes we were asked to choose and write about something that represented us--a metaphor, our theme, our philosophy of leadership. I chose Sankofa (San-KO-fa). I learned about Sankofa as a classroom teacher while writing an instructional unit on African folktales. Sankofa is a mystical, imaginary, West-African bird which flies forward while looking backwards, holding a "nugget" (not seen here) in its mouth which symbolizes the wisdom in learning from the past. The Sankofa symbol is from a group of Adinkra (a cotton fabric made in Ghana) symbols which as a whole express love, wisdom, power, peace, beauty and respect. Adinkra symbols were originally used solely by royalty and the spiritual leaders of West Africa for very important sacred ceremonies and rituals. I have learned from the exploration of my past in this autoethnographic study that Sankofa fits how I see the future.

The word "Sankofa" is derived from the language of the Akan people who live in Ghana, the Ivory Coast, and parts of Togo, in West Africa. "…SANKOFA is derived from the words SAN (return), KO (go), FA (look, seek and take)." Sankofa reflects the Akans' belief that the past provides a guide for planning the future. They believe that as we march forward, the precious stones or nuggets (lessons learned, victories) from the past must be carried forward on the march if progress is to be made (http://www.africawithin.

com/studies/sankofa.hmt). I chose the Sankofa bird because of its unmatched ability to achieve what seems impossible—flying forward while looking backward. Sankofa reminds me of who I am and what this study has meant to me; that I am the sum of all my experiences, to keep the good as I go forward and leave the bad in the past, to remember the lessons I've learned, and know that with God all things are possible.

Cultural Capital

Earning this advanced degree will give me cultural capital in the Black community, but when the average White person sees me it will be the farthest thing from their minds that I have achieved such a goal. Cultural capital is a term with origins in Sociology. It is defined as the "skills, education, norms, and behaviors acquired by members of a social group that can give them economic and other advantages. The accumulation of cultural capital is one route to upward mobility (www.dictionary.com)." The Black community will applaud my efforts because an advanced degree carries with it something of which the whole community can be proud. bell hooks (1994) stresses that for Black people, education's most important goal is the gift of freedom. It will also say to others in the Black community that if I did it, so can they. That they too have the ability and the "stuff" it takes. In the Black community education brings hope … hope for a better future. For a long time I have felt that for Black people in America education is a "way out" of second-class citizenship. Many times since--in times of frustration--I have questioned that assumption, but to me "hope springs eternal" in every situation. There are still too many instances when educated African Americans are seen as less capable and less desirable because of the color of their skin and the racial history of Blacks and Whites, no matter how qualified we are. At times we must be overly qualified for a job that a White person can obtain with merely half the training and half the preparation. For a country which claims to be the epitome of all things that other countries desire, America has a lot of work to do in the equity arena. In my own community, the more education you have the more cultural capital and respect you gain. I believe this is mostly true because the Black community knows that for members of the average Black family, getting an education requires much sacrifice, especially a college or advanced degree. In the realm of the academic community, accomplishment is also respected. It is encouraging too that there are many African American writers and educators whose work is referred to as "experts" in their field. My desire is to some day, with additional study and research, join their ranks.

"Mysterious Ways"

Some would say the Universe was cooperating with me while writing my story. I say it was God working in mysterious ways "behind the scenes" for me. Over the past year there have been many significant events which have occurred in relation to my general topic, providing me with information and additional resources for my research which I had not expected, and reminding me that race impacts my life each and every day in one way or another. The first was the speaker who came to one of my doctoral classes and I discovered he and his staff were trying to make a revolutionary change at a neighboring high school by beginning to look at everything they do through a race and equity lens beginning with detracking, which in real terms meant "desegregating" the freshman year at his high school. Although it was more than fifty years after my own high school experience, my life was still being drawn to an educational situation where racial inequities existed. I was able to fulfill my educational leadership internship hours and responsibilities with this dynamic leader. The fact that this is a White man, who has literally put himself in the "line of fire" for what he believes to be the right thing, restores my faith and hope in humankind. It reminds me of " ...the moral imperative" expressed over a century ago by educator John Dewey when he said: "What the best and wisest parent wants for his own child, that must the community want for all its children" (Childress, Doyle and Thomas 2009, 3).

Secondly, I was invited to an event celebrating Dr. Martin L. King where I was honored to hear a dynamic speech from Rev. Bernice King as she spoke about her father, civil rights, and race relations in America to nearly 400 high school students. We spoke briefly after her speech, and I told her of my involvement in the 1960s Civil Rights Movement and the march from Selma to Montgomery where I was a protestor while her father led the way. She told me to continue the fight and gave me an autographed copy of her book, *Hard Questions, Heart Answers*, which has been a great resource in my research.

Also, while I was conducting research for this study, the Dr. Martin L. King, Jr. National Monument was completed. After many years of fundraisers—concerts and dinners, and contributions by peoples from all walks of life including big business, the 120 million dollar King National Memorial Monument (MLK Memorial) was completed in October, 2011. The monument sits between Presidents Lincoln and Jefferson on the National Mall in Washington, D.C. and honors "the life, the dream, and the legacy" of Dr. King. The theme for the memorial came out of Dr. King's 1963 "I Have a Dream Speech" when he said "Out of the mountain of despair a stone of hope" (http://www.mlkmemorial.org). The memorial is made of large pieces of beautiful white granite imported from China. One large piece of granite has been cut into three pieces. The middle piece contains the 30-foot-tall sculpture of the partial image of Dr. Martin L. King, Jr. which appears to be hewn out of the "Mountain of Despair" into the "Stone of Hope" as they have been designated. The sculpture was created by Chinese Master Sculptor, Lei Yixim and his team. Visitors to the memorial must symbolically pass through the mountain (despair) to get to the stone (hope). The, the address of the National Monument is 1964 Independence Avenue—a reference to the 1964 Civil Rights Act for which Dr. King and the civil rights protesters fought so vigorously, and President L. B. Johnson (LBJ) signed into law. Before this study I knew little about LBJ, but I now have a deep respect for him and the battles he fought to help in the fight for social justice and racial equality.

At the October 6, 2011 dedication ceremony for the MLK

Memorial, Nikki Sutton, White House blogger, reported President Obama's keynote address which included these remarks:

> Our work is not done. And so on this day, in which we celebrate a man and a movement that did so much for this country, let us draw strength from those earlier struggles. First and foremost, let us remember that change has never been quick. Change has never been simple, or without controversy. Change depends on persistence. Change requires determination. It took a full decade before the moral guidance of *Brown v. Board of Education* was translated into the enforcement measures of the Civil Rights Act and the Voting Rights Act, but those 10 long years did not lead Dr. King to give up. He kept on pushing, he kept on speaking, and he kept on marching until change finally came (http://www.whitehouse.gov/blog2011).

President Obama's speech was fittingly entitled "We Will Overcome." A few months later, in celebration of what would have been Dr. Martin Luther King, Jr.'s 83rd birthday on Martin Luther King Day, January 16th, 2012; the National Memorial Foundation Project laid a wreath at the foot of the "Stone of Hope" in a public ceremony.

In an earlier chapter I spoke of Holy Angels Church where I was a member for nearly twenty-five years. What I did not talk about was the church where I am currently an active member. This church is a family-oriented Pentecostal church. Something spectacular happened at the 2012 celebration of Martin Luther King (MLK) Day in conjunction with my church. When I joined this church it had been under the leadership of one pastor for more than 40 years and had grown to nearly 20, 000 members. They call us a mega-church, which some interpret in a negative manner because of its size, but for me it is a positive, nourishing, environment with many opportunities for growth. The church is known all over the City of Chicago because our church service is broadcast each Sunday morning and because the pastor was outspoken against gangs and crime, and in 1966 marched with Dr. King against segregation in housing and education. He also helped to bring new and better housing into the church community. He was a dynamic speaker and had many political connections in the City (2010 Funeral Program booklet). The story at the church was that if you called him and he was not at the church to answer, he would always call you back. How does someone do that with a church as large as this? It happened to me personally, so I believe it. He served his fellow man in and outside of the church, until his death in 2010. I value the time that I had with him as my pastor. I learned to be a better Christian and a better human being under his watch. His son, my current pastor, is striving diligently to maintain all of the programs and the positive environment his father fostered.

The spectacular thing that happened on MLK Day 2012 was that the 200-voice Sanctuary Choir, of which I am a member, performed with the Chicago Sinfonietta at North Central College in Naperville, Illinois. The audience was majority Caucasian, the choir is 100% African American, and the Sinfonietta is a multi-cultural group under the direction of newly appointed Taiwanese Maestro, Mei-Ann Chen. The Chicago Sinfonietta was created in 1987 by Maestro Paul Freeman, an African American, because he felt there was "lack of opportunity for minority classical musicians, composers, and soloists." The orchestra has an excellent reputation and has performed in "Germany, Austria, Italy, Switzerland and the Canary Islands" and is known for performances that "stretch the boundaries of classical music presentations" (http://www.chicagosinfonietta.org). The fascinating thing was to see Maestro Chen directing a gospel choir, somewhat different from a classical orchestra, and she was wonderful! Her passion and fire spread to the orchestra, the choir and the audience as we performed the undeniably gospel, "Total Praise", by singer and songwriter, Richard Smallwood, and we received a standing ovation. Dr. King would have been so proud to see all of us, from many races and nationalities, working together to produce such beautiful music as a tribute to God first and then to him. I felt hope rising up inside me, and I thought to myself, "It really can be done." We *can* overcome racism, prejudice, and bigotry if we work together for a common goal. God was certainly working in mysterious ways in Naperville, IL that night!

Another great civil rights' milestone occurred as I conducted research for this dissertation—the Freedom Riders celebrated their 50th Anniversary. The Freedom Riders were a group of about 450 mostly young, Blacks and Whites, men and women, who in 1961 volunteered to work with the Congress of Racial Equality (CORE), one of the civil rights organizations of that day, to break the Jim Crow laws regarding interstate transportation. United States Congressman, John Lewis, Representative from Georgia since 1987, was one of those riders. They traveled from Washington D.C. through the Jim Crow South sitting side-by-side—Black and White. Blacks were expected to sit in the back of the bus and bus stations and train stations had separate waiting rooms for Whites and "Colored" as well as separate washrooms and water fountains. I remember as a child, traveling by Greyhound bus with my mother and stopping in Effingham, Indiana where the washrooms and water fountains had Jim Crow signs and Blacks couldn't sit at the lunch counters. I was a sophomore in Lincoln High School in Missouri at the time of the Freedom Riders with little knowledge of what was happening in the Jim Crow South. Missouri isn't usually considered "the South", but Jim Crow was well established there as well. In the book, *Freedom Riders,* author Raymond Arsenault (2011) explains what the Freedom Riders accomplished:

> Fifty years ago, during the spring and summer of 1961, the Freedom Riders set out to change the world. Amazingly, they did so by simply boarding a bus, not as blacks or whites restricted by an outmoded system of racial discrimination, but as free and full citizens of a democratic nation. ... [They] knew that federal law and the Constitution of the United States protected their right to travel together, even in the

Deep South where local law and custom mandated racial separation. But they also knew that they might be injured or even killed for trying to exercise their right (ix).

With sacrifices, "courage and commitment", the freedom riders were "redefining the limits of dissent" and help to set the stage for what we experienced while integrating Charleston High School in 1962 and the years of civil rights struggles ahead.

There has also been a national conversation recently about a book entitled, *The Help,* which I believe women of all colors in book clubs all over America, have read. The book is a story about race relations in the South in the 1960s during the Civil Rights era. The "help" are the Black women who left their houses and their children on a daily basis to clean the houses of White women and to care for—in some cases practically raise—their children, yet these Black women were, for the most part, treated as less-human and humiliated at the whim of the White women for whom they worked. Subsequently, a movie was made based on the novel and several of the Black actresses in the film were nominated for Academy Awards. The book and the movie brought a lot of attention to racism in the South at that time and serve not only as entertainment, but also as a history lesson for young and old, Black and White. One of the aspects of the book and subsequent movie that I appreciated is that it showed Blacks and Whites working together, courageously, to expose the inequality these Black women suffered inside the homes of White women. Both the book and the movie provided historical information for my research.

One of the Black actresses, Octavia Spencer, won the Oscar for Best Supporting Actress (2012). I'm reminded here of the Declamatory Contest in high school where I won 2nd Place, which should have been 1st Place, because I believe both women were absolutely excellent and should have won, (Viola Davis was nominated for Best Actress), but what would America think and do if two Black actresses won Oscars in the same year? Reflecting on Critical Race Theory again, as I have done throughout this study, causes me to consider whether or not someone in Hollywood, somewhere, said "…but we can't have that!"

Another movie, *Red Tails,* produced by White billionaire filmmaker, George Lucas of *Star Wars* fame, tells the story of the Tuskegee Airmen, a group of brave Black US airmen who struggled and overcame many racial barriers in order to pilot airplanes in WWII for this country. The tails of the airplanes they flew were painted red as the title of the film indicates. It separated the Black squadrons from the others. Likely in order to provide more authenticity, Lucas chose a Black director, Anthony Hemingway, for the film, and hired a few less-known young Black actors, as well as two of the best known African American actors, one with an Academy Award, to star in this movie. A January 2012 USATODAY.com report (http://www.usatoday.com/life/movies/news/story/2012-01-04/george-lucas-on-red-tails-tuskegee-airmen) quoted Lucas as saying "I have only one agenda, and that's for a lot of young people to see this movie … I think kids who see this, be they black or white, will walk out thinking (the Airmen) were cool." The truth is the treatment of the Tuskegee Airmen was another example of *the insanity of racism in the United States.* The Airmen experienced racial discrimination in America's armed forces as did Blacks in every area of their lives during World War II when Jim Crow segregation laws were in full swing. A fuller story of my alma mater, Tuskegee Institute, and the Tuskegee Airmen is found in Chapter Four of this work.

Adding to that, the Oprah Winfrey Show included a segment on "Racism in America" in its final season. This show helped to keep the conversation on race alive for a while in the minds of the general public, at least in the millions of people reported to be regular viewers of Oprah's show; although for those who live with it in one form or another every day, *racism never goes away.* It is my belief that Oprah Winfrey, talk show host extraordinaire, more than anyone else in recent history, has helped to narrow the racial divide. People all over the world, from every nation and tribe, know and love Oprah through her show which aired on television for more than twenty-five years. While in a restaurant in Dublin, Ireland a few years ago, when the Oprah Winfrey Show was in full-swing, I carried on a brief conversation with one of the customers sitting near me who soon learned I was from the United States, and in the next breath asked if I knew Oprah. She seemed a little disappointed when I said I didn't. Should I have known Oprah since we are both Black and live in the United States?

The Oprah Winfrey Show is reported to have been seen in 140 countries around the globe. She has helped countless numbers of people of all races, and yet I wonder if they really see her as a brilliant, creative "African American" woman, or just someone who had a great show and helped a lot of people—colorblind. I'm sure she too has met with discrimination at some point in her life and there are those who because of their hate for Black people would not value the person she is and what she has done for America. When we elected our first Black President, Barack Obama, some naïve White people may have thought racism had been eliminated, but that couldn't be further from the truth. His election was a-dream-come-true for some, for others it was their worst nightmare. In addition, although I know it took a diverse group of people to put him in office; it seems that he has been under more scrutiny than any other living president before him. The major difference between President Obama and any other US President is that he has the blood of an African father running through his veins, and no matter how intelligent, how personable, how commanding he is—he is still Black in America. Never in the history of America has anyone ever stood up during a President's speech, regardless of whether they agreed with him or not, and called him a liar, and before the joint session of Congress—until there was a Black President. It was not America's proudest moment. Thank God for the Americans, Black, White, Brown, and otherwise who understand that skin color is not a predictor of greatness or failure, or the "measure of a man", woman, boy or girl.

"The Mouse Story" (a fable) by an anonymous writer, was sent to me during this time by a friend, through electronic mail and speaks to how we as human beings are all connected, regardless of race or nationality. It articulates how we need one another especially in time of trouble, in order to survive. Fables were written to teach us lessons about life. Dr. M.L. King spoke to this experience when he said:

> The ultimate measure of a man is not where he stands in moments of comfort and convenience, but where he stands at times of challenge and controversy ... In the end, we will remember not the words of our enemies, but the silence of our friends ... He who passively accepts evil is as much involved in it as he who helps to perpetrate it ... He who accepts evil without protesting against it is really cooperating with it (http.www.brainyquote.com/martin_luther_king).

"The Mouse Story"

(A Fable)

A mouse looked through the crack in the wall to see the farmer and his wife open a package. "What food might this contain?" The mouse wondered. He was devastated to discover it was a mousetrap. Retreating to the farmyard, the mouse proclaimed the warning: "There is a mousetrap in the house! There is a mousetrap in the house!"

The chicken clucked and scratched, raised her head and said, "Mr. Mouse, I can tell this is a grave concern to you, but it is of no consequence to me. I cannot be bothered by it."

The mouse turned to the pig and told him, "There is a mousetrap in the house! There is a mousetrap in the house!" The pig sympathized, but said, "I am so very sorry, Mr. Mouse, but there is nothing I can do about it but pray. Be assured you are in my prayers."

The mouse turned to the cow and said "There is a mousetrap in the house! There is a mousetrap in the house!" The cow said, "Wow, Mr. Mouse. I'm sorry for you, but it's no skin off my nose."

So, the mouse returned to the house, head down and dejected, to face the farmer's mousetrap alone. That very night a sound was heard throughout the house -- like the sound of a mousetrap catching its prey. The farmer's wife rushed to see what was caught. In the darkness, she did not see it was a venomous snake whose tail the trap had caught. The snake bit the farmer's wife. The farmer rushed her to the hospital, and she returned home with a fever. Everyone knows you treat a fever with fresh chicken soup, so the farmer took his hatchet to the farmyard for the soup's main ingredient. But his wife's sickness continued, so friends and neighbors came to sit with her around the clock. To feed them, the farmer butchered the pig. The farmer's wife did not get well; she died.

So many people came for her funeral; the farmer had the cow slaughtered to provide enough meat for all of them. The mouse looked upon it all from his crack in the wall with great sadness. So, the next time you hear someone is facing a problem and think it doesn't concern you, remember—when one of us is threatened, we are all at risk. We are all involved in this journey called life. We must keep an eye out for one another and make an extra effort to encourage one another.

The lesson:

- *Each of us is a vital thread in another person's tapestry;*
- *Our lives are woven together for a reason.*

This moving story reminds me of the way some Americans deal with racism because they haven't experienced it themselves and don't see it as their problem. Dr. King said in his *Letter from Birmingham Jail* (1963), "Injustice anywhere is a threat to justice everywhere" (http://www.mlkonline.net/jail), so what isn't your problem today could be your problem tomorrow. What I take from the story and Dr. King is, if we work together we can solve our problems. That is, if you see racism in America as a problem for us all, you will not ignore it, but use your resources, time, and energy to help eradicate it … "equipping ourselves and others to challenge racial inequalities, … rather than accepting racial disparities as normal …" (Pollack 2008, xx).

"All God's Children"

I'm sure the trauma I experienced in high school has left me with remnants of resentment. I have forgiven all those involved in the inhuman ways they treated us who came to Charleston High School to pursue a better education than we were getting at the all-Black high school, but realistically, I can not forget it. I have internalized the lessons I've learned from it and put it behind me, but it is part of my journey—a piece of the puzzle that is me. Sankofa says look at your past and learn from it. I have learned from my experiences with racial hatred how important it is to treat every human being with respect and honor. I know the cliché, "We are all God's children", is not an original one, but I keep coming back to it when all other explanations fail me as to how I should respond to someone who hates and mistreats someone else because they are different—not another species, but of another skin color or another culture, or of another religion or sexual orientation. Those who hate are the victims themselves because they lack understanding. To me, there is no other logical explanation. Consider how boring the world would be if everyone looked alike and thought alike—how rich a world where people and cultures are different, diverse—how much there is to learn from others unlike ourselves who can offer a perspective different than our own. I pity those who have built a prison of hate and narrow-mindedness for themselves. Jesus Christ said in Matthew 5: 44-47a of the Holy Bible (NLT)—

> But I say love your enemies! Pray for those who persecute you! In that way, you will be acting as true children of your Father in heaven. For he gives His sunlight to both the evil and the good, and He sends rain on the just and on the unjust, too. If you love only those who love you, what good is that? … If you are kind only to your friends, how are you different from anyone else?

A Few Battles Won, Still …

Yes, a few battles against racism have been won. In years past, segregation in housing and employment has improved and in some schools academic tracking has been eliminated. However, the employment celebration was short-lived, especially for Blacks, when the United States experienced what economists call "The Great Recession" from 2007-2009. Thousands of Americans lost their jobs and many lost their homes, and the US in 2012, still has not fully recovered from high unemployment rates and housing foreclosures. John Roberts, in July, 2011 reported for Foxnews.com that the "Black middle-class is eroding" and for African Americans the "The Great Recession" has been more like the "Great Depression" (www.foxnews. com/blackunemployment). According to a September, 2011 report by Annalyn Censky for CNN online, the US Labor Department reported Black unemployment rates *rose* to 16.7% in August 2011, while White unemployment rates *fell* to 8% (http://money.cnn.com/2011/08/08/ news/economy/ jobs unemployment rate/index.htm). Given the fact that institutional racism is still at work everywhere and at all times, Critical Race Theory tells me the reality that Black unemployment is double that of White unemployment is not surprising. It is common knowledge in the Black community that Blacks are always "the last hired and the first fired." In that same CNN report, Algernon Austin, director of the Race, Ethnicity, and the Economy program at the Economic Policy Institute is quoted as saying 'Even when you compare black and white workers, same age range, same education, you still see pretty significant gaps in unemployment rates ... so I do think the fact of racial discrimination in the labor market continues to play a role.' (The Economic Policy Institute website, http://www.epi.org, states that it is a not-for-profit, non-partisan, think tank headquartered in Washington, D.C., created in 1986 to widen discussions about the US economy to include the needs of the low-and middle-income workforce).

Because I can clearly see, as President Obama said in his speech at the MLK Memorial program, that the "work is not done", I am seeking avenues by which I can continue the race and equity work I started so many years ago as a sixteen-year old high school student. Throughout conducting this study I have read numerous books and articles on race relations, White privilege and power, racial disparities and discrimination, Critical Race Theory and Culturally Relevant Pedagogy. Now, I feel the need to share what I have learned with others and encourage them to also work towards racial harmony. I consider it a great opportunity to bring forth my story as one which educators and students alike can read alongside secondary documents they may already have, and possibly through their understanding of my authentic story, my exploration, new knowledge will be gained.

Concluding Thoughts on Educational Equity

I hear it over and over again, "everyone has a story." Included in that, everyone has a race story—what we grew up believing about race and how race has impacted our lives, or not impacted them. I believe if we knew one another's stories we would understand each other better and be more tolerant of differences. In *Courageous Conversations about Race*, Glenn Singleton and Curtis Linton (2006) suggest that we first "examine their own personal, local, and immediate circumstances related to race" (74). They believe that in order to fully understand "race" it is necessary for each individual to look at their own "racial existence."

I am hopeful that my work will inspire those who read it to tell their own "racial story." And that they will be able to find a safe environment where they can share it with friends and colleagues, especially when in cross-racial settings. Everyone has a unique story which carries with it lessons for life. For some sharing their own racial story will offer opportunities to release past hurts and pent up hostilities, for others it will offer an opening to see how much they have in common with someone whom they never expected to have anything in common. Singleton and Lipton (2006) refer to what they call a "racial autobiography" where people can write about and reflect on how race is impacting their individual lives currently and right where they are. They declare, "Racial autobiographies are a tool for developing and deepening personal understanding of and insights around race" (75).

I think back to a few years ago when educators and business organizations all over America and the world were reading what was called the #1 best seller, *Who Moved My Cheese?: An Amazing*

Way to Deal with Change in Your Work and in Your Life, by Spencer Johnson, MD (2002). The book talked about change and how it affects us. Sometimes change is good and sometimes not so good, but in order to grow we must accept it, adjust to it, and try to turn loss into gain. I taught a summer class for teachers based on the book where they could receive professional development credit for it. The book was a quick read, short and simple. We read, discussed, analyzed, compared and wrote several essays based on the lessons the four fictional characters learned when someone "moved their cheese"—a metaphor for something that was changed which they didn't expect or did not necessarily want changed, but had to learn to embrace. In a school system as large as Chicago's, something is changing all the time and teachers more than anyone, must deal with those changes and how they impact them and their students, and so this was a relevant topic that gave the teachers who registered for the class an opportunity to explore their feelings about some of the changes they had experienced since becoming a teacher. I did not realize how powerful this class would be. There were approximately twenty teachers in my class—a diverse mixture of Black, White, Hispanic, male, female, high school and elementary school teachers. An interesting thing happened in one class which touched all us emotionally. The assignment was to write about a time who someone moved your cheese and how you experienced it. It could have been a work or personal experience. When the assignment was due, teachers who volunteered where asked to share their stories out loud with the class. Some teachers told stories of new principals and being moved from a class or classroom where they felt most comfortable, or about other teachers they were being "forced" to work with, or students that had been assigned to them whom they didn't connect with such as a teacher who was moved from first grade to sixth grade, and a myriad of other ways in which their "cheese" had been moved. One of the men in the class read his story of pain when he had been "let go" from a school where he had spent most of his teaching career, where he got along with everyone and loved his job, but found out he had to leave the school he loved for some reason which he chose not to disclose.

He spoke about how broken-hearted he was. His voice cracked and he began to wipe his eyes as he shared the story with the class. Everyone in the class was tearing up by the time he finished. He spoke of how he came out triumphant after adapting to the change, and ended up in a better place than he had been before and made new friends.

Another man told the story of his divorce and how he had been devastated by it. It was mind-blowing that these teachers were willing to share personal hurts and losses which they had not shared with colleagues before, but in class they felt they were in a safe environment with people who would listen to what they had to say and not judge. We crossed racial barriers because we shared the same challenges, joy, and pain. We left with a better understanding of each other and how different people deal with the same Issue differently. Occasionally, I see one teacher of Middle-eastern descent, who was in that class and she always has a big hug and a smile for me.

I tell this story now because I think the same camaraderie can be developed around sharing race experiences. Glenn Singleton (2006), who co-authored *Courageous Conversations about Race*, first developed a seminar entitled "Beyond Diversity: A Foundation for Deinstitutionalizing Racism and Eliminating Systemic Racial Disparities" in 1995. This seminar offered educators the opportunity to join their peers in an "unparalleled", job-embedded, professional development experience around "educational equity." The School Improvement Network and Pacific Education Group (PEG) have adapted this seminar into a "transformative online experience which guides you in thoughtful, compassionate exploration of race and racism, challenging you to grapple with how these two forces influence the culture and climate of our schools." Educators and other stakeholders have an opportunity to "identify and address policies and practices that negatively impact achievement for students of color and serve as barriers to all students receiving a world-class education" (http://www.schoolimprovement.com). I would recommend this seminar for school communities as a first step toward achieving equity.

Faculty and staff members at Middleton District High School

have onsite professional development by an affiliate from PEG of which Singleton is the founder. "The Beyond Diversity" training has helped set the stage for the equity work now taking place at the school. Addition professional development based on the *Courageous Conversations about Race* text has offered a framework and a guide for the superintendent and leadership team to follow. Although there have been some obstacles, there have been monumental successes. This school would serve as a good role model for others who are working towards becoming "courageous racial equity leaders who will tackle inequities" as they find them and vow to serve all students (*Courageous Conversations* Summit packet, 2011).

As I worked towards completing this autoethnographic project, the opportunity came to attend the Summit for Courageous Conversations about Race in San Francisco, California. "The Summit for Courageous Conversations annually brings together dedicated leaders for racial equity from across the nation to discuss systemic racism and its impact on opportunity and achievement for all students" (http://www.ed.gov). Several members of the Middleton District High School (pseudonym) equity team at the high school where I was a participant observer for my leadership internship were planning to attend, and so I joined them. I went along to gain a better understanding of the background for the equity work the superintendent, faculty, and staff have been doing at the high school for the past two to three years. I wasn't quite sure of what to expect, but after I had spent three days with people of various colors and nationalities—Black, White, Hispanic, Asian, Native American, whose main focus was racial equity in their schools, I felt a renewed hope that the work they do will lead to a more equitable education for students of color in America's schools. I remember thinking, "Every teacher, every administrator, should attend a conference like this", especially those who teach minority students. Those who don't, more than likely will, sometime in the not too distant future because the student population is becoming more and more one of students of color (Darling-Hammond 2010, Howard 2006). And so, one of my recommendations towards ending racial inequality in schools is that in addition to educators, all stakeholders—students, parents, community members, and school boards should attend such a conference where race, racism, institutional racism, and racial disparities are being discussed in an honest, open, fashion to push the equity and excellence agenda forward.

There were approximately three to four hundred people in attendance at the summit in San Francisco—students, teachers, principals, and superintendents representing every state in the United States including Alaska. It was good to see that students were being given a voice in the discussions about race. I remember thinking that more students need to be included in the courageous conversations in schools all over the country. There were break-out sessions with titles such as "No Child Is Born a Racist: The Impact of Systemic Anti-Racist Student Leadership Development on Students, Schools, and Communities", "Cultural Proficiency As An *Inside-Out* Change Process", "Let's Get Real about Racism: What People of Color Can't Say and Whites Won't Ask", "Living in the Middle: The Experience of Asians and Latinos along the Black-White Continuum", and "Transforming Instruction by Making Formative Assessments Culturally Relevant" (Summit packet, 2011).

The keynote and featured speakers were national figures such as Linda Darling-Hammond (2010), author of *The Flat World and Education: How America's Commitment to Equity Will Determine Our Future* and Professor of Education at Stanford University; Antonia Darder (1991), author of *Culture and Power in the Classroom* and Professor of Ethical and Moral Leadership at Loyola Marymount; Jeff Duncan-Andrade, author of two books and numerous articles on the conditions of urban education and Glenn Singleton (2006), co-author of *Courageous Conversations about Race,* founder of the Pacific Education Group, which sponsored the Summit, and the developer of the aforementioned, "Beyond Diversity" seminar designed to help educators "identify, define, and examine the powerful intersection of race and schooling" (summitforcourageousconversation.com). The common focus of the summit was the inequality in America's schools.

On the opening page on the Summit for Courageous Conversations web site these disquieting statistics appear:

- In 2010, a study released by the Council of the Great City Schools stated that by fourth grade, only 12% of Black male students read at or above grade level, while 38% of White males do. By eighth grade, the numbers fall to 9% for Black males, and 33% for Whites.
- The Alliance for Excellent Education recently reported that barely half of African American and Latino students graduate from high school, with Latinos graduating at 56% and African Americans at 54%, as compared to their White counterparts at 77%.
- National Scholastic Assessment Test (SAT) scores have revealed that low-income White students consistently outperform middle and upper income Black and Latino students.

The statistics are stark and revealing, and our task as educators is undeniable: We must continue to engage in honest, unapologetic conversations about racial disparities in education and effective ways in which to unlock the untapped potential of children of color (summitforcourageousconversations.com).

I was able to speak to Linda-Darling Hammond, one of the keynote speakers, who I saw later in the day in the hotel coffee shop. We talked about her key note address which was taken from her latest work (2010), *The Flat World and Education ...,* and also about my dissertation work around the impact of my experiences with racial hatred, which she encouraged me to complete, and said it was an important story to tell. I also attended a workshop which was led by Russlynn Ali, the assistant secretary for the US Office for Civil Rights (OCR). She assured summit participants that the OCR is doing what it can to "ensure equal access and promote educational excellence for all children" through its vigorous enforcement of federal civil rights laws (http://www.ed.gov).

Survival Skills for All Students

I also advocate that all students should be taught the Seven Survival Skills which Tony Wagner (2008) speaks of in *The Global Achievement Gap*. They are: critical thinking and problem solving, collaboration across networks and leading by influence, agility and adaptability, initiative and entrepreneurialism, effective oral and written communication, accessing and analyzing information and curiosity and imagination. The question is, will *all* students be privy to the teachers and resources they need to learn these skills? Teachers everywhere in every school must examine their instructional and leadership practices, and share, learn, and question if those practices are equitable. And even though I agree with Wagner that there are some teachers who are still using instructional practices that are or soon will be obsolete, I believe there are more and more educational leaders, both Black and White, such as those I heard speak and attended workshops with at the Courageous Conversation Summit who are forward-thinking, transformative leaders, who try their very best each day to make a positive difference in the life of a child. Many succeed. They will continue to push for equity and excellence in schools all over the nation.

In order for our children and teens to learn the survival skills needed to successfully navigate the 21st Century, they need quality teachers. The research has shown that the most important characteristic in a student's success is the classroom teacher. Over the past five years I have supervised nine pre-service teachers who have completed their student teaching requirements in a Chicago public school. All of these teacher-interns were White, but in each case but one, the student population was majority Black or Hispanic. It was apparent that they did not connect with these students except on a surface level. There was no evidence that they had ever been taught anything about culturally relevant pedagogy. It was not in any of their documents as a requirement or in few if any of the lessons they planned for these students. One intern used a term that might be considered derogatory in a Black school, and I explained it to her as best I could.

I however, had specific behaviors to look for as it appeared in their paperwork, and I believe schools of education and college professors should do more to prepare teachers to teach students who are not like them and have had a different cultural experience. The quality of teacher preparation programs is extremely important in the fight for racial equity. All teachers need training in teaching students of color. Students must be "seen" and their cultures must be validated. There should be no "hidden curriculums" for minority students where teachers have "low expectations and negative beliefs" about students' abilities to achieve at high levels (Ladson-Billings, 1994). With the new teacher evaluation systems currently being put into place in some states, merit pay, and more teachers entering the National Board Certification process, perhaps we can look forward to the day when teaching practices in the US will show remarkable improvements and be a source of pride. Although student achievement is the work of the whole "village", not just teachers alone, I remain optimistic.

Writing this autoethnography has been a wonderful, rewarding experience. To be able to tell my story in this format was awe-inspiring. I was not restricted in my writing style which made for a more honest and open representation of myself and the events which have unfolded in my life. The "latest and still emergent [qualitative] approach" (Patton 2002, 84), autoethnography, has allowed me to record my memories and reflections in poetry, in prayer, in fiction (fable), as well as in a series of vignettes that capture vestiges of my past, a few which I had long since forgotten. Prior to learning that my lived experiences and "introspections" (Patton 2002) as a "racialized" (Delgado and Stefancic, 2001) American were considered valuable to the academic community, I had thought of dissertation work as a laborious task that I may or may not have felt passionate about, but which had to be done in order to reach the goal in the field of education which I had set for myself. Instead it has been one of the most engaging and enlightening experiences of my life.

One very poignant discovery that was made during my research was that I uncovered my own name, along with the other Black students who were enrolled in Charleston High School, written for all eternity in a three-hundred page court document under the legal case title: *Johnnie Davis v. Board of Education of Charleston Consolidated School District Number 7 of Mississippi County, Missouri*, United States District Court, Eastern District of Missouri, Southeastern Division, which I located in the National Archives in Kansas City, Missouri. This is a historical document dated October 8, 1962, which verifies me as one of the students who helped to integrate Charleston High School in Charleston, Missouri. When I actually saw my name on several pages of this court document, I was extremely excited, but also sad because of the memories it stirred, and then I realized my name in this court document is a part of history. Millions of people will never know my name, but for the Black and Brown students who are now enrolled in Charleston High School and in all schools in that Missouri district catapulted by what we did back then, it was something important and life changing! In the future, and as part of my legacy, my grandchildren and great grandchildren will be able to research this court case and find their grandmother's name as a pioneer for school integration in her home state. Perhaps it will give them the incentive and the courage to become fighters for racial justice as well. That is my hope.

Using autoethnography as my qualitative method of study has allowed me to explore my past, my now, my future, and my interactions with others along the way. I have looked at my culture and my community, and reflected on what my next chapter in life will be. The work I have done here has given me voice. So many other African Americans born and living in the same space and time have had similar experiences, but their voices will never be heard except through me. It has broadened my knowledge of self and has encouraged me to speak as and for Black Americans today who would like to know and feel what it's like to be respected and appreciated for the talents we have, and the contributions we have made towards the building of America and American life. Regardless of the many changes we need to make towards equity for all of America's people, this is still our home. We owe it to our children and generations to come to fight to make America what we want it to be—what it claims to be. The fight begins with each of us, Black activists and White allies, who desire equity for ourselves and others. It's an everyday personal fight! There is no time to rest! "Racism is the day-to-day wearing down of the spirit. Anti-racism is the day-to-day goin' after the little things" (Oprah Winfrey). Singleton and Linton (2006) make the following statement at the conclusion of *A Field Guide for Achieving Equity in Schools: Courageous Conversations about Race* as a call for achieving equity in our schools. I believe we can also apply these same words to eradicating racism and racial inequities wherever they are found. It seems fitting for this glorious work:

> If, as a nation, we develop communities in which people can speak honestly and productively about racism and heal from its hurts, we can change biased practices and attitudes. If we can communicate love and caring to [one another and to] our students and help them [and others] recover from racism and internalized racism, they will be much more likely to achieve their full ... potential. If we do all this, we will accomplish more than reducing the achievement gap. We will create a better society (270).

It Has Become Clearer ...

Through many hours of research and reflection while conducting this self-study, I have experienced a myriad of emotions: I have cried. I have laughed. I have questioned. I have wondered, and some things have become clearer to me—clearer through my own reflections and through the wisdom imparted by others. Ralph Waldo Emerson, noted American poet, philosopher, and novelist, who was also a minister, was known for greeting his friends with the question, "What has become clear to you since we last met?" Historians say his objective was to encourage and challenge them to reflect on "the progress of their thinking." Who originally coined the phrase is unclear. Some sources say it was Benjamin Franklin (http://www.dictionary-quotes.com). In any case, when thinking about the evolution of my own thinking, I capture below a number of things which have become clearer to me now regarding the past, the present, and the future as over the past three years in which I have sought to obtain an advanced degree and conduct research for my study of lived experiences with racial hatred and discrimination.

The past:
It has become clearer to me that ...

- God has always been with me. I felt His presence even as a small child.
- In 1962, as a student at Charleston High School, I was where He intended me to be.
- What I and the other students did when we integrated Charleston High School was historical. Students of all races now attend the same schools in Charleston, MO. The sad thing is that Black teachers lost their jobs, and most of those jobs have never been regained in that district.
- My mother was a strong, wise and courageous woman.
- Racial hatred and intolerance coming from anyone of any race or color is an unfortunate and scary thing.
- There are many passionate and "privileged" White people who continue to fight for social justice and equality for minority and poor people because they believe it's the right thing to do.
- My African ancestors were strong, intelligent, and creative people. And so am I.
- There are people of other "races" in America who have also experienced racism, e.g. innocent Japanese Americans were rounded up and put in internment camps after the Japanese bombed Pearl Harbor in 1941. Some lost their homes; others lost their jobs and were separated from their other-race loved ones.
- "Race" labels were constructed by privileged and powerful White men to separate and isolate people and make themselves look and feel superior to others.

The present:

It has become clearer to me that …

- Everyone has a story—many which will never be told.
- We all have crosses to bear—most of us will or have experienced pain of one kind or another, no matter what our skin color.
- Trials really do come to make us strong. They prepare us for handling future difficulties for which we would otherwise be unprepared.
- Even now there is some residual pain when reliving my teenage experiences with racial hatred.
- There are many things about my African American culture that I love: our strength, our spirituality, our creativity, our intellect, our determination, our rainbow of skin colors, our varied styles of fashion--hair and dress.
- Race impacts my life on a daily basis—where I live, the people with whom I associate, the church I attend, the insurance rates I pay … and every other event or happening in my life.
- Fear is sometimes disguised as hate or intolerance.
- As long as we live, we are still works in progress.
- When you are open to what God has destined, your closest ally may be someone you least expect, even someone of another race.
- There are still racially segregated schools in the US one-half century after the Supreme Court declared segregation illegal in *Brown v. Board of Education (1954)*, but not much is being said or done about it.
- There are schools in America similar to those in South Africa where the poverty-stricken student population is nearly 100% African American or 100% Hispanic, and they are called "apartheid" schools. These schools have been forgotten and have been called the "shame of the nation" (Kozol 2005).

- There are many African Americans who have stories similar to mine who will never have an opportunity to tell their stories in a public format. This work can serve as a voice for them.
- There are young African Americans and those of other races who have little knowledge of the devastating history of racial segregation in America, the progress which has been made and the work for equality which needs to continue. I hope my story finds it way to these young people somehow.
- There are people alive today who do not realize they are racists.
- Love does not have to be reciprocal; I can love you even if you don't love me.
- Some people believe racism ended when Barack Obama was elected the first Black president of the United States. They are wrong.
- There are good and kind people of all races all over this nation, all over this world.
- To be "colorblind" is to do a disservice to the other person because it fails to recognize and honor his/her individual cultural heritage.
- I am blessed to have my name appear in a historical document, while hundreds of others who participated in the Civil Rights Movement will remain nameless for eternity.
- "There is more than one story if we look for it; there is always more than one reality in any human experience" (Critical Race Theory).
- There are people who are still fighting for equity and excellence in America's schools and are not afraid to speak out about it, sometimes putting their own careers at risk.
- If someone is to begin a "courageous conversation" with others about race, it might as well be me.
- I should not strive to be just like someone else because then there would be no need for one of us (Colin Powell).
- Sometimes "your greatest adversities can become a catalyst for change" (Lisa Osteen).

- "Our greatest glory is not in never falling, but in rising every time we fall" (Confucius).
- "Success is to be measured not so much by the position that one has reached in life as by the obstacles he has overcome" (Booker T. Washington).
- No one can make me feel inferior unless I give them permission to do so (Eleanor Roosevelt).
- "Forgiveness is freedom" ("Kinyarwanda" film).

The future:
It has become clearer to me that …

- My story is an American history story.
- I am the sum total of all my experiences—the good and the bad, the past and the present. We are who we are because of our experiences.
- One day my grandchildren will know of my involvement as a social activist and be proud.
- I am a teacher and I will always seek to teach someone something.
- I am a life-long learner because I believe there is always something else to learn.
- Wherever I go, my story goes with me, and I will tell it to whomever will listen, hoping it will make a positive difference in how they respond to racism.
- A new understanding of an old situation can produce change.
- A school cannot call itself "excellent" until all students in that school have access to high quality instruction and are succeeding in reaching their highest potential.
- I now have the credentials to be a transformative leader—perhaps in a Historical Black College or University where I was first a student—to "pay it forward."
- There is still equity work to be done, and as an educator I can influence others to see schooling through a race and equity

lens and understand how racial disparities affect academic achievement.

- I should reach out to those whose culture is different from mine in hope of developing cross-cultural/cross-racial relationships which will help with racial understanding and healing.
- Change in the area of educational equity is needed, but none of us can make the change alone.
- I have a few more stories which I would like to tell regarding my experiences as an African American living in a racist society.
- I will encourage other African American women to seek advanced degrees.
- I hope to add my voice to the existing pool of educational literature on racism in America and the power of forgiveness.
- Forgiveness helps to heal wounds which nothing else can heal.
- Forgiveness is letting go of resentment and hurt.
- Forgiveness is your freedom; my freedom.
- Forgiveness is the fortress which protects us from bitterness.
- Forgiving allows me to be forgiven.
- Forgiveness allows me to *love* and …

Love is patient and kind. Love is not jealous or boastful or proud or rude. It does not demand its own way. It is not irritable, and it keeps no record of being wronged. It does not rejoice about injustice but rejoices whenever the truth wins out. Love never gives up, never loses faith, is always hopeful, and endures through every circumstance (1 Corinthians 13: 4-8) NLT.

A Closing Prayer
2012

Heavenly Father,

Show us your loving kindness.

Forgive us for the ways in which we hurt one another.

Help us to make *our* country a place of which we can *all* be proud.

Although we may have come here by different routes,

This is *our* home.

You deemed it so.

Teach us to love and not fear,

for it is fear which causes intolerance.

We are *all* your children.

Bless us today I pray.

God, bless our America.

Do it through Your Son, Jesus Christ.

Amen

REFERENCES

Appiah, K. and Gates, H., Eds. (2003). *Africana: The encyclopedia of the African and African American experience: The concise desk reference.* Philadelphia: Running Press.

Aquila, E. (2010). Teaching secrets: when the kids don't share your culture. *Teacher Magazine.* Retrieved from http://www.edweek.org/tm/article.

Alexander, M. (2010). *The new jim crow: Mass incarceration in the age of colorblindness.* New York: The New Press. Additional information retrieved from http://www.newjimcrow.com.

Alridge, D. P. (2008). The educational thought of W.E.B. DuBois: An intellectual history. New York: Teachers College Press.

American Heritage Dictionary online. http://ahdictionary.com.

Anderson, L. (2006). Analytic auto-ethnography. *Journal of Contemporary Ethnography, 35* (4), 373-395.

Anderson, S.L., Attwood, P.F., and Howard, L. C. (Eds.). (2004). *Facing racism in education* (3rd ed.). Cambridge, MA: Harvard Education Publishing Group.

Arsenault, R. (2011). *Freedom riders* (abridged edition): *1961 and the struggle for racial justice.* New York: Oxford University Press.

Ayers, W. (1989). *The good preschool teacher: Six teachers reflect on their lives.* New York: Teachers College Press.

Ayers, W. (2001). *To teach: The journey of a teacher* (2nd ed.). New York: Teachers College Press.

Banks, R. (2011). *Is marriage for white people? How the African American marriage decline affects everyone.* New York: Penguin Group.

Barton, D. (2004). *Setting the record straight: American history in black and white.* Aledo, TX: WallBuilder Press.

Bellinger, Whitney (2007). Why African American women try to obtain 'good hair'. University of Pittsburgh at Bradford. *Sociological Viewpoints*, 65.

Bennets, L. (2011, October 3). Surviving Clarence. Interview with Anita Hill for Newsweek Magazine.

"Beyond Diversity" seminar. Retrieved from http://www.schoolimprove ment.com.

Boyatzis, R. and McKee, A. (2005). *Resonant leadership.* Boston: Harvard Business School Press.

Brant, (Ed.) R. S. (2000). *Education in a new era.* Alexandria, VA: ASCD.

BrainyQuotes.com. (2010). Martin L. King, Booker T .Washington, Eleanor Roosevelt, Confucius. Retrieved from http://www.brainyquote.com.

Bridges, R. (2000-2004). Retrieved from http://rubyebridges.com.

Briggs, A. and Coleman, M. (2007). *Research methods in educational leadership and management.* Los Angeles: Sage Publications.

Brown v. Board of Education of Topeka I, 347 U.S. at 495 (1954).

Brown-Jeffy and Cooper, J. E. (2011). Toward a conceptual framework of culturally relevant pedagogy: an overview of the conceptual and theoretical literature. *Teacher Education Quarterly, Winter.* 65-84.

Brown, J. L. & Moffett, C. A. (1999). *The hero's journey: How educators can transform schools and improve learning* .Alexandria VA: ASCD.

Bury. C. and Na, J. (2011, August 9). Marilyn Monroe and her panties catch eyes in Chicago. Retrieved from http://abcnews.go.com.

Censky, A. (2011, September). CNN online, the US Labor Department report. Retrieved from http://money.cnn.com/2011/08/08/news/ economy/ jobs unemployment rate/index.htm.

Chang, H. (2008). *Autoethnography as method.* CA: Left Coast Press.

Chicago Sinfionetta. Retrieved from www.chicagosinfionetta.org.

Childress, M., Doyle, D., and Thomas, D. (2009). *Leading for equity: The pursuit of excellence in Montgomery County Public Schools.* Cambridge, MA: Harvard University Press.

Caviness, Y. G. (2002). Single moms, strong sons, *Essence Magazine,* November, 216-218.

Charleston High School (2012). Retrieved from http://www.education.com.

Coia, L. and Taylor, M. (2007). From the inside out and the outside in: Co/ auto-ethnography as a means of professional renewal in C. Kosnik et al. *Making a difference in teacher education through self-study* (19-33). Amsterdam: Springer.

Collins, J. (2001). *Good to great.* New York, NY: HarperCollins.

Collins, J. (2005). *Good to great and the social sectors: A monograph to accompany good to great.* Boulder, CO.

Collins, P.H. (2000). *Black feminist thought: Knowledge, consciousness, and the politics of empowerment* (2nd ed.). New York: Routledge.

Congressman John Lewis to receive 87th Spingarn Medal (2002, May/June). *New Crisis, 109*: 3, 58.

Cuban, L. (1993). *How teachers taught: Constancy and change in American classrooms.* New York. Teachers College Press.

Darling-Hammond, L. (2010). *The flat world and education: How America's commitment to equity will determine our future.* New York: Teachers College Press.

Davis, Johnnie, et al. v. Board of Education, et al. No. S 62 C 51. US District Court, Eastern District of Missouri, Southeastern Division.

Declaration of Independence. Retrieved from www.usconstitution.net.

Decuir, J. T. and Dixson, A. D. (2004). So when it comes out, they aren't surprised that it is there: Using critical race theory as a tool of analysis of race and racism in education. *Educational Researcher,* 26-30.

Delgado, R. and Stefancic, J. (2001). *Critical race theory.* New York: University Press.

Della Cava, M. (2012, January 4). George Lucas' Red Tails salute Tuskegee Airmen. Retrieved from (http://www.usatoday.com/life/movies/news/story/2012-01-04/ george- lucas-on-red-tails-tuskegee-airmen).

Delpit, L. (1995). *Other people's children: Cultural conflict in the classroom.* New York: The New Press. Delta Sigma Theta Sorority. Retrieved from http://www.deltasigmatheta.org.

Dictionary of Quotes (2008-2012). Retrieved from http://www.dictionary-quotes.com. WordPress.

Donaldson, G. A. Jr. (2006). *Cultivating leadership in schools: Connecting people, purpose and practice.* New York: Teachers College Press.

DuBois, W. E. B. (1970). The freedom to learn. In P.S. Fonder (Ed.), *W. E. B. DuBois speaks.* 230-231. New York: Pathfinder. (Original work published 1949).

Duncan-Andrade, J. M. R. (2009). Note to educators: Hope required when growing roses in concrete. *Harvard Educational Review, 79* (2), 181-194.

DuSable Heritage Association. Retireved from http://www.dusableheritage.com.

Ellis, C. (2009). *Revision: Auto-ethnographic reflections on life and work.* Walnut Creek, Left Coast Press.

Ellis, C. & Bochner, A. (1996). *Composing ethnography: Alternative forms of qualitative writing.* Walnut Creek, Ca: Alta Mira Press.

Esposito, J. and Swain, A. N. (2009). Pathways to social justice: urban teachers' uses of culturally relevant pedagogy as a conduit for teaching for social justice. *Perspectives on Urban Education*, 38-48.

Essence Magazine (2012). The 99% solution. *42*: 9, 48.

Etherington, K. (2004). *Becoming a reflexive researcher: Using ourselves in research.* Great Britain: Athenaeum Press.

Farrell, T. (2004). *Reflective practice in action.* Thousand Oaks, CA. Corwin Press.

Foeman, A. K. and Nance, T. (1999). From miscegenation to multi-culturalism: Perceptions and stages of interracial relationship development. *Journal of Black Studies, 29*: 4, 540-557.

Folan, K. L. (2010). *Don't bring home a white boy and other notions that keep black women from dating out.* New York: Gallery Books.

Fullan, M. (1991). *The new meaning of educational change* (2nd ed). New York: Teachers College Press.

Fullan, M. (2008). *The six secrets of change: What the best leaders do to help their organizations survive and thrive.* Jossey-Bass., CA.

Goodman, A. H. (2008). Exposing race as an obsolete biological concept. Mica Pollock, (Ed.) *Everyday antiracism: Getting real about race in school* (4-7). New York: The New Press.

Gropman, A. (2007). In recognition of their unique record: Tuskegee Airmen awarded the Congressional Gold Medal. *Air Power History,* Summer, 47-51.

Haberman, M. (1995). *Star teachers of children in poverty.* Lafayette, IN: Kappa Delta Pi.

Hamilton, M. L., Smith, L. and Worthington, K. (2008). Fitting the methodology with the research: An exploration of narrative, self-study and auto-ethnography. *Studying Teacher Education,* 4:1, 17-28.

Hinchey, P. H. (1998). *Finding freedom in the classroom.* New York Peter Lang.

Holt, N. (2003). Representation, legitimation, and auto-ethnography: An auto-ethnographic writing story. *International Journal of Qualitative Methods,* 2(1).

Harris-Perry, M. V. (2011). *Sister citizen.* New Haven: Yale University Press.

Harvard Education Review (2009). *Education and the Obama presidency,* 79 (2).

Hayden, T. (2010). The tribe of SNCC. *Nation, 290*:18, 6-8.

Hill, A. (2011). *Reimagining equality: Stories of gender, race, and finding home.* Boston: Beacon Press.

Hinchey, P. H. (1998). *Finding freedom in the classroom.* New York: Lang Publishing.

Holley, D. R. (2004). Is brown dying? Exploring the resegregation trend in our public schools. *New York Law School Law Review, 49,* 1085-1107.

Holy Angels Church (2011). Retrieved from http//:www.holyangles.com.

Holy Bible (1984). New International Version. Grand Rapids: Zondervan Bible Publishers.

Holy Bible (1996). New Living Translation. Wheaton: Tyndale House Publishers, Inc.

Holy Bible (2004). King James Version. Thomas Nelson, Inc.

Hooks, B. (1994). *Teaching to Transgress: Education as the Practice of Freedom.*New York: Routledge.

Howard, G. R. (2006). *We can't teach what we don't know: White teachers, multiracial schools.* New York: Teachers College Press.

http://www.numberof.net.

https://www.britannica.com/biography/Ruby-Bridges

http://www.ucdoer.ie/index.php/Education Theory/ Epistemology and Learning Theories

http://www.WordIQ.com.

Humphreys, M. (2005). Getting personal: Reflexivity and auto-ethnographic vignettes. *Qualitative Inquiry, 11*: 6, 840-860.

Hyland, N. E. (2009). One white teacher's struggle for culturally relevant pedagogy: The problem of the community. New York: The City College of New York.

Irvine, J. (2010, April). Culturally relevant pedagogy. *The Education Digest,* 57-61.

Jackson, J. (2011, October). Rainbow PUSH television program.

Jackson, J. (1997). *American Bandstand: Dick Clark and the making of a rock 'n' roll empire.* New York: Oxford University Press.

Jealous, B. T. (2010). Retrieved from http://www.thenewjimcrow.com.

Jetter, A. (2005). Raising super men. *Health Magazine*, July-August, 114-119.

Jim Crow signs. Retrieved from http//www.dobsonproducts.com.

Johnson, S. (2002). *Who moved my cheese?: An amazing way to deal with change in your work and in your life.* New York: Penguin Putnam, Inc.

King, B. A. (1996). *Hard questions, heart answers: Sermons and speeches.* New York: Dell Publishing Group.

"Kinyarwanda" (2011). Retrieved from http://www.kinyarwandamovie.com.

"Kinyarwanda" (2011). Retrieved from http://www.indiewire.com.

Knight, M.B. and Melnicove, M. (2000). Africa is not a country. Brookfield, CN: Millbrook Press.

Kozol, J. (2005). *The shame of the nation: The restoration of apartheid schooling in America.* New York: Three Rivers Press.

Kozol, J., Tatum, B. D., Eaton, S. and Gandara, P. (2010). Resegregation: What's the answer? *Educational Leadership, 68*:3, 28-31.

Ladson-Billings, G. (1994). *The dreamkeepers: successful teachers of African American children.* San Francisco, CA: Jossey-Bass.

Ladson-Billings, G. (2005). The evolving role of critical race theory in educational scholarship. *Race Ethnicity and Education, 8*: 1, 115-119.

Landsman, J. (2001). *A white teacher talks about race.* Lanham: MD. Rowman & Littlefield Publishing Group.

Landsman, J. and Lewis, C. (2006). *White teachers/diverse classrooms.* Sterling, VA: Stylus.

Lawson, S. F and Payne, C. (1998). *The civil rights movement, 1945-1968.* New York, Oxford: Rowman & Littlefield, Publishing, Inc.

Lee, S. (2005). *Up against whiteness: Race, school, and immigrant youth.* New York: Teachers College Press.

Lindsey, R., Robins, K. and Terrell, R. (2009). *Cultural proficiency: A manual for school leaders (3rd ed.).* Thousand Oaks, CA: Sage.

Linn, R. L. and Welner, K. G. (Eds.) (2007). Race-conscious policies for assigning students to schools: Social science research and the Supreme Court cases. Washington DC: National Academy of Education.

Lisa Osteen Quote (2012). Retrieved from www.joelosteen.com.

Loving v. Virginia (1967). Retrieved from http://www.encyclopediavirginia.org/ loving_v_virginia_1967.

Lucado, M. (2010). *Outlive your life: You were made to make a difference.* Nashville, TN: Thomas Nelson.

Margaret Burroughs' Legacy poem. Retrieved from http://peoplesworld. org/dr-margaret-burroughs.

Martin Luther King, Jr.'s Letter from Birmingham Jail (1963). http://www. mlkonline.net/jail.

Martin Luther King, Jr. Memorial (2012). http://www.mlkmemorial.org.

Martin Luther King, Jr. Quotes. http.www.brainyquote.com/martin_luther king.

Marzano, R., Waters, T., and McNuttty, B. (2005). *School leadership that works.* Alexandria, VA: ASCD, Aurora, CO: McRel.

Mazel, E. (1998). *And don't call me a racist!* Lexington, MA: Argonaut Press.

McCourt, F. (2005). *Teacher man: A memoir.* New York: Scribner.

Medterms.com (2011). Online medical dictionary. Retrieved from http://www.medterms.com.

Meier, D. (2000). Progressive education in the 21st century: A work in progress. In Ronald Brandt (Ed.), *Education in a new era* (211-228). Alexandria, VA: (ASCD).

Merriam-Webster Dictionary online (2010).

NAACP chairman Julian Bond's eulogy of Rosa Parks. *Crisis*, Nov/Dec 2005, Vol. 112 Issue 6, 68.

National Memorial Project Foundation (2006-2011). Martin Luther King, Jr. National Memorial. Retrieved from http://www.mlkmemorial.org.

National Park Service-Department of the Interior. Historic places of the civil rights movement. Retrieved from http://www.nps.gov./nr/travel/civilrights/al4.htm.

Oakes, J. (2005). *Keeping track: how schools structure inequality (2nded.)* New Haven: Yale University Press.

Obama, B. (2004). *Dreams from my father: A story of race and inheritance.* New York: Three Rivers Press.

Obama, B. (2006). *The audacity of hope.* New York: Vintage Books.

Obama, B. (January 10, 2008). Remarks of Senator Barack Obama: The great need of the hour. Retrieved from http: //sweetness-light.com/archive.

Obama, B. (2011). Retrieved from http://www.BarackObama.com

O'Neil, J. (1992). On tracking and individual differences: a conversation with Jeannie Oakes. *Educational Leadership, 50:* 2, 18-21.

Okun, T. (2010). *The emperor has no clothes; Teaching about race and racism to people who don't want to know.* Charlotte, NC: Information Age Publishing.

Orfield, G., Frankenberg, E. & Siegel-Hawley (2010). Integrated schools: Finding a new path. *Educational Leadership, 68:*3, 23-27.

Patton, M. Q. (2002). *Qualitative research & evaluation methods.* Thousand Oaks: Sage.

Payne, C. M. (2008). *So much reform, so little change.* Cambridge, MA: Harvard Education Press.

Payne, L. (2002). The night I stopped being a Negro. In Bernice Singley, (Ed.) *When becomes real: Black and white writers confront their personal histories* (37- 49). Chicago, IL: Lawrence Hill Books.

Perry, T. (2003a). Up from the parched earth: Toward a theory of African Americanachievement. In T. Perry, C. Steele, & A. Hilliard, (Eds.), *Young, gifted, and black: Promoting high achievement among African American students* (1- 10). Boston: Beacon Press.

Peshkin, A. (2001). Angels of vision: Enhancing perception in qualitative research. *Qualitative Inquiry, 7:* 2, 238-253.

Pilgrim, D. (2011). Ferris State University, Museum of Racist Memorabilia, (ferris.edu).

Pitts, L. Jr. (2002). Crazy sometimes. Bernice Singley, (Ed.) *When race becomes real: Black and white writers confront their personal histories* (21-27). Chicago, IL: Lawrence Hill Books.

Pleasants, H. (2008). Showing students who you are. Mica Pollock (Ed.). In *Everyday antiracism: Getting real about race in school.* (70-73). New York, London: The New Press.

Pollock, M. (2008). No brain is racial. *Everyday antiracism: Getting real about race in school.* (9-11). New York, London: The New Press.

Ponterotto, J., Utsey, S. and Pendeson, P. (2006). *Preventing prejudice: A guide for counselors, educators and parents.* Thousand Oakes, CA: Sage Publications.

Reed-Danahay, D. (1997). *Auto/Ethnography.* New York and London: Berg.

Reeves, D. (2002). *The daily disciples of leadership: How to improve student achievement, staff motivation, and personal organization.* San Francisco, CA: Jossey- Bass.

Reis, E. (1999). Interview with Beverly Daniel Tatum. Techniques: Making education and career connections, *74*:2, 42-45.

Rhodes, S. (2009, March 11). Prison v. college. Retrieved from http://www.ncbchicago.com.

Roberts, J. (2011, July 28). African American middle class eroding as unemployment rate soars. Retrieved from www.foxnews.com/blackunemployment.

Rossman, G. B. and Rallis, S. F. (2003). *Learning in the field: An introduction to qualitative research.* Thousand Oakes, CA: Sage Publications.

Rubin, B. C. (2008). Grouping in detracked classrooms. *Everyday antiracism: Getting real about race in school.* (90-95). New York, London: The New Press.

Salley, C. (1993). *The black 100: A ranking of the most influential African Americans, past and present.* New York: A Citadel Press Book.

Sankofa. Retrieved from http://www.africawithin/studies/sankofa.htm.

Scherer, M. (2011). Taking it to the streets. *Time, 178*: 16, 20-24.

Singleton, G. E. and Linton, C. (2006). *Courageous conversations about race.* Thousand Oaks, CA: Corwin Press.

Singleton, G. E. and Linton, C. (2011). *Courageous conversations about race summit packet.* San Francisco, CA.

Singley, B. (Ed.) (2002). *When race becomes real: Black and white writers confront their personal histories.* Chicago: Lawrence Hill Books.

Smith, C. (2011, November 11). Sewickley memorial to honor Tuskegee Airmen. Retrieved from http://www.pittsburghlive.com.

Smith, M. L. (2004). *Political spectacle and the fate of American schools.* New York: Routledge.

Smith, T. J. (2010). Introduction to paradigms of research: Epistemology power point. Chicago: IL: National Louis University.

Steinhauer, J. (2011, September1). G.O. P. vs. Obama: Disrespect or just politics. New York Times online newspaper.

Stockett, K. (2009). *The help.* New York: Berkley Books.

Sue, D. W. (2003). *Overcoming our racism: The journey to liberation.* San Francisco, CA: Jossey-Bass.

Sutton, N. (2011, October 16). President Obama at the Martin L. King, Jr. Memorial dedication: We will overcome. Retrieved from http://www.whitehouse.gov/blog2011.

Tatum, B. D. (2002). Choosing to be black—the ultimate white privilege? Bernice Singley, (Ed.) *When becomes real: Black and white writers confront their personal histories* (215-224). Chicago: Lawrence Hill Books.

Tatum, B.D. (2004). Family life and school experience: factors in the racial identity development of black youth in white communities. *Journal of Social Issues, 60*:1, 117-135.

Tatum, B. D. (2007). *Can we talk about race? And other conversations in an era of school resegregation.* Boston: Beacon Press.

Taylor, S. L. (1993*). In the spirit.* Essence Communications, Inc.

The Economic Policy Institute. Retrieved from http://www.epi.org.

The Editors of Black Issues in Higher Education. (2005). *Selma-Montgomery voting rights march.* Hoboken: Wiley & Sons, Inc.

The Jossey-Bass reader on educational leadership (2007). San Francisco: Wiley and Sons.

The Legends of America. Retrieved from http://www.legendsofamerica. com/il-cairo.html.

The Sentencing Project (2010). Retrieved from http://www.thesentencing project.com.

The Summit for Courageous Conversations about Race (2011). Retrieved from http://www.ed.gov.

The Summit for Courageous Conversations about Race (2011). Retrieved from the summitforcourageousconversations.com.

Tomlinson, C. and McTighe, J. (2006). *Integrating differentiated instruction and understanding by design.* Alexandria, VA: ASCD.

Trevino, J., Harris, M., and Wallace. D. (2011). *Contemporary Justice Review, 11:*1, 7- 10.

Turck, M. (2009). *Freedom song: Young voices and the struggle for civil rights.* Chicago: Chicago Review Press.

Tuskegee Institute and Tuskegee Airmen. Retrieved from http://www. Tuskegee.edu.

Urban, W. and Wagoner, J. (2000). *American education: A history.* Boston: McGraw Hill Companies, Inc.

US Bureau of Justice Statistics. http://bjs.ojp.usdoj.gov.

Wagner, T. (2008). *The global achievement gap: When even our best schools don't teach the new survival skills our children need - and what we can do about it.* New York: Basic Books.

Wagner, T. and Kegan, R. (2006). Change leadership: A practical guide to transforming our schools. San Francisco, CA: Jossey-Bass.

Walker, V. S. (1996). *Their highest potential.* The University of North Carolina Press: USA.

Wall, S. (2006). An autoethnography on learning about autoethnography. *International Journal of Qualitative Methods, 5*(2), 1-12.

Webb, J. (2010). Diversity and the myth of white privilege. *The Wall Street Journal*, July. Retrieved from http://www.djreprints.com.

Weiser, W. and Norten, L. (2011, October 3). Voting law changes in 2012. Retrieved from http://www.brennancenterforjustice.org.

West, C. (1994). *Race matters.* New York: Vintage Books.

"West Side Story" Lyrics. Retrieved from http://www.westsidestory.com.

What has President Obama accomplished in the last three years (2012)? Retrieved from http://www.BarackObama.com.

Wheelock, A. (1992). The case for untracking. *Educational Leadership, 50*:2, 6-10.

Whittle, C. (2005). *Crash course: imagining a better future for public education.* New York: Riverhead Books.

Williams, R. W. (2012). http://webdubois.org.

Winfrey, O. (2011). The Oprah Winfrey Show.

Wise, T. (2002). White like me, race and identity through majority eyes. Bernice Singley, (Ed.) *When race becomes real: Black and white writers confront their personal histories* (pp. 225-240). Chicago, IL: Lawrence Hill Books.

Woodson, C. G. (1999). *The mis-education of the Negro.* Trenton, NJ: Africa World. www.dictionary.com.

Younge, S. Jr. Retrieved from http://www.encyclopediaofalabama.org.

Made in the USA
Las Vegas, NV
28 January 2022

42482664R00152